American Religious Democracy

American Religious Democracy

Coming to Terms with the End of Secular Politics

BY BRUCE LEDEWITZ

Westport, Connecticut
London

Library of Congress Cataloging-in-Publication Data

Ledewitz, Bruce, 1975–
    American religious democracy : coming to terms with the end of secular politics /
Bruce Ledewitz.
        p.   cm.
    Includes bibliographical references and index.
    ISBN 978–0–275–99460–0 (alk. paper)
    1. Church and state—United States.   2. Religion and state—United
    States.   3. United States—Religion.   4. Religion and politics—United States.   I. Title.
    BR516.L388   2007
    322′.10973—dc22   2007000053

British Library Cataloguing in Publication Data is available.

Library of Congress Catalog Card Number: 2007000053
ISBN-13: 978–0–275–99460–0
ISBN-10: 0–275–99460–0

First published in 2007

Praeger Publishers, 88 Post Road West, Westport, CT 06881
An imprint of Greenwood Publishing Group, Inc.
www.praeger.com

Printed in the United States of America

The paper used in this book complies with the
Permanent Paper Standard issued by the National
Information Standards Organization (Z39.48–1984).

10 9 8 7 6 5 4 3 2 1

To the men of Yeshiva and Mount Hermon, who taught me to love;
to Robert Taylor, who taught me to learn;
and to Patt, who freed my voice.

Contents

Acknowledgments

This book is no individual accomplishment. My friends, family, and colleagues have suffered through my many attempts to find a publisher and I thank them for their patience, as well as forgive them for their lack of patience. They as well as I would like to thank Praeger for taking a chance on an unproven author. My particular thanks to my editor Suzanne Staszak-Silva, who, due to my lack of experience, had to explain everything to me. I wish to thank Duquesne University, my home since 1980, and its President, Charles Dougherty, for the 2006 Presidential Scholarship Award that greatly eased the final preparation of this book. I want to especially thank the Law School—the current Dean, Donald Guter, and the former Dean, Nicholas Cafardi—for the support of the Duquesne Summer Writing Program in 2004 and 2005, which allowed me to write the two law review articles that introduced versions of many of the ideas contained in this book. The editors of those journals have kindly granted permission for the use of those articles here. "Justice Harlan's Law and Democracy," 20 *Journal of Law and Politics* 373 (2004), forms the foundation of Chapter 8 and I have relied on "Up Against the Wall of Separation: The Question of American Religious Democracy," 14 *William & Mary Bill of Rights Journal* 555 (2005), throughout the book. The final, panicked, stages of preparation of the manuscript would not have successfully concluded without the intelligent and thorough hand of my research assistant, Jesse Leisawitz; and, as usual, nothing at all would have gotten done without the hard work and caring competence of my secretary, Kathy Koehler. Over the years I have benefited from the dedication of the staff of Duquesne's Center for

Legal Information and its able Director, Frank Liu; from the dedication of the librarians of the Gumberg Library at Duquesne University; from the support of the former Abrahamic Institute; and from my students. To all of these and many more, here unnamed, my gratitude.

INTRODUCTION

Coming to Terms with American Religious Democracy

Bruce Ledewitz

Metaphorical walls do not fall as dramatically as physical ones. So it will be hard to name a moment of which one could say, before, the wall of separation between Church and State was standing; afterward, it was gone. In popular understanding, the wall is largely down. In the courts, the wall is breaking apart. In academia, the wall is only starting to fall. This book is partly a chronicle of the fall. Mostly, it is a bridge to the post-fall world.

Just as the Iraqi negotiators wrangled over the role of Islam under the new constitution of Iraq, so we in America have been wrangling for years over the proper role of religion in American political life. On November 3, 2004, with the reelection of President George W. Bush, the American people finally decided that government should, and would, endorse religion. The people decided in that election that some type of religion would establish a basis for American public life. And that has been the case since 2004. That religion is not exactly Christian, or even Judeo-Christian. It might be called ethical monotheism, or something close to that. But it does now form the basis of political life in America.

Three questions emerge from this decision. First, is it legitimate for government to endorse religion? Second, assuming that it is legitimate, how far and in what forms should such endorsement go? Finally, how should secular voters and others who disagree with government endorsement of religion, come to terms with a political system in which religion is endorsed?

The answers I give to these three questions are based on a particular view of American democratic life. This book presents a vision of organic democracy, in which these sorts of questions are decided by the people in a diffuse, evolutionary manner. The people of the United States have decided the first question in the affirmative and are in the process of answering the second one. Secular voters, who are my primary audience in this work, must decide the third matter—how to come to terms with this new political/theological reality. I hope they will see religious democracy as an opportunity for a political and religious renewal.

The watershed event in the 2004 election was not defined solely by the reelection of President Bush. There were also somewhat enlarged Republican majorities in both houses of Congress. The exclamation point for the change was the March 2005 spectacle surrounding the death of Theresa Marie Schiavo. The statute that was passed in response to Schiavo's condition, the Relief of the Parents of Theresa Marie Schiavo Act, and the process by which that statute was passed, demonstrated the dominating influence of religious voters. In this singular and dramatic event, religion played the key role.

Religion's newfound presence is not confined to politics. There was a time that mainstream television would not feature this society's majority religion, Christianity. In 2005, however, ABC broadcast a respectful and serious examination of the resurrection of Jesus and NBC a show— *Revelations*—that seemed to imitate aspects of the well-known *"Left Behind"* book series, by suggesting that the current age may be the biblically predicted end-times. A few months earlier, ABC broadcast several hours examining the roots of early Christianity. Aside from these planned events, the three major broadcast networks, and really all of the media, covered in great depth the death of Pope John Paul II and the election of Pope Benedict XVI—even greater depth than such events usually warrant. For two weeks, the Catholic Church dominated the airwaves.

What do the secularists say about religiously motivated voting in the 2004 election? Some say that religiously oriented voting was a media creation and that political matters have not changed all that much since 2004. This was the view expressed by Mark Danner in the *New York Review of Books* in January, 2005: "[A]n army of self-interested commentators, self-appointed spiritual leaders, and television pundits hot for a simple storyline had seized on the answers to a clumsily posed exit poll question ... and used those answers to transform the results of the 2004 election into a rousing statement of Americans' disgust with abortion, promiscuity, R-rated movies, gay marriage, late-night television, and other 'Hollywood-type' moral laxity."[1] Dick Meyer wrote in the "Moral Values' Myth," in the *Pittsburgh Post-Gazette*, of "how one dodgy question in an exit poll wrongly became the story of how Bush won."[2] Meyer was referring to the now famous exit poll result that 22 percent of voters ranked moral values as their top voting issue.

There is some truth in this denial. Religion has always played a large part in American political and legal life. Justice Joseph Bradley, for example, purported to speak for God, in his concurrence in *Bradwell v. Illinois* in 1873, in which the United States Supreme Court upheld a state statute denying women the right to practice law. Justice Bradley wrote, "The paramount destiny and mission of woman are to fulfill the noble and benign offices of wife and mother. This is the law of the Creator."[3] The 2004 presidential election, influenced as it was by religion, was not a complete break with the American past.

In addition to the centrality of religion in the past, the religiosity of the American people in the present can be overstated, as the generally negative public reaction to the Schiavo statute suggested. A *Time Magazine* poll showed that 75 percent disapproved[4] of federal intervention into the issues of continued nutrition and hydration for Terri Schiavo. The Republican Party was even criticized over the Schiavo intervention by Republican representative Christopher Shays of Connecticut on this point. He said, "This Republican Party of Lincoln has become a party of theocracy."[5]

Nevertheless, religion is a political force today in a way that it has not been during the past fifty years. Religion has made a political and even a cultural breakthrough that would have been hard to predict during the mid-twentieth century. Imagine predicting in the 1960s that in February 2005, *Time Magazine* would run a story naming "The 25 Most Influential Evangelicals in America"[6] or that the *New York Times* would run a story on September 25, 2005, observing that Hollywood moviemakers "have tried to strengthen their connection with religious and social conservatives."[7]

When I say that America is now a "religious democracy," I mean simply that a substantial number of voters in America now vote the way they do for what they consider to be religious reasons and that, as a result of their voting, government policy is changing to reflect their religious commitments. In other words, George Bush might just as well have said out loud during the 2004 campaign, "Vote for me because I am a Christian and I will carry out policies that you and I believe are consistent with the Christian faith." Actually, Bush had previously done something like this. In the third televised debate during the primaries in 2000, candidate George Bush was asked what political philosopher had most influenced him. He responded, "Christ." Bush's answer was not insincere vote mongering. I'm sure he meant what he said. But his statement was a sign to the faithful to vote for him as a Christian. That was religious democracy in action. In 2004, the call for religious votes won him reelection.

Once President Bush was reelected on these terms, he tried to carry out those promised Christian policies. As Republican Senator Rick Santorum of Pennsylvania once said, "elections have consequences."[8] This is the political system we now have—one premised on religion. It appears we will have religious democracy for the foreseeable future.

This definition does not seem particularly radical. Of course, voters vote for religious reasons, as for other reasons, and, of course, government policy changes as a result of their preferences. But this seemingly obvious fact was opposed very expressly by what I call secular democracy. The first tenet of secular democracy was the denial that government could endorse religion. Religion was conceptualized as occupying a different realm from that of political life. That meant many things, including denying that government could legitimately act to promote religion and religious values. Secular democracy no longer expresses the mainstream commitment of the American people, but one can still hear its echoes every time religious policies are promoted in the public square. Secularists often now claim that they do not oppose religious values. But this retreat is just accommodation to the reality of the ballot box. The cry of "theocracy" is raised whenever government policies are pursued on religious grounds. For example, the anti-Bush campaign that was aimed at massive demonstrations on October 5, 2006 was organized around four issues: "war," "torture," "Katrina," and "theocracy." Liberals don't accept religion in public life.

Religious democracy is not confined to the Republican Party, but it is centered there. Election statistics are presented in a later chapter. For now, it is enough to note that though some voters for Senator Kerry no doubt also voted on religious grounds, the more important religion was to a voter, the more likely that voter was to vote for President Bush.

The advantage that religious democracy gives to the Republican Party does not mean that the Republican Party coalition will win every election. On certain issues, religious voters will overreach and secular voters, along with the majority of voters who cannot be readily defined in these terms, will reject the "religious" position. At other times, the Republican Party will perform badly in office and will lose elections for reasons having little to do with religious issues. The off-term elections of 2005 showed new strength for the Democratic Party and the Republicans may lose control of one or both houses in 2006. Nevertheless, an important underlying Republican electoral advantage will remain because of religious voters. That advantage will continue until the Democratic Party can contest religious votes.

Thus, religious democracy is not religious hegemony. Despite the concerns of Kevin Phillips in his recent book, *American Theocracy*,[9] we do not have theocracy in America. We have democracy that endorses religion and religious values. In religious democracy, religious voters are an important, indeed crucial, and legitimate force in American political life. Their concerns will not always prevail, but, from now on, their concerns will be addressed by American politics. No longer can any national political figure credibly assert that religion has no place in American political life. This is American religious democracy.

When I presented this thesis in an earlier form, one critic called this a straw man argument. No one denies that voters vote on religious grounds.

No one denies that government policy is affected thereby. One need only look at Prohibition and certain forms of anti-Communism in the 1950s.

In order to finally bring some peace to the American culture wars, it is necessary to be very clear on this point. Millions of Americans absolutely deny to this day that it is legitimate for voters to attempt to legislate God's will as they see it in the *Bible*. On the eve of the Connecticut Senatorial Primary in 2006, *New York Times* columnist Frank Rich thought it appropriate to call for Joe Lieberman's defeat in part on the ground of Lieberman's "incessant *Bible* thumping"[10] in the 2000 election. Rich did not even think it necessary to criticize the positions Lieberman was invoking the *Bible* to support. Quoting the *Bible* is the sin.

Secularism still opposes the presence of religious language in the public square. This can be seen in certain forms of secular opposition to proposed State constitutional amendments banning gay marriage. There is all the difference in the world between opposing an anti-gay marriage constitutional amendment on the ground that it is discriminatory, versus opposing it on the ground that it is being proposed by "*Bible* thumpers." The former position deals with the matter itself. It does not focus on the motivation of the amendment's supporters. The latter criticism aims at a perceived illegitimate and inappropriate religious motivation. The political worldview of secular democracy insists that policies should not be promoted on the basis that they are God's will.

Secular democracy is in steep decline politically today. But it did achieve a short-lived cultural dominance in the 1960s and 1970s and it still lives today in the hearts of many Americans. These secular voters hope to use constitutional values in political debate, and in litigation, to avoid certain religion-based policies, such as bans on gay marriage and education vouchers, certain rituals, such as public prayer and Christmas crèches, and certain forms of character formation, such as religious training in public schools. At the very least, they hope to force all of these proposals to mask their religious grounding and to proceed as if they were secular proposals.

Secularly oriented Americans also have an overall constitutional theory. They believe that the framers of the original federal Constitution already decided that America cannot have religious democracy. They decided the matter when they prohibited an establishment of religion in the First Amendment. For these Americans, nonestablishment means that religion is to have no public role.

It is not likely that the generation who adopted the Constitution and the Bill of Rights intended to prohibit public expression of religion. But even if they did, America could still be a religious democracy. A Constitution in a democratic society cannot determine that society's fundamental arrangements. Every generation must decide its fundamental arrangements anew, although of course influenced by what has gone before. The framers of the original Constitution could no more keep America secular against our will than they could keep America capitalist. A Constitution that could do those things would not allow true democracy. Some people believe that original meaning is the benchmark for the Constitution, that such meaning does not change, and that the framers prohibited the religious political system that America now has. To such people, I can only say that in the 2004 presidential election, the people amended their Constitution to allow for religious democracy.

This book explores this new terrain of American religious democracy. Part I describes the change that has taken place from secular democracy to religious democracy. It describes the current political and constitutional landscape of religion in America.

Part I also asks whether secularism could present a coherent political viewpoint. Part of the reason we are no longer a secular democracy is that political and religious life are intimately connected. It was inevitable, therefore, that we would become what we now are–a religious democracy.

Part II engages religious democracy and asks how far it will, and should, go. If government is now free to endorse religion, how religious a democracy will America become? What kind of religion is being promoted? Christian? Monotheistic? What sort of religiously influenced public school curriculum is being promoted? Until now, the hostility of secular voters to religion has prevented debate on the particular public policies that religious voters are promoting.

Some readers will suggest at this point that the limit of religious democracy will be set by judicial interpretation of the Constitution. After all, the Constitution does not change. I asserted above that the people in effect amended the Constitution in the 2004 election. But that is not literally true, of course. There has not been a constitutional amendment repealing the separation of Church and State, so how can something new, like religious democracy, exist? Isn't such a thing unconstitutional?

The first chapter in Part II of the book, Chapter 8, takes some time to describe how a constitution changes. Constitutional interpretation is not a technical matter to be dominated by experts. Constitutional interpretation is an organic process that, at least as regards broad terms like Establishment and Free Exercise of Religion, follows the mood and commitments of the American people. The American people have decreed religious democracy and the courts are now following them. This understanding of constitutional interpretation was best annunciated by U.S. Supreme Court Justice John M. Harlan, whose famous formulation to that effect in *Poe v. Ullman* is highlighted in Chapter 8.[11]

Despite the level of political influence religious voters now have, the parameters of religious democracy have not yet been set. The rest of Part II sets forth some of the questions that religious democracy will have to answer in the coming years. Religion will certainly play an important political role in America for the foreseeable future. But, precisely what kind of role will that be, and what will be the place of minority religious believers in American political life?

Aside from the role of minority religious believers and the unfolding of American religious democracy, there is an even larger question hovering over our political future. The final question this book addresses is what secular voters—those who object to the trend of religion in American public life—should do about religious democracy. Part III of the book addresses political secularism itself. Religious democracy in America is unhealthy today, but not because it is religious. The problem is that America is currently divided, or perceived to be divided, into political groupings of "pro-God" and "anti-God" coalitions. Not surprisingly, given this formula, the pro-God party—the Republican Party–tends to win national elections. The problem with that outcome, aside from the electoral fallout, is that this stark division between the religious and the secular leads, on both sides, to self-righteousness, bitter division, and a narrowing of religious and political possibility in America.

This religious divide between the Republican and Democratic Parties is not absolute, of course. There are plenty of religious believers who vote for Democrats and there are many nonbelievers who vote Republican. But although it is not absolute, the division is real. The reason that this simplistic labeling has stuck, and has been so electorally effective, is not just smart politics by the Republicans. Nor is the religious perception just a matter of the policy divisions between the parties on issues like abortion, stem-cell research, and gay marriage. Rather, the reason the parties seem to divide on religion is that there is an important segment in the Democratic Party, and indeed in America itself, that thinks of itself as secular and as antireligion.

Part III of the book addresses these secular voters. Despite national antireligious rhetoric, this book denies that there is much actual secularism among the American body politic. Mostly because of ignorance by secular voters, the notion of religion has been restricted in secular political understanding to a particular, and narrow, interpretation of the *Bible*. That interpretation is then taken to be the essence of religion and is then opposed by those who reject that narrow interpretation. But they do not reject this interpretation as bad religion, but as religion in general, all of which then must be kept out of political life. There are liberal religious voices who understand this, but they have not played much of a role in American political life

What is needed in American religious democracy to break this logjam is not secularism, but more and better religion. What is needed is the recognition by secular voters that they have their own connection to biblical religion and that they are believers, albeit often not Jewish or Christian believers. Secular voters must be helped to see how large and beautiful a tent religion actually is. That is not a political strategy, though it would have political effects. It is a religious task. America is now a religious democracy. What I hope to accomplish in writing this book is that America, already a religious democracy, may become a better one.

PART I

THE COLLAPSE OF AMERICAN SECULAR DEMOCRACY

Recently, a friend of mine, upon hearing that I was writing about religious democracy, asked, "Isn't that an oxymoron?" This question reflects a general assumption in certain educated American circles that secular democracy is the norm and that religious democracy is the phenomenon that must be analyzed and justified. Thus, it is second nature for many Americans to refer to our political system as a "secular constitutional democracy," as Rabbi David Novak did in an article in 2004.[12]

A substantial number of Americans also assume that religion in political life is, by definition, undemocratic, maybe even antidemocratic. University of Houston Law Professor David Dow flatly states, "religious ideology, any religious ideology, is inherently undemocratic."[13] Many Americans would therefore deny that something like religious democracy is even possible.

The background assumption for these feelings is, to put the matter simply, that religious people are felt to answer to a higher authority than the will of the people. Thus, if their religion tells them to violate the norms and laws of a democratic system, they are bound to do so. In like fashion, religion furnishes believers with norms that are absolute, whether or not the believer is able to persuade others. In that sense, the religious believer can be said to be outside normal democratic life. As Noah Feldman described this position in his widely read book, *Divided by God*,[14] secularism argues that, given our diversity, the best way to keep the democratic conversation going is to agree to a "precondition of politics" that religious reasoning be kept out of political policy debate.

These are the assumptions, widely accepted still in certain American circles, that have collapsed as effective democratic rhetoric in America. They are no longer electorally winning arguments. What happened to secular democracy in America? Is secular democracy possible in principle, in America or anywhere else?

These are real questions. But for someone like me, who grew up with secular political assumptions, it is hard to take these questions seriously. It is hard to accept, as Richard John Neuhaus argued in his book, *The Naked Public Square*,[15] that it is secular democracy rather than religious democracy that should be thought of as in question. In American society, he wrote back in 1984, with its biblical tradition, "[t]he state . . . cannot be 'strictly secular' and still be deemed morally legitimate."[16] Yet, it is Neuhaus, rather than secularism, who expresses our current political reality.

This change to religious democracy is not absolute. Religion has always been influential in American life, including political life. Conversely, even after 2004, religion is not the main determinant of American life, only one such. The change to religious democracy is not so much that we will now be religious as that we will not be secular. With the election of 2004, the hope that religion could be banished from political life ended as a serious political possibility in America. The question addressed in Part I is, what are the foundations and implications of that change?

CHAPTER 1

The Presidential Election of 2004

Right after the 2004 presidential election, Thomas Friedman, a liberal *New York Times* columnist, described the election in dramatic fashion. He had been on his way to vote when a "constitutional convention broke out."[17]

In terms of religion and public life, something about the 2004 presidential election felt very different. Friedman was describing that different feel. There were objective markers in the election's aftermath that suggested an important role played by religion in the voting. An exit poll reported that 22 percent of the voters ranked moral values as their top voting issue and of those voters, 80 percent voted for President Bush. That would mean that almost 18 percent of the voters overall voted for President Bush on this basis. This would be an important political role for religion. Many people, hearing of this poll result, assumed that "moral values" could be taken as a reference to religion.

The presidential election also reflected institutional religious preferences by the voters. In a dramatic divide, given such a close election, weekly churchgoers—41 percent of the 2004 presidential voters—voted for President Bush, 61 percent to 39 percent. Seventy-eight percent of white evangelical voters—23 percent of the electorate—and 52 percent of Catholic voters—27 percent of the electorate—voted for President Bush. In other words, though the nation was closely divided in the 2004 presidential election, those who could be termed religious voters were not nearly so divided.[18] They supported President Bush.

There were other issues on various state ballots in 2004 that also sounded religious and moral themes. Adding to the perception of the election as a kind of moral/religious referendum, eleven States adopted proposals banning gay marriage: Arkansas, Georgia, Kentucky, Michigan, Mississippi, Montana, North Dakota, Ohio, Oklahoma, Oregon, and Utah. Every state where the issue was on the ballot adopted an antigay state constitutional amendment by double-digit margins.

Even before the voting began, there was a feeling in America that the election might be decided along a national religious divide. Before the election, Professor David Domke criticized President Bush for promoting his identification as more religiously pious than his political opponent.[19] The weekend before the election, both candidates went to the churches. In fact, John Kerry went to two churches on the Sunday before the election.

The political importance of religion in the 2004 election lay not in the mere existence of these voting patterns, for patterns like these had existed before. The change lay in the clearly delineated intention of the Bush campaign to win the presidential election specifically by using these religious patterns—an apparently successful strategy. It was widely reported that Karl Rove, President Bush's main election strategist, considered the goal of turning out four million more evangelical voters in 2004 than in the 2000 presidential election, to be the key to winning for President Bush. Rove was of the view that four million evangelical voters stayed home in the 2000 election and that most of them would have voted for Bush.

A changed national political mood after the voting reinforced the impression of a new role for religion in American political life. Religious groups on the political right were emboldened, with numerous local Christian groups pushing for action on cutting-edge social issues like abortion and same sex marriage. Ed Vitagliano, for example, asked in the *American Family Association Journal*, "Will the Church see the results of the 2004 election as a vindication of power politics, or as a window of opportunity to impact a morally degenerating culture with the gospel?"[20] And, in the aftermath of the election, evangelical groups in Ohio began planning a sort of takeover of the Ohio Republican Party.

Liberals, on the other hand, engaged in a kind of secular retreat—maybe surrender would be a better word—after the 2004 election. The most powerful such postelection symbol was the announcement by Senator Hillary Rodham Clinton in January 2005 that she "has always been a praying person."[21] It may very well be that Senator Clinton has always been such a person, but it does not seem likely that she would have made this announcement except for the results of the 2004 election. Other liberal icons were also in retreat. Burt Neuborne, for example, sounded ready to abandon public prayer cases altogether: "[S]eriously, as long as all religions are treated equally, do you really view such exercises in religious symbolism as a threat to our way of life?"[22]

There were some denials at the time that the election had turned on religious lines. And since then as well, it has been claimed that the famous

22 percent moral values poll result was inaccurate and misleading. Among those observers who denied that much, if anything, had changed in terms of politics and religion were columnists David Brooks and Charles Krauthammer. But their arguments might have resulted from their discomfort that they were Jewish neoconservatives who were suddenly part of a political coalition driven by a conservative Christian agenda. Theirs was an isolated view.

It has also been said that the media took a simplistic analysis, made it the whole story of the 2004 election and then the perception became the reality, as politicians reacted to the erroneous media account of the 2004 election. But the media do not have that kind of power. When a story told by the media has as much traction as this religious story, there is something there besides spin. Democratic Party politicians feared the political power of religious voters after the 2004 election because they knew there was something real there—not a media creation.

The most persuasive demonstration of the political power of religious voters in the post-2004 election atmosphere was the large congressional majority that supported the Terri Schiavo legislation. The vote in the House was 203 to 58. In the Senate, opposition literally disappeared. The bill passed in the Senate without objection, on a voice vote, with only three Senators, all Republican, present. This remarkable piece of intimidation illustrates the political power of religious voters at that time. President Bush rather publicly returned to Washington from vacation to sign the Schiavo bill, even ordering his staff to awaken him so he could sign the bill immediately after passage.

Certainly the politicians who voted for the Schiavo legislation had reasons for doing so in addition to gaining the support, or avoiding the anger, of religious voters. Some of them no doubt sincerely believed that Schiavo was not in a vegetative state and/or that her husband could not be trusted to protect her and act in her best interest.

But these sincere beliefs by themselves would not have been enough to make this bill law. The federal Schiavo legislation was very unusual. The bill reversed the normal assumptions of American federalism by allowing a federal judge in a civil context to revisit issues already decided by a judge in State court. We just do not do this in American law. All the more remarkable, this was done by a Republican Party majority, who are normally supportive of states' rights.

Of course this power of religious voters has not remained at the zenith it enjoyed right after the 2004 election. As I write about these issues in mid-2006, the poor course of the war in Iraq, and other setbacks, have weakened the Republican Party coalition that seemed so strong two years ago. In addition, the bright Republican Presidential nomination prospects of Senator John McCain, long considered a political opponent of some religious figures, suggests that even in the Republican Party, the dominance of religious voters has waned.

The point is not that religious voters are all-powerful, but that they are very powerful. That has not changed since 2004. Senator McCain, for example, for all his maverick qualities, was careful to go to Liberty University on May 13, 2006, to deliver a Commencement Address, despite having labeled the University's founder, Reverend Jerry Falwell, an "agent of intolerance" during the 2000 primary election campaign. Neither Senator McCain nor Senator Clinton, the current frontrunners, has any intention of running for President against religious voters, if it can be helped. Religion is now a permanent part of the politician's calculus. In this sense, there are no longer any secular national politicians in America.

The particular policy and political consequences of this power will depend on what religious voters want. Certainly such voters want to elect persons who, like themselves, are religious. This explains the strong support for President Bush, himself a self-identified born-again Christian. This political support should not be thought of as necessarily Christian. An Orthodox Jew like Senator Joseph Lieberman of Connecticut might do very well with these religious voters.

Nor should it be thought that political support for candidates like President Bush is a matter purely of religious identification. That was the interpretation put forward, for example, by the liberal magazine, *The New Yorker*, which wrote about the 2004 election result as if religious voters who supported President Bush did not quite know what they were doing:

> The 80 percent of the evangelical voters who supported President Bush did so against their own material (and, some might imagine, spiritual) well-being. The moral values that stirred them seemed not to encompass botched wars, or economic injustices, or esnvironmental depredations; rather, moral values are about sexual behavior and its various manifestations and outcomes, about family structures, and about a particularly demonstrative brand of religious piety. What was important to these voters, it appears, was not Bush's public record but what they conceived to be his private soul. He is a good Christian, so his policy failures are forgivable.[23]

Where this analysis went wrong is that among some of these religious voters, ending the Estate Tax and antigovernment rhetoric were not necessarily inconsistent with religious values. So these matters were not policy failures to be overcome or disfavored policies to be overlooked, but were often additional reasons to support President Bush. Many religious voters thought President Bush had a pretty good record.

Religious voters also want to end the "activism" of judges, especially federal judges. This was a repeated theme in the support for the nomination of Chief Justice John Roberts among religious groups. Former Senate Majority Leader Tom Delay, for example, addressed Justice Sunday II on

August 14, 2005, which was televised to churches nationwide, as follows: "All wisdom does not reside in nine persons in black robes."

It is odd that an issue like "judicial activism" should sound in religious terms in American politics. Obviously, religious voters do not mean by the term "judicial activism" the tendency of the Court to strike down Congressional enactments on federalism grounds, or the questionable constitutional protections given by the Court to corporations and to commercial advertising. "Judicial activism" is a code for abortion, gay rights, limits on establishment of religion, and, more generally, the tendency of the courts to identify fundamental rights where religious voters see only immorality. As renowned liberal law professor Burt Neuborne wrote, "The 2004 election saw the Democrats' 50-year practice of successfully advancing Enlightenment values through the courts instead of through the political process come home to roost."[24]

In December 2004, shortly after the election, National Public Radio ran a story about the continuing culture war in America that illustrated this point. Repeatedly, ordinary religious people who want public policy to mirror their religious values expressed hostility toward "judges" and the way "judges are running the country," making decisions at odds with the wishes of the majority of the American people. In June, 2005, in a story by Russel Shorto in the *New York Times Magazine* about antigay marriage organizers in Maryland, this same point was made by Laura Clark, a typical apolitical parent turned antigay activist: "She believed that what happened in Massachusetts could happen in Maryland. 'My first reaction was frustration,' she said, 'knowing that this was a legislative issue and the court in Massachusetts had overstepped their bounds.' "[25]

The fight over the judicial nomination filibuster in the United States Senate in the spring of 2005 stemmed in large part from just this concern by religious voters over the judiciary. It was widely felt that the abolition of the judicial filibuster would have allowed President Bush to select candidates for the federal judiciary who would change the way judges act—at the very least, overruling *Roe v. Wade*[26] and preventing judicial endorsement of gay marriage. The religious hostility to the judiciary explains why the Family Research Council program supporting an end to filibusters in judicial nominations described Democrats conducting these filibusters as "against people of faith." It also explains the strong reaction to the federal judicial decisions that, in effect, dismissed the Schiavo case, despite the passage of that extraordinary federal legislation. At the time, House Majority Leader, Tom DeLay practically threatened the federal judges involved: "[T]he time will come for the men responsible for this to answer for their behavior."[27]

Religious voters are also, no doubt, committed to seeing more religious symbolism in public life, more public support for private religious education and more religious instruction in public schools. This means more symbolic religious expression cases, more voucher issues and more litigation about prayer in the public schools.

Religious voters are likely to get their way eventually, although the Supreme Court has been closely divided on certain religious issues. The Supreme Court's decision in *Elk Grove Unified School Dist. v. Newdow*,[28] essentially ducking the case, no doubt reflected the dilemma confronting the liberal Justices on the Court that upholding the words "under God" in the Pledge of Allegiance was inevitable in the current political climate. In June 2005, the Court divided 5–4 in two Ten Commandments cases, upholding a display in Texas[29] and striking down courthouse displays in Kentucky,[30] which is as close as the Court can get to splitting the difference on a legal issue. It is not yet clear how Chief Justice Roberts and Justice Samuel Alito will affect this division on the Court. But it is clear that leaders among religious voters expect the new Justices to have an impact in their direction. There is no reason to doubt the accuracy of their expectation.

Does the increased influence of religious voters mean that agnostics and atheists cannot be considered viable candidates for national and, in many places, statewide offices? Yes, of course it means that. That should have been clear when Howard Dean's candidacy for the Democratic Party nomination for President unraveled, in part because Dean was considered too unreliable in religious matters. Dean was not perceived as comfortable with religion from the start of his candidacy, when he described Job as his favorite book of the New Testament and stated, "I don't want to listen to the fundamentalist preachers anymore" in March 2003.[31] Ultimately, that perception became a serious political liability. It is not clear that an Abraham Lincoln, who did not belong to any religious denomination, could be a serious contender for the presidential nomination today, certainly not for the Republican Party nomination. Of course, religion was a political problem for Lincoln too, who once wrote, "[I]t was every where contended that no Christian ought to go for me, because I belonged to no church."[32] Today, however, Lincoln's problem would be far worse.

But isn't the reality that agnostics and atheists are so politically disfavored totally at odds with the Establishment Clause? Does not the fact that atheists and agnostics cannot win national, or even statewide, elections "send a message to no adherents that they are outsiders, not full members of the political community . . ." as Justice Sandra Day O'Connor famously described the test for Establishment Clause violations in her concurrence in *Lynch v. Donnelly*?[33] Isn't all this an endorsement of religion, which Justice O'Connor's Establishment Clause jurisprudence specifically aimed at preventing and which a bare majority of the Court has adopted? Finally, doesn't disfavoring the nonbeliever ordain a de facto religious test, in violation of Art. VI, cl. 3 of the Constitution, which prohibits religious tests for public office?

Yes, all of the above is true. Indeed, it is precisely the point. The un-reviewable actions of religious voters have created a religious democ-racy in America that is inconsistent with a certain interpretation of the Constitution. And it does not really matter whether a majority of the Supreme Court agrees with the voters. Religious voters now effectively control this aspect of our democracy.

How is American politics changed by all this? There is more to the change than simply the 2004 election result. What was repudiated in the 2004 election was the wall of separation between Church and State. The very concept of a secular society was rejected. This was a cultural and religious, as much as a political, matter and it was so understood by reli-gious voters and their leaders. In one particularly dramatic example, Bob Jones III wrote a public letter of congratulation to President Bush after the 2004 election in which he stated, "You owe the liberals nothing. They despise you because they despise your Christ."[34]

Fairly or not, the political left in America has been associated with dis-dain for ordinary people, especially disdain for the religious beliefs of or-dinary people. The leadership of this secular elite is part of what was de-feated in the 2004 election. In May 2005, in the *New York Review of Books*, Thomas Frank described this political reality:

> For more than thirty-five years, American politics has followed a populist pattern as predictable as a Punch and Judy show and as conducive to en-lightened statesmanship as the cycles of a noisy washing machine. The an-tagonists of this familiar melodrama are instantly recognizable: the average American, humble, long-suffering, working hard, and paying his taxes; and the liberal elite, the know-it-alls of Manhattan and Malibu, sipping their lat-tes as they lord it over the peasantry with their fancy college degrees and their friends in the judiciary.[35]

Frank quotes Republican Senator Sam Brownback at the 2004 Repub-lican convention speaking at a private meeting of evangelical Christians, a meeting that received a great deal of publicity despite being billed as media-free: "He took on the tone of affronted middle-American victim-hood, complaining to a roomful of Christian conservatives that 'the press beats up on you like there's something wrong with faith, family and free-dom' and exhorting them to 'win this culture war.' For the conservative rank and file, this election was to be the culture-war Armageddon, and they were battling for the Lord."[36]

Popular resentment of secular leadership now seems to have blossomed into a crucial part of a narrow, but dependable, Republican Party national governing majority. Of course, there will be electoral setbacks to the Re-publican coalition and, presumably, poor performance in economics and foreign policy will cost votes in future elections. High gas prices and the continuing Iraqi War may undo the current Republican majority in Congress in the 2006 election cycle, for example. Nevertheless, religious voting that favors the Republican Party is now a settled feature of American political life, giving the Republicans a constant electoral edge.

The significance and dramatic nature of this political change is hard to overstate. In a short twenty years, America has gone from Richard John Neuhaus's well-known reference to the "naked public square,"[37] hostile to religion, through Stephen Carter's description of the public square as "formally open,"[38] with religion treated only as a hobby,[39] to the practical exclusion from the public square of arguments grounded on nonbelief—on atheism or agnosticism. This latest exclusion from the public square admittedly has the democratic advantage that the reason atheists do not get a hearing is simply that most Americans disagree with them on religious matters. But it is still exclusion of the secular. Political and constitutional analysis should acknowledge today's changed political reality and not repeat arguments about exclusion of religion that no longer apply. In no sense are religious voters now persecuted outsiders in American political life.

Religious voters and their leaders do not always acknowledge the new political reality that the naked public square has been filled in with religion. For example, in 2005, Senator Rick Santorum was quoted in a *New York Times Magazine* feature article speaking as if religious voters were still on the outside of political life: "How is it possible that there exists so little space in the public square for expressions of faith and the standards that follow from a belief in a transcendent God?"[40] On one level, this protest makes no sense, since the Republican Party coalition now controls the entire federal government—the White House, the Congress, and the Supreme Court–in large part because of religious voters. There is therefore as much space for faith in the public square as Senator Santorum and his allies say there should be, since they now in effect make the rules. And the same is true of alleged discrimination against Christianity in America. After the 2004 election, Columnist Burt Prelutsky wrote that his fellow Jews were pushing an anti-Christian agenda: "The dirty little secret in America is that anti-Semitism is no longer a problem in society—it's been replaced by a rampant anti-Christianity."[41] Why would Prelutsky write such an inaccurate statement? A political coalition influenced, if not dominated, by Christians now controls the entire federal government. It is a strange time to claim there is a national, rampant anti-Christianity.

Does this political change mean that fundamental constitutional arrangements concerning religion will also change? If the Constitution prohibits the establishment of religion, why does it matter what a majority of the American people think about it? The voters may be able to elect candidates based on religious affiliation, but they cannot amend the

Constitution. As one recent law review article put it: "Though 'We the People' established the Constitution and may amend it, the people themselves are not the arbiters of the Constitution's meaning. The Constitution does not establish a people's Court or a people's Committee by which the people definitively decide the Constitution's meaning."[42]

The image of the Constitution as unchanging may be reassuring rhetoric, but it in no way describes how the Constitution actually has been interpreted. In practice, the Constitution comes to mean what the people want it to mean. John Rawls said this memorably, if perhaps too bluntly:

> The constitution is not what the Court says it is. Rather it is what the people acting constitutionally through the other branches eventually allow the Court to say it is. A particular understanding of the constitution may be mandated to the Court by amendments, or by a wide and continuing political majority, as it was in the case of the New Deal.[43]

We may thus expect that if there has been a revolution concerning the role of religion in American political life, there either already has been or soon will be a similar revolution in constitutional interpretation of the Establishment and Free Exercise Clauses of the Constitution.

It is not clear that the role of religion was ever in real eclipse in America. Certainly religion plays a more prominent role in public life today than it has at any time since World War II. But was American political life ever secular? The French social theorist Bruno Latour once wrote a book about the meaning of modernity. Latour concluded that we have never been modern, which he used as the title of the book. By the same token, in asking about the change from secular democracy to religious democracy, we have to at least leave open the question whether we have ever been secular.

The final fallout from the new religious/political reality after the 2004 election is that it changed the context for the traditional, internal Christian debate about the relation of the Church and public life. In his book, *The Moral Tradition of American Constitutionalism*, H. Jefferson Powell argues that the most appropriate political response for a Christian living in the democratic West, and in America particularly, is a strong anti-Constantinianism: "The equation of constitutional with theological ethics repeats the Constantinian error of confusing Caesar with God."[44] Speaking theologically, Professor Powell would say, there can be no Christian constitutionalism, nor Christian State, nor even any Christian political policy.

In theory, probably few Christians would disagree with Professor Powell. But this agreement is irrelevant. In the 2004 election a sizeable group of religious voters, primarily and almost exclusively Christian, achieved an impressive degree of political/governmental power in

America. They achieved this power self-consciously as Christians, that is, as the Church. It is, therefore, not possible for the rest of America to think in anti-Constantinian terms. The rest of us cannot think of public life without seeing the Church as a powerful component in it. The rest of us can only decide whether we are rivals or allies of this Christian accomplishment. It is not for the rest of us to declare for Christians whether their political power is theologically legitimate. It is not for the rest of us to say whether Christians should have done what they did. Fellow Christians must debate that issue within the Church. In the political realm, there is no debate. Events have left anti-Constantinianism behind. The rest of us must regard the Church, the Church universal and not any one church, of course, as wholly involved in the exercise of profane political power in America. That is the legacy of the 2004 presidential election.

CHAPTER 2

The Establishment and Content of the American Secular Consensus

In 2004, *New York Times* columnist David Brooks wrote a farewell to the American secular consensus:

> Like a lot of people these days, I am a recovering secularist. Until September 11, 2001, I accepted the notion that as the world becomes richer and better educated, it becomes less religious.[45]

Brooks did not mean that he had personally become more religious in light of the events of 9/11. He meant that he had assumed until the 9/11 attacks that religion would decline in worldwide significance over time as income and education increased. In this expected process of secularization, he wrote, eventually "science replaces dogma and reason replaces unthinking obedience."[46] Brooks assumed religion was not going to be important in the future and, along with many others, was shocked by the continuing power of religion manifested by the 9/11 attacks.

The doctrine that religion declines with the rise of income and education is known as the secularization thesis. The secularization thesis may be more simply stated as asserting that religion declines with modernization. That belief was the first and foundational element of what we may call the "American Secular Consensus." It was a claim about history, more specifically about the inevitable movement of history away from religion.

The secularization thesis has not turned out to be true in America. But it certainly seemed true from the perspective of, as the science writer David Brin put it on his Web site, "five decades of confident post-WWII secular consensus."[47] Brooks assumed that he was like a lot of other people. Prior to 9/11, his crowd had been unthinkingly secular.

The secular consensus no longer dominates American legal and political thought. Secularism has collapsed as a consensus. There are still many Americans who believe in the tenets of secularism and fully expect secular thinking to triumph eventually. Indeed, despite political reversals, some people still hope that the courts will pull a secular victory from electoral defeat. But even these secularists would have to admit that the context of religion and public life in America has changed since 2004, in favor of religion.

For our purpose here, however, it is sufficient to note that a secular consensus did apparently dominate American public life for a period of time and to consider what its elements were at the time of its ascendancy. The secular consensus rested primarily on three pillars. Historically, it was assumed that religion was a sort of vestigial matter that was destined to pass away. This had been David Brooks' assumption until 9/11. Politically, it was assumed that religion and religious doctrine could not legitimately serve as a ground of public—that is, government—action. Religion could not be a reason for policy. This is the view associated with John Rawls in his early work, *A Theory of Justice*.

In addition to the historical and political, there was a legal side to the secular consensus. The legal manifestation of the secular consensus was the wall of separation between Church and State. This doctrine of American constitutional law was understood in what we can call the "*Lemon* era" to prohibit government from promoting religion or religious belief.

When these three assumptions are put together, the result is the secularist dream of a public life without religious language and symbolism. Government was to be neutral with regard to religion and not to promote or endorse it. Religion was to be relegated to the personal and, thus, private life. There it would eventually dissipate. This secular dream emerged, as Noah Feldman shows in his book, *Divided by God*, after World War II and succeeded as accepted constitutional doctrine in an astonishingly short time. By the 1960s and more or less since then, this form of separation of Church and State has been enforced by the Supreme Court to greater and lesser extents. It was this dream of true separation of religion and public life that was repudiated in the 2004 presidential election.

The historical assumption of the secular consensus—the secularization thesis—is not usually stated bluntly in America. But Professor Dow described it, with admirable candor, in 2001: "Two primary forces will stand in the way of the creation of a single world, and what is peculiar is that while one of these forces is on the wane, the other has of late attracted articulate and thoughtful defenders. These two forces, of course, are nationalism and religion. But the days for both of these counter-revolutionary forces are numbered."[48]

The belief in the secularization thesis has been a widespread Western phenomenon. Secularism did not emerge as a uniquely American phenomenon, nor was it a post-World War II event. Secularism had been building in the West since the scientific revolution of the sixteenth and seventeenth centuries, which, in the words of British historian Herbert Butterfield, "overturned the authority . . . of the middle ages" and the classical world. In the seventeenth and eighteenth centuries, many Enlightenment thinkers advocated the establishment of a secular society. By 1881, the philosopher Friedrich Nietzsche could announce in *The Gay Science* that "God is dead." Nietzsche did not mean that God had ceased to exist, but rather that the process of secularization was complete. No longer could God serve to guarantee a foundation for our values. Thus, in the West, one could look at a broad movement leading to a secular end point.

The founding generation that wrote our Constitution was heir to the Enlightenment. They participated in this movement toward a secular society. That statement will strike some as tendentious since there has recently been a lot of argument in American law and politics about what the framers meant by the Establishment Clause and just how Christian or deistic or religious or agnostic the founders were. The reason the founders are serving as cannon fodder in our culture wars is that the movement toward secularization was a change over a long period of time. The framers of the Constitution, and other influential American leaders of the time, were, for the most part, comparatively nonreligious for that age. Many of them probably did expect the trend away from orthodox Christianity to continue. Nevertheless, hardly anyone of that time could be considered secular in the sense we mean that term today. Our frame of reference has changed. For example, even the most radical deist of that age would have rejected the pure materialism of some versions of modern Darwinian thought.

The process of gradual secularization in America reached its zenith sometime during the latter half of the twentieth century. It was a very high societal watermark. In the shadow of the 2004 presidential election, it is astounding to remember just how well established secularism seemed to be in America a mere thirty years ago. The constitutional symbol of this secular age was the test for the separation of Church and State enunciated in *Lemon v. Kutzman* in 1971.[49] Under that test, every government action had to have a secular purpose or it was unconstitutional. This was the absolute victory, at least conceptually, of a secular Constitution.

In a more personal vein, secularism in the 1970s was so obvious as a background that it was invisible in certain institutions. Exactly when the secular consensus became conventional wisdom, at least among American coastal elites, is not clear, but that consensus had thoroughly solidified by the time I entered law school in 1974. I know this mostly by the absence of the topic of religion during my law school experience. I cannot remember a single discussion of religion in any course during my years at Yale. In fact, I cannot remember any discussion of religion even outside of class. We students understood without really thinking about it that, following John Rawls, religious arguments were not legitimate in public discourse. It would have been inconceivable for a student at Yale Law School in the mid-1970s to refer to God as in any way relevant to the law.

Rawls represented the overwhelmingly dominant political theory of law school culture at that time. Rawls insisted that liberal democracy could only be secular. He wrote that "government has neither the right nor the duty to do what it or a majority . . . wants to do in questions of morals and religion. Its duty is limited to underwriting the conditions of equal moral and religious liberty."[50] While these words do not sound antireligious, they would have had the effect of banishing religion and religious sentiment from the public square. The reason for this is that it is religious motivation that determines policy choices for a truly religious person. If government may not legitimately pursue a religious end, we end up with secular government.

The consequence of student acceptance of Rawls' antireligious views was not a feeling of censorship, even among students like myself who had fairly religious backgrounds. In 1974, religion in the public square was not an issue in the way it is today. We students did not think about religion in a public sense.

Strangely, this monolithic secular worldview was in place in the period of the mid- and late 1970s, just when the modern political phenomenon of the religious right was beginning to emerge. That coming political change did not matter to the secularists at Yale.

Nor was this secular orientation dependent on any particular political belief. Conservative law students were either business oriented or libertarian, but, in either case, remained secular in their fundamental worldview. The competitor to Rawlsian liberalism thus was not religion, but either economic analysis of law or some form of libertarian thought or a mix of both. Naturally, some law students practiced their religion. But religion had no relationship to law and government. It was regarded as a private matter, separate from law.

I had thought that perhaps my experiences at law school were idiosyncratic. I received unexpected confirmation in a November 20, 2005, article by Rinker Buck in the Hartford Courant about Samuel Alito's years at Yale Law School, from 1972 to 1975, which overlapped mine. Though Alito is described in the story as personally religious, and though his prizewinning writing about the Establishment Clause "release time" cases showed his strong interest, religion seemed to play no role in his public life as a student. The two Yale constitutional law professors mentioned in the story,[51] Robert Bork and Charles Reich, though opposites in political views and social styles, were both altogether secular in their thinking.

They were both secular despite the difference between Bork's originalist conservatism and Reich's Woodstock-spiritual-new-consciousness.

The secular consensus of the 1970s was either a false impression at the time or did not last very long. By the 1980s, even in law, the role of religion had become much more significant. In 1983, Robert Cover published his famous article, "Nomos and Narrative,"[52] which examined the political and legal crises inherent in conflicts of conscience, especially conflicts of religious conscience. Cover's article led to what Suzanne Stone called a "startling increase of citations to Jewish sources"[53] over the following decade in legal research. Then in 1984, Richard John Neuhaus published *The Naked Public Square: Religion and Democracy in America*,[54] which directly challenged the assumptions of the secular consensus and argued for the place of religion in public discourse. In law, religion was fully in play at that point.

This intense engagement of law and government with religion had actually been building throughout the 1970s. Robert Cover's book, *Justice Accused: Antislavery and the Judicial Process*, published in 1975, (New Haven: Yale University Press), raised the same sorts of issues concerning the conflicts of conscience in terms of antislavery judges, as "Nomos and Narrative" did later. A large body of legal writing in the 1970s broadly addressed law and religion in what was called the "New Literature in Law and Religion."[55] Similarly, Neuhaus was writing in part in reaction to the victory of the religious right associated with the election of Ronald Reagan in 1980.

In contrast to the secularization thesis, the political assumption of the secular consensus never enjoyed the wide and easy acceptance of its historical counterpart. It was not realistic to expect to convince people that they had no right to express themselves in a religious way in public debate. Nevertheless, this political assumption had considerable support within academia and other highly secular communities. Ronald Dworkin in his influential 1977 book, *Taking Rights Seriously*, rejected reliance on moral authority as a ground for political action, "[w]ith the possible (though complex) exception of a deity."[56] Stanford law professor, and former Dean, Kathleen Sullivan, wrote in 1992 that religion had to be confined to a private sphere. The reason for this necessity was not that religion was particularly controversial. The reason was that the Constitution had made a decision about the allowed political role for religion: "True, abortion, like religion, is divisive and controversial, but not all divisive and controversial questions have been privatized by the Constitution; only religious questions have."[57] Thus, Sullivan could refer, as if it were a simple fact, to the "the establishment of the secular public order"[58] in the United States, under the Constitution. In the face of the political changes in America since the 2004 presidential election, people do not write like this anymore, at least in serious legal and political discourse.

This notion of privatization of religion has to do with giving "reasons" for public action. Secularists like Sullivan think of public debate as if there were a referee enforcing debate rules. This all-powerful referee would not allow the players in the political "game" to invoke religious reasons on behalf of their proposed course of public action. Thus, in this fantasy, a person could be against abortion, but that person would not be allowed to claim that abortion should be outlawed because the *Bible* says so. For a long time, it apparently did not occur to people like Sullivan that there was no such referee; nor, of course, could there be, given the rights of free exercise of religion and freedom of speech.

In accordance with the political assumption that religion could not be a reason for public action, the secular consensus attempted to ground the legal system as a whole in nonreligious sources. On the political left, this effort meant finding a ground for rights in secular liberal values. For example, David Douglas, exemplifying the secular consensus, responded as follows in a book review of Neuhaus' book, *The Naked Public Square*: "The Christian, Jew and traditional Native American cannot be united by religion, but only by America's fierce and longstanding adherence to the fundamental principles of liberalism—the ideology of individuals' freedom and inherent worth—and democracy—the philosophy of self-governance and majority rule."[59]

This effort to separate public action from any religious framework of values still goes on. A recent example is the attempt by Ohio State law professor Edward Foley to ground human rights in a theory of reciprocity, specifically without reference to God. That this was a serious secular effort is demonstrated in Foley's title, *Jurisprudence and Theology*.[60] Another, even more recent, example is Alan Dershowitz's new book, *Rights from Wrongs: A Secular Theory of the Origin of Rights*.[61] The point of this work is to try to give a foundation for law outside any religious tradition.

The same effort to ground law outside religion was made on the political right. Though it may come as a surprise, the secular consensus was in law as pervasive on the right as on the left. It may even be more surprising that the most prominent exponent of the secularization of American law was, and remains, that darling of the religious right, Justice Antonin Scalia.

On the political right, the nonreligious ground for law is the Constitution itself, treated as a historical and linguistic "given" without regard to underlying issues of right and wrong or truth and falsehood. Thus, in the most obvious example of secular conservative thought, there is said to be no constitutional right to abortion because the subject of abortion is not "in" the Constitution. As Justice Scalia once stated in arguing against recognition of a constitutional right to die, "the Constitution says nothing about the matter."[62]

This positivist mode of constitutional analysis is associated not only with Justice Scalia but also with other conservative icons, such as former federal judge Robert Bork and the late Chief Justice, William Rehnquist. This way of looking at things yields results that many religious voters desire, such as overruling *Roe v. Wade*. Thus, this conservative jurisprudence has led today to a contingent and temporary alliance of religious voters with secular, conservative, constitutional jurisprudence.

But this alliance of religious voters and conservative jurisprudence is an unholy one. Pope Benedict XVI, then Cardinal Ratzinger, in his 2003 book, *Truth and Tolerance*, writes of the religious basis of Anglo-American constitutionalism: "Man has rights on the basis of his creation, rights that must be brought into effect, that justice may prevail."[63] This is what the Declaration of Independence meant in asserting that men are endowed with inalienable rights. It is just this kind of religiously based natural law that conservative jurisprudence expressly rejects.

From a religious perspective, the problem with protecting the right to abortion is not that this right is not "in" the Constitution, as Justice Scalia asserts, but that it is violence against human beings. That does not necessarily mean that laws allowing abortions would be unconstitutional. Positive law could trump natural rights. One could even have a constitutional right to abortion, but only if, like slavery in an earlier age, the right were expressly given. This is a form of natural law thinking.

The secular quality of conservative constitutional jurisprudence will become clear once *Roe* is overturned. When the pro-life movement one day asks that the unborn be protected by the courts against pro-choice legislative majorities, they will be told by some later-day Scalia that protecting the unborn is also not "in" the Constitution.

Actually that day, in a sense, has already come. In a debate in the magazine *First Things*, in January 2003, Robert Bork excoriated Nathan Schlueter for arguing that, properly interpreted, the Constitution not only did not contain a right to abortion, but its reference to deprivations of "life" in the fifth and fourteenth amendments means that the life of the unborn must, in fact, be protected. Thus, at least some pro-choice legislation in a post-*Roe v. Wade* world would be unconstitutional.

Bork denigrated Schleuter's argument as the " 'heart's desire' school of constitutional jurisprudence" and called this position "absurd." Bork did not deny that "value judgments . . . are subject to rational discourse" but, revealingly, Bork warned against sacrificing law's integrity to "moral passions." "Moral passions" are not subject to reason and one may suspect that Bork feared that a values jurisprudence would inevitably descend into mere personal preference.[64]

These examples of the secular grounding of law, on the right, and the prohibition of all public religious discourse, on the left, are not precisely the same phenomena. Some jurisprudential conservatives celebrate religious reasoning in political public life. They just refuse to use religiously based reasoning in interpreting the Constitution. But moral skepticism cannot be so easily restricted. There is either truth or there is not. If there is truth, judges would have to be permitted to reason toward it and, in some instances at least, rely upon it. In this sense, liberals and conservatives share the assumption of skepticism toward religious reasoning in the public realm.

Was there a widespread political assumption in the 1970s that religion could not ground public action? Most Americans, after all, continued to live and vote within religiously oriented viewpoints at that time, as now. The *Bible* did not lose its authoritative status for them. They presumably continued to consider religion a valid reason for supporting or opposing public policy.

But the point of American secular democracy was not that it ever achieved actual success in banishing religion. It succeeded in offering a coherent constitutional vision through its requirement of government neutrality. This jurisprudential success lent weight to opposition to political organizing by religiously oriented voters.

The commitment to secular democracy can still be seen in the use of the term "theocracy" to oppose not particular policies but the motivation of the religious people who propose them. Kevin Phillips' book, *American Theocracy*, is a good example. In most of the book, Phillips criticizes the policies of American overreliance on oil and various forms of debt. These are policies. When it comes to religion, however, it is not the policies of the religious right that he criticizes, but mainly the fact that these policies are pursued in an effort to carry out God's will. Phillips writes, "For the first time, the United States has a political party that represents ... true-believing frequent churchgoers."[65]

Phillips' statement is misleading. American political parties have always represented the views of religious people because that is what most Americans have always been. Nor, prior to World War II, would anyone have been surprised that religious values would form a basis for public policy. It would have been more accurate for Phillips to have said that, in the 1960s, America developed for the first time a truly secular political party, one dedicated to the separation of religion from public life—the Democratic Party—and that in response, the American people chose to endorse religion and reject the secularization of the public square.

Another example of continuing secular opposition to religion in the public square is the reaction to proposed state constitutional amendments to ban gay marriage. I strongly oppose these amendments and support legislative efforts to legalize gay marriage. Much of the opposition to these State constitutional amendments, however, is premised on the notion that it is illegitimate for people to try to legislate biblical norms, not because they are bad policy, but because the norms emerge from an interpretation of the *Bible*. That is the political assumption of the secular consensus in action.

The final pillar of the secular consensus was a legal/constitutional assumption that was centered in a certain interpretation of the Establishment and Free Exercise Clauses of the Constitution. Here, we are not asking, as above, about religious understanding in the interpretation of the Constitution in general, but rather, what the Constitution specifically requires in terms of the relationship of religion and public life. The secular consensus read the constitutional founding as establishing, if not a "Godless Constitution," as Isaac Kramnick and R. Laurence Moore called it in their 1995 book,[66] at least a Constitution with a clear distinction between the sacred and the secular spheres of life. Between the two, there is said to be a wall of separation. Public life thus falls into the secular sphere, both as wise policy—the political aspect of the secular consensus, and as constitutional imperative—the legal face of the secular consensus.

The legal doctrine in which the wall of separation between Church and State comes into clearest focus is in the interpretation of the Establishment Clause. The Establishment Clause of the First Amendment prohibits Congress, and now by extension, State and local government, from creating an "establishment of religion". This language was originally meant to proscribe a national, official church. Some of the States had official churches—Connecticut and Massachusetts, for example—and the First Amendment was not originally expected to have any effect on those.

The Establishment Clause was later interpreted in such a way as to operationalize the wall of separation. The two doctrines that accomplished this result were the so-called *Lemon* test announced in *Lemon v. Kurtzman* in 1971 and the endorsement test associated with Justice O'Connor's concurrence in *Lynch v. Donnelly* in 1984.

The *Lemon* test required, among other things, that government have a secular purpose for its actions rather than a religious purpose, so that a government program that sought to convince schoolchildren to believe in God or put the phrase "In God We Trust" on legal tender in order to express a national commitment to do God's will would be unconstitutional. This requirement of a secular legislative purpose was most recently the determining factor in striking down the Ten Commandments courthouse displays in *McCreary County v. ACLU*. The Court admitted in *McCreary* that the purpose test from *Lemon* has rarely been dispositive, but it was so in this case.

Under the endorsement test, government may not endorse religion. Probably the best-known application of this formulation of the Establishment Clause was *Wallace v. Jaffree* in 1985, in which the Court found Louisiana's silent prayer provision for public schools unconstitutional as an endorsement of religion. The test requires, as then-Justice Rehnquist critically observed in dissent in *Wallace v. Jaffree*,[67] "neutrality on the part of government between religion and irreligion." The reason that government may not endorse religion, according to Justice O'Connor, is that such endorsement "sends a message to nonadherents that they are outsiders, not full members of the political community, and an accompanying message to adherents that they are insiders, favored members of the political community." Justice Rehnquist's dissent denied that the "Establishment Clause of the First Amendment, properly understood, prohibits any such generalized 'endorsement' of prayer."[68]

All of the elements of the secular consensus are obviously under attack today from a variety of sources. Nevertheless, its legal assumption of separation is still common in law and political life. American Law professors, in particular, have been slow to change their understanding of the role of religion under the Constitution. Even those legal thinkers who argue for a larger role for religion in the public square do so hesitatingly, with an eye on the premises of the secular consensus. For example, in 1985 Columbia law professor and well-known legal theorist Kent Greenawalt wrote a law review article justifying reliance on religious reasoning in public policy. He wrote, "[W]hen issues cannot be settled on rational secular grounds, it is hard to see why legislators should give weight to nonreligious judgments of value and not to religious ones."[69] Putting the matter that way, however, suggests that religious views are a second-class ground of government policy, to be relied upon when there are not really rational grounds for action or inaction. Though not totally prohibited from public debate, religion sounds disfavored.

Michael J. Perry, one of the nation's leading authorities on the relationship of morality to law, suggested in a title of a law review article in 2000 that "Political Reliance on Religiously Grounded Morality is not Illegitimate in a Liberal Democracy."[70] But Perry felt he had to add in the article itself that "some religious believers—Christians—have good reason to be wary about relying on one kind of religiously grounded morality—biblically grounded morality—in deciding whether to oppose laws or other public policies that grant official recognition to same-sex unions."[71] This is to take away with one hand what the other hand had just granted. Professor Perry has also argued that resort to such religious decision-making does not violate the Establishment Clause, which was a change from Perry's earlier position. As is the case with Kent Greenawalt, while public religious argument is not rejected, it is only nervously endorsed.

Ronald Thieman, Professor of Theology and former dean of the Harvard Divinity School, wrote *Religion in Public Life* in 1996.[72] The book was intended to help open up space for religion in public life. But in the book, Professor Thieman could only bring himself to say that religious voices should be free to participate in political life insofar as they embrace the values of freedom, equality, and mutual respect. That sounds fair, of course, but it is a test we would never impose on any nonreligious political polemic, and further, it is one that many nonreligious political participants would have a hard time satisfying.

Finally, Noah Feldman's important new book on Church and State—*Divided by God*—which aims to endorse the use of religious language in the public square, characterizes as a "reasonable concern" the secular fear that "Christians might organize against non-Christians, or religious people might marginalize the nonreligious."[73]

But this is just another example of holding religious people to a higher standard than everyone else. Republicans organize against Democrats. Democrats marginalize Republicans. That is the way politics works.

Feldman adds:

> If I assert in public debate that God, speaking through the *Bible*, has instructed me to oppose abortion or capital punishment, then perhaps there will be nothing the other side can say to me to change my mind.[74]

Again, this argument unfairly attributes a general problem uniquely to religion. It is just difficult to change the minds of people. It is not true that religion particularly interferes with democratic debate.

In these examples, friends of religion in the public square unintentionally participate in second-class treatment of religion in American political life. These authors, though sympathetic to religion, reflect the assumptions of the secular consensus. The fact that that these assumptions are embraced by the friends of religion just shows how secular legal academia has been.

The final support for the secular consensus, one more foundational than the others, and less often expressly articulated, was the supposed superiority of reason and rationality over the nonrational, over the emotional, and over matters of faith and spirituality. A recent example of the supposed hostility of science to religion is the book, *Breaking the Spell* by Daniel Dennett.[75] Dennett tries to undermine religion—Freeman Dyson in reviewing the book describes Dennett's view of religion as a "load of superfluous mental baggage which we should be glad to discard"—by showing that it is a "natural phenomenon" that should be subject to scientific study. Religion is just a natural thing that people do. Of course no one is stopping Dennett from studying religion. But his approach to religion makes as much sense as claiming that food cannot be a source of meaning for human life because it is natural for all people to eat.

This superiority of a limited type of reason can be asserted by the secular even in the face of the acknowledged burdens of our society, which purports to be organized around just such rationality. Thus in 2005, Francis Fukuyama in the *New York Times Book Review* section, criticized Max Weber's famous portrayal of modernity as an "iron cage" in the following words: "One must wonder whether it was not Weber's nostalgia for spiritual authenticity—what one might term his Nietzscheanism—that was misplaced, and whether living in the iron cage of modern rationalism is such a terrible thing after all."[76]

This is a remarkable statement by Fukuyama. He is claiming that even if we do actually live in an iron cage, our cage is at least a rational and secular one and is, therefore, to be preferred to whatever Weber was yearning for. Fukuyama attributes Naziism and Communism to religion because they "were based on passionate commitments to ultimately irrational beliefs."[77] Considering the seriousness of blaming religion for those calamities, it must follow that, for Fukuyama, anything would be better than to be subject to religion and religious authority.

Fukuyama is plainly wrong to attribute these totalitarianisms to religion. Communism was largely a product of Marx's enlightenment thinking, rather than religious thinking. Fukuyama should have been taking some secular blame for the crimes of Marxism. The only religious aspect to Marx's thinking was his dedication to a better world—his Messianism. But messianic hopes are not confined to religious people. Certainly Marx himself would have denied that his thinking was grounded in the irrational. He thought his thinking was scientific and so did his followers.

Nazism, unlike Communism, can be thought of as antimodern. But Naziism was still not a religious movement. The Nazis persecuted religious believers. And even if it is justly said that the churches should have done more to oppose Hitler, believing Christians were in no sense a mainstay of the regime. It would make more sense for Fukuyama to blame the industrialists in Germany and, by extension, capitalism, for the rise of Nazism, rather than religion.

Fukuyama's premise that religion is irrationalism is earnestly resisted in Pope Benedict XVI's book, *Truth and Tolerance*, mentioned earlier. Pope Benedict argues that not only is biblically based religion, and much other religion as well, not irrational, but that our religions are grounded in the claim that they are true. And they make these claims of truth with the knowledge that the reliability of their truth claims must be subject to demonstration. Religion is not empirical science and does not verify matters the same way that science does. But religion is, nevertheless, a form of knowing. Religion is not primarily about feeling or ethics. Thus, in its final assumption—that religion is irrational—the secular consensus is challenged, as it is elsewhere. Indeed, as we see in the next chapter, the secular consensus is increasingly on the defensive today in American public life.

CHAPTER 3

Cracks in the Foundations of the American Secular Consensus

The secular consensus is collapsing today. Historically, the secular story is just not unfolding. Religion is not disappearing, either in America or elsewhere. Politically, the secular consensus cannot counter, nor account for, religious voters speaking and voting out of religious commitments and attaining thereby a great deal of political power. The secular consensus is collapsing in law, as accepted constitutional doctrines are weakened or rejected and the Court allows the separation of Church and State to become blurred. The secular consensus is also collapsing as a confident worldview. There is no longer the past assurance that clear thinking modern people reject religion. And, finally, and most fundamentally, the secular consensus is collapsing in terms of democratic acceptance. In the election of 2004, the American people chose religion as a basis of public life. That is why we now have religious democracy in America.

Of course many Americans, millions in fact, are still committed to the tenets of the secular consensus. But even among this group, the old confidence is waning. Even here, it is clear that a secular way of public life has ended, and something new is beginning. The battle for a true separation between Church and State has been lost.

The condition of the secular consensus today is reminiscent of an earlier deep change in American public life. The state of the secular consensus is remarkably similar to the eve of what is known as the Constitutional Revolution of 1937. At that moment, a combination of constitutional doctrines, primarily due process limits on state economic legislation and restrictions on Congress's Commerce power were blocking the public desire for dramatic action to combat the effects of the Depression. Prior to 1937, Supreme Court decision-making had been based upon a national private property and economic liberty consensus. That conservative approach led to a series of decisions throughout the early twentieth century that limited the power of Congress to regulate the national economy and also limited the powers of state legislatures to regulate local economic activity. The period in which these due process decisions inhibited state regulation became known as the Lochner era, in reference to the 1905 case of *Lochner v. New York*,[78] in which the Supreme Court held unconstitutional New York's sixty-hour/week and ten-hour/day limitations on employment in a bakery.

These lines of cases were transformed in a judicial instant in 1937, in a pair of cases decided only weeks apart. First, the Court upheld a state minimum wage law in *West Coast Hotel Co. v. Parrish*,[79] in the course of which the Court overruled several of its earlier due process cases. Then, two weeks later, the Court upheld Congress's power to impose federal labor law on large-scale manufacturers in *NLRB v. Jones & Laughlin Steel Corp.*[80]

A pattern similar to the Constitutional Revolution of 1937 and its aftermath may be emerging now with regard to the secular consensus. As in the period before 1937, there has been growing popular and theoretical dissatisfaction with the Supreme Court's basic orientation. Then, it was dissatisfaction with an economic theory. During the last thirty-five years, it has been dissatisfaction with the theory of the separation of religion and public life. A majority of Americans, including people who were not particularly religious, began to oppose the commitment of the Supreme Court to making our democracy secular.

Just as the private property/economic liberty consensus of the early twentieth century had not been a product of only judicial decisions, so too the secular consensus had been a generalized cultural phenomenon since World War II. In both instances, though, the country as a whole began to move in a direction different from that of the Court. For a long time, and in the face of growing popular opposition, the Court maintained its view that government must practice religious neutrality and must reflect secular purposes. But with the election of President George W. Bush in 2000, the Court's decisions began to change. Now that President Bush has been reelected, in large part running against judicial resistance to an expanded role for religion in American public life, we might expect a radical reformulation of constitutional doctrine from the Court. Later personnel changes would then symbolize and finalize these likely changes. In the spring of 2005, Chief Justice William Rehnquist died and Justice Sandra Day O'Connor retired from the Court. Because of his advanced age, Justice John Paul Stevens may also be expected to leave the Court fairly soon. On a closely divided Court, these changes would be expected to alter the outcome of cases in the realm of Church and State as well as other areas.

How have we reached this point at which we seem to be teetering on the brink of a major change in the constitutional relationship of religion and public life? How did the secular consensus lose its dominant position?

The major historical assumption of the secular consensus is that the United States would become less religious as it became wealthier and better educated. Though the secularization thesis has been criticized, it probably reflected the view of most postwar sociologists.

However, despite rising income, the United States has not become less religious since World War II. Nor has there been much, if any, correlation between rising levels of education and decreased religious commitment. Buffalo Law Professor Rebecca French summarized the American religious context in 2003: "Church membership is up over the past century, attendance and belief in God have remained stable, religious contributions have stayed at their 1955 level and the rate of belief and activity has generally increased with education."[81]

Poll numbers admittedly fluctuate, depending on the survey. A CNN poll in 2002, for example, found that between 1939 and 2002, church membership was down but church attendance was up.[82] Overall, though, there has been no noticeable drop in recent years in how many people go to church, believe in God, or say that God is important to them.

What is even more significant in a political sense is not whether there is decline, but the magnitude of the level of remaining support for religion in America. Belief in God in a *Newsweek* poll in 2000 was reported at 94 percent.[83] That level of belief is so high that even if there were some erosion in it, a political party identified as pro-God would always have an enormous electoral advantage, especially if the opposing party were viewed as anti-God.

An attempt can be made to explain away and minimize the apparent resistance of religion to the pressures of modernity in the United States. Perhaps religious commitment is just talk. Many people say they go to Church, for example; but do they? More people get divorced, gamble, and have premarital sex in America today than prior to World War II. These are not behaviors usually associated with religious commitment. Does this mean that religious belief has in fact waned in some sense, even if polls seem to suggest the contrary? Maybe polls, or even measuring conduct such as church attendance, are not the proper ways to evaluate religion in America.

Furthermore, most people would probably agree that American culture, as a whole, is coarser than it had been earlier in the twentieth century. Ariel Levy's new book, *Female Chauvinist Pigs*[84] and Pamela Paul's new book, *How Pornography is Transforming Our Lives, Our Relationships and Our Families*,[85] document how widespread, and how damaging, pornographic female images of sexuality have become in American culture in recent years. American culture does not seem to reflect religious values. And certainly, the culture reflects religious values to less of an extent than it did in 1950, even granting the enormous decrease in racial and gender oppression, and other forms of bigotry, in recent years. Where is the social effect of religion?

These are reasonable objections to the idea that America continues to be a religious society. But these objections address the kind of religious resurgence that is occurring in America rather than whether there is one. In part, the new energy in religious movements in America comes from opposition to just these cultural changes. And it may well be that church-going Christians and other religiously involved people participate in the same sinful activities that their neighbors engage in. Religious Americans may gamble, drink, get divorced, and read dirty books. That does not make them secular.

The resurgence of religion, against the expectations of the secularization thesis, can also be marked by the terms in which religious arguments are made in political debate. Religious political arguments in the American public square are increasingly made in unapologetically religious terms rather than by what is called the "cut flower" approach, covering the roots of religious concerns with purely secular language.

Sometimes religious argument is difficult to distinguish from any other kind of argument because there may be no clear delineation between religious concerns and nonreligious concerns in a particular policy dispute. But in other contexts, religious concerns are evident. For example, in the continuing debate about stem cell research, both sides talk about valuing human life. The foundation of that language is in religious values. Indeed, that kind of language came into the public square from the pro-life movement.

In a more obvious example of the resurgence of religious language in the public square, the invocation of God in public debate is now commonplace. Indeed such invocations can be quite embarrassing, like the willingness of people to attribute Hurricane Katrina to any number of human sins that God was aiming to punish.

The increasing presence of religious language in the public square predated the 2000 and 2004 presidential elections. President Clinton invoked God regularly in his speeches. Here is what Melissa A. Dalziel found in a 1999 review of Clinton's rhetoric: "In 35 of the 49 speeches posted on the website which President Clinton delivered from 1993–1998, Clinton closes his address with a 'God bless' of some sort. In eight of the fourteen speeches in which he does not close with 'God bless,' there are references to God in the speech, either explicitly or through references to the *Bible*. That leaves only 6 of 49 speeches in which there is absolutely no reference to God. Three of those six addresses were given in foreign countries. Therefore, the President of the United States has recognized a Judeo-Christian God in 94% of his recent speeches to the American people."[86]

The Naked Public Square seems to be fully clothed in religious garb. Despite all expectations, religion is publicly vibrant. The secularization thesis has proven false in America.

The political assumption behind the secular consensus was that religion cannot properly serve as a ground for public action. To give a religious reason as an argument for policy—for example, to say that "prostitution is condemned in the *Bible* and therefore should be illegal"—would be "anticonstitutional," as Michael Berg put it in 1995.[87] Berg admitted that such a religious argument is constitutionally protected, but, at the same time, he asserted that such an argument "offends constitutional values." At about the same time, the book *The Godless Constitution* by Isaac Kramnick and R. Laurence Moore[88] was similarly arguing that asking people for votes on the basis of God's will violates at least the spirit of the First Amendment and the prohibition of religious tests for office in Article VI.

It is a sign of just how far and fast the secular consensus has faded that arguments like these already sound dated only ten years later. It is quite obvious now that religious talk in the public square is accepted. The people who oppose this phenomenon either keep quiet or have no influence. Their dream of a secular public square now seems quaint.

An illustration of the new religious situation, in which religious justifications for government action are routinely offered, appeared in a *Los Angeles Times* article in August, 2005. The reporter, Stephanie Simon, described a dozen congressional aides who had gathered every Monday for the prior six months in the House speaker's private dining room. These aides were being taught by "conservative college professors," "televangelists," and "devout members of Congress," to "mine the *Bible*" for God's teachings on a variety of policy debates. The article describes these meetings as "the vanguard of a bold effort by evangelical conservatives to mold a new generation of leaders who will answer not to voters, but to God."[89]

Aside from the unfairness of this description—the students are not being taught to take power by force and therefore they will in fact answer to the voters rather than just to God—the article does show that people are quite free now to advocate policies on the basis of God's will. Barry Lynn, executive director of Americans United for Separation of Church and State, was quoted objecting to these meetings on the ground that, in America, "we are not to turn the Holy Scriptures of any group into public policy."[90]

What does someone like Lynn want? Unless democracy is to be repealed, voters, and therefore politicians, must be free to advocate policies on whatever basis the voters decide. Some voters favor a ban on gay marriage and on abortion because they think this is God's will. Maybe Lynn believes that such motivations are illegitimate. But after 2004, such motivations are plainly common in politics. Whatever the Establishment Clause forbids, the founders of our constitutional democracy did not ban reliance on religious reasons for public policy. In terms simply of policy prescriptions, a Christian Democratic Party in the European sense—one that would promote public policy in accord with the Christian tradition— would not be an affront to America's founding. Certainly it would not be an affront to democracy.

In any event, I do not mean to argue that case here. It is enough to note that the Evangelical movement is proceeding with its political efforts. Any observer of the American scene is aware that the secular consensus reflected by Lynn's comment lacks the authority to control, combat, or even really influence such matters in American political life.

A related assumption of the secular consensus is that religion should be regarded as a private matter, one that primarily concerns a person's personal relationship with God, rather than something that influences the outcomes of policy debates. Jeffrey Hart, emeritus Professor of English at Dartmouth College, wrote in 2005 that "Jesus teaches little or nothing about politics. His focus is inward, to the purity of the soul."[91]

The view that religion is inward rather than public is not the position of secularists alone. Until the rebirth of evangelical political involvement, this was the view of many notable religious leaders, as well. In 1965, for example, Jerry Falwell criticized Protestant ministers for their involvement in the civil rights movement on just this basis—that they were failing to win souls for Christ in their hurry to change society's laws.

This attitude toward religion—that it is a private orientation—is certainly not the dominant understanding of religion in America today. On the political right, a whole religious agenda is being pursued, from abortion, to gay marriage, to abstinence-only forms of sex education. Perhaps more surprising, similar religious efforts are now spilling over to the left side of the political spectrum. Jim Wallis's book—*God's Politics*—for example, argues strongly for what would be considered left-wing public policies on the basis of Wallis's understanding of the Christian tradition.[92] Wallis calls those who think religion should be restricted to a private sphere, "secular fundamentalists." Wallis begins from the point of view that religion matters in American policy debate today and argues for his own understanding of the direction in which religious influence should be moving America. A number of nascent religious/environmental movements are also springing up. And, of course, the model for these recent progressive religious movements is the Reverend Martin Luther King, Jr.

Not only is this idea of private religion not followed today, but it is also not a convincing reading of the *Torah*—the Jewish term for the *Old Testament*—or the *Gospel*. The *Torah*'s central story is about God's victory over Egyptian slavery. Slavery is a social, political, and economic matter. There is nothing inward about it. In terms of the *Gospel*, while Jesus did not confront Rome directly, he did confront the Jewish religious and political authorities, and was executed by Rome. This means, at the very least, that he was seen as a political threat by someone. Jesus was not executed because he purified souls.

The legal assumption of the secular consensus was that the Constitution ordained liberal, secular government. Supreme Court decisions were an important foundation of that legal assumption. In recent years, however, judicial support for the separation of Church and State has lessened. That case law is presented in Chapter 7. Here, I just want to glance at the Court's decisions to show that they are no longer a reliable pillar of the secular consensus.

Admittedly, the Court's movement has not been unidirectional. There have been recent cases in which the Court has allowed the government to disfavor religion. In the two most important such cases, the Court abandoned the protections of the Free Exercise Clause for religious believers in *Employment Division v. Smith*[93] in 1990 and the Court refused to overturn Washington State's exclusion of theology study from its State grant program in *Locke v. Davey*[94] in 2004.

In *Smith*, a drug rehabilitation organization fired two workers who had ingested peyote for religious purposes as part of religious worship at the Native American Church. There was not any dispute in the opinion about the sincerity of this religious use of the drug. In a majority opinion departing from the Court's prior holdings, Justice Scalia held that practitioners of religion can never claim a constitutional exemption from a generally applicable law, such as a general prohibition on drug use.

The *Smith* decision proved very unpopular, both among the public and Congress. Congress tried to overturn the *Smith* decision by passing, with large bipartisan majorities, the Religious Freedom Restoration Act of 1993. In 1997, in *City of Boerne v. Flores*,[95] the Court held the statute unconstitutional as a violation of the separation-of-powers.

Smith certainly was in some sense antireligious, as suggested by the presence of Justice Stevens as a member of the five-vote majority. So, if religion is enjoying such popularity today, why hasn't *Smith* sparked more opposition? Why, for example, are Supreme Court nominees not asked about overturning it during Senate hearings?

Probably the reason that *Smith* is not more of a focal point in public discourse is that the decision only has an effect when direct political action fails to protect religious believers. Not only was Oregon free, despite *Smith*, to grant a religious exemption from prosecution under its peyote law, it did so in 1991. Exemption can be granted under any generally applicable law that interferes with religious belief. So the fact that *Smith* remains the law without much obvious opposition may have more to do with its intermittent application than with the role of religion in American life.

This same potential recourse to the political system probably explains the continuing viability of *Locke v. Davey*. Very few states disfavor religion in the way Washington does and the voters there can change the program, although they need to amend the State Constitution to do so. Nevertheless, *Locke* was decided by a strong 7–2 vote, in the teeth of precedent protecting religion from formal discrimination. So, the Supreme Court cannot be said to have granted religion a completely protected status in its recent decisions.

On the other hand, where government wishes to benefit religion, the Court has been quite receptive to arguments that such benefits do not violate the Establishment Clause. For example, the Court in recent years has allowed more government aid to religious schools. The Court issued broad decisions in 1997 and 2000 that overruled several precedents that had constricted the aid government could give to religious schools. In the most important recent government aid to religion case, *Zelman v. Simmons Harris*,[96] in 2002, the Court approved educational vouchers that can be used at religious schools, and in so doing, probably ushered in a new era of indirect government aid to religion.

Outside the aid to religion cases, the Court has held repeatedly that government must offer resources to religious groups on a nondiscriminatory basis and that doing so is not a violation of the Establishment Clause. Given the pervasiveness of religion in American life, these decisions ensure a presence for religion in government institutions.

Perhaps the most important cases in terms of the Court's role as champion of the secular consensus are cases concerning the use of religious language and symbolism by the government. When the Court dismissed the challenge to the words "under God" in the Pledge of Allegiance because of a lack of standing by the plaintiff, in 2004, the Court sidestepped an opportunity to clarify whether the new judicial willingness to allow government-religious institutional interaction will also apply to symbolic religious expression cases. But the Court will undoubtedly uphold the Pledge of Allegiance when there is a proper case.

The Court did split in the *Ten Commandments* cases in 2005, upholding a display on the Texas capital grounds in *Van Orden v. Perry*,[97] while in *McCreary v. ACLU*,[98] the Court struck down such displays in Kentucky courthouses. Each case was decided 5–4, indicating a very close split on the Court that will depend for its resolution on the votes of Chief Justice John Roberts and Justice Samuel Alito. We cannot be certain of the Court's future trend. But right now the Court is not reinvigorating Establishment Clause limits on what government can do. The Court has at least lost its position as guarantor of the secular consensus. It is not clear anymore that government must be neutral as to religion.

The secular consensus also assumed that reason, in the form of science and instrumental rationality, would come to dominate over religion. Therefore, it was also significant to the undermining of the secular consensus that important cultural and intellectual figures were seen to be taking religion seriously. As John Roberts—not the Chief Justice—wrote in *Radical Philosophy* in 2003: "If the 'turn to ethics' has shaped much recent continental philosophy, the 'turn to religion' has not been far behind."[99] The most important such event in intellectual terms was Jacque Derrida's famed turn to religion in the period prior to his death. That turn was not without ambiguity of course. John Caputo's book about this subject—*The Prayers and Tears of Jacques Derrida*[100]—was aptly subtitled *Religion without Religion*. Nevertheless, at the very least, Derrida reintroduced into Western intellectual life the centrality and inevitability of the religious question. The impact of Derrida's thinking can be seen in the reaction of the American critic—certainly not religious himself—Stanley Fish. Fish wrote in 2005, "When Jacques Derrida died I was called by a reporter who wanted to know what would succeed high theory and the triumvirate of race, gender, and class as the center of intellectual energy in the academy. I answered like a shot: religion."[101]

Popular culture has also not left religion behind. There is a yearning for religion in quite unexpected places in our culture today. One example of this is the alternative music singer Anthony. Anthony has been described as "androgynous" and he does push gender barriers. In no sense is he traditionally religious. Yet his song, "Hope There's Someone," which was released on his second album, in 2005, contained this lyric: "Hope there's someone/Who'll take care of me/When I die; will I go?/Hope there's someone/Who'll set my heart free . . ." Could the human yearning for God be set forth any better? I've read that Anthony used to sing while dressed up as God at the Pyramid Club in New York City in the 1990s. That sounds pretty religious although, to be fair, he also would dress as Charles Manson. Anthony's references to God and religious imagery express something that cannot be approached in purely secular vocabulary. That continuing gap between the secular and the sacred defines the limit of secular thinking.

In American legal circles—a much more insular world, but one that influences American political life—there has also been a modest turn to religion in recent years. For one thing, although they dabbled in postmodern nihilism, American legal thinkers were frightened by its implications. So, Yale Law Professor Arthur Leff wrote in 1979 in a well-known law review article that without "supernatural grounding" everything with respect to right and wrong is "up for grabs."[102] He concluded with a poem about the necessity of resisting evil all the same but then could not resist the cynic/postmodern relativist's question, "Sez who?" Leff ended the poem with a plea, "God help us."[103] Samuel Calhoun, law professor at Washington and Lee University, has recently returned to Leff and concludes, I think rightly, that Leff was not "serious" in this last call, and that Leff was not seriously seeking God.[104] But the call can be serious whether the author meant it to be or not. In any event, Leff shows that religion is needed even if Leff assumes that religion is impossible. This conclusion is not consistent with the assumptions of the secular consensus. The secular consensus never imagined that the defeat of religion would turn out to be a tragedy.

The mirror image of Leff, at Yale and elsewhere in the American legal landscape, was the consistent use of religious history, language, and metaphor by admired liberal law professor Robert Cover. Cover wrote widely about religious themes or religiolegal themes and was at home using classic Jewish sources. Cover was part of a renaissance among Jewish academics in law and related disciplines that attempted to connect Jewish sources to American legal and political issues. A massive illustration of this movement is the four-volume work, *The Jewish Political Tradition*, the first volume of which appeared in 2000.[105]

Christian thought in American law is undergoing a similar, limited, resurgence. The resurgence is limited because it is not happening on the left. Despite the example of the religious foundations of the civil rights movement, there is not a significant, left-wing Christian revival in American law. Perhaps the reasons for the lack of a Christian Left in law are the apparent biblical opposition to abortion and gay rights. Whatever the reason, the powerful witness of William Stringfellow, a Christian activist lawyer in Harlem in the 1960s, has not left much of an imprint in American law today.

Outside the traditional left, however, there is growth in Christian lawyering. The influence of Stanley Hauerwas, the creation of new religious law schools, the growing religious lawyering movement, and various law and religion organizations, bespeak religion taken much more seriously today than it was thirty years ago.

More broadly, the collapse of the secular consensus seems to reflect a broad popular decision that religion is needed in public life. The future will probably show that the fundamental reason the secular consensus collapsed was that it did not "take" in a democratic sense. This idea of democratic "taking" or support is how Richard John Neuhaus described the national reaction to *Dred Scott* in 1856.[106] In that case, the Court overturned the Missouri Compromise in a tragic attempt to resolve the national slavery issue. Neuhaus writes of Dred Scott: "That decision did not 'take' democratically; it did not resolve but only exacerbated the issue it intended to settle."[107]

In this organic sense, the secular consensus was unable to convince the American people that the role of religion in public life should be severely restricted. Indeed, the real problem for the secular consensus was that religion was never as unpopular among the American people as it was among a relatively small but influential portion of the population. We can see in the fallout of the 2004 presidential election that, at least for now, whoever controls the religious high ground in American public life will tend to dominate politically.

What is the meaning of this democratic rejection of the secular consensus? It was not merely a political failure, to be remedied by more effective public relations. The Democratic Party and its supporters are not just an attractive candidate or two away from reinstituting the cultural dominance of the secular consensus. The collapse is permanent and its meaning complex. It turns out there is a necessary religious element embedded in American democracy that the secular consensus overlooked. That necessary element could not ultimately be suppressed.

CHAPTER 4

Religious Elements in American Constitutional Democracy

Why did the secular consensus fall apart? Part of the reason the secular consensus failed was that religion and constitutional democracy are not as easily separated as the secular consensus assumed. Of course, if that is the case, secularists should be willing to look to religion as foundational to democracy.

Obviously, views differ widely today about the proper relationship between religion and democracy. With apologies for compressing the thought of the following authors, it is possible to construct a kind of continuum of the centrality of religion in political life across American legal and political thinking. At one point on the American continuum, people like Kathleen Sullivan seek to ban religion from the public square. According to this perspective, all of our public debates would be cast in secular terms. Another view, a little less hostile to religion, is reflected by Robert Audi's book, *Religious Commitment and Secular Reason*.[108] Audi argues that religious and secular morality can be integrated, but that in a religiously pluralistic context like ours, secular rationale must be offered in justification of at least coercive legislation. Paul Salamanca offered a more sympathetic position in regard to religion at a symposium in 2003,[109] in which he suggested that all religions—he was comparing Islam today in America with Roman Catholicism in an earlier period—have illiberal tendencies, since they all insist on a particular vision of the good life. Yet American liberal democracy can live with all of them. Religion and politics can also be thoroughly mixed. Marci Hamilton, for example, criticizes the view that religion is distinct from politics and links the theologies of the founding generation to the governing structure of the Constitution.

(This is a view of religion from Hamilton more benign than her recent diatribe against the conduct of churches in the book *God vs. the Gavel*).[110] In a view somewhat hostile to secularism, Paul Campos argues that Rawlsian public reason is empty and incapable of encountering other forms of understanding—forms that could be called religious.[111] Thus, according to Campos, liberal thinking ends up as "secular fundamentalism," which is also the term used by Jim Wallis. Finally, in this brief list, there are arguments like those of Franklin Gamwell in his 2000 book, *Democracy on Purpose: Justice and the Reality of God*,[112] in which Gamwell argues that moral and political principles demand a divine purpose. There would be no place in this understanding for purely secular political life.

As we move along this continuum, secular thinking is thrown increasingly into question and the religious foundations of political life are embraced. The best description of the failure of the secular consensus in our time is Marci Hamilton's suggestion that one cannot readily separate political from religious commitments. In a 2004 article, Hamilton criticized the "false notion that religion is distinct from politics."[113] Of course, it is a fundamental axiom of the secular consensus that religion and politics can be kept apart—and should be. But if that premise is mistaken, then the assertion that religion and politics should be kept apart is irrelevant. One cannot be bound to do that which cannot be done.

To illustrate the connection of politics and religion, we can look at major themes in American political life that look like forms of religious commitment. Given these "religious" themes, the instability of the secular consensus probably was inevitable. The problem is not, as secularists suppose, that religious people are using the political system to attain religious ends. Rather, American political life may be expressing religious themes inherently, even apart from any attempt at religious indoctrination. If that is the case, the goal of separation between Church and State could never have been attained.

It can be argued that political and moral commitments that look religious can still be grounded in secular rather than religious foundations. Even if that is so, however, it is no support for the secular consensus. Our major political commitments, even if they can be derived outside any religion, were not so derived originally, but came to us from the Jewish and Christian traditions. The religious origins of these themes do not disappear simply because religion and democracy later diverged. Nor is the further development of these themes unaffected by their religious origins.

These points are illustrated with some examples.

SELF-EVIDENT TRUTH

Aside from the content of truth proclaimed in the Declaration of Independence, the nature of the claim of truth itself is a core American political commitment. The Declaration of Independence states famously: "We hold these Truths to be self-evident." But secularism in certain forms challenges the very notion of Truth.

This epistemological skepticism is common in American academic thought. It can be considered a part of secular life, although not that many secular voters actually share this perspective. Certainly an absolute challenge to Truth could have no place in American political life. No politician in America could credibly stand up and say, "There is no Truth."

Our religions are committed to announcing the truth of human existence. This is so even of a nontheistic tradition like Buddhism. It is even more clearly the case in the classic monotheist traditions, such as Judaism, Christianity, and Islam. Jesus said in the *Gospel of John* that we will know the truth and the truth will make us free.[114] The *Old Testament, Deuteronomy* 32, describes God as follows: "He is the Rock, his work is perfect; for all his ways are justice; a God of truth and without iniquity, just and right is he."[115]

These religious claims do not have a direct relationship to politics. As Pope Benedict XVI has written, "The one single correct political option does not exist."[116] Truth in political life must always be relative in a sense.

Nevertheless, there were for the framers—and for Pope Benedict too, of course—certain truths that endure and are not relative, even in political discourse. In the Declaration of Independence, some of these foundational truths are set forth.

Not only is the notion of Truth grounded in religion, but its self-evident quality is as well. This "self-evident" quality of truth is but a reprise of The Letter of Paul to the Romans, 2:15: "They show that what the law requires is written on their hearts . . ." The prophet Jeremiah foresees the new covenant that will be written "upon their hearts."[117]

Self-evident truth was the American political beginning point. Thus, America was grounded in religious thinking at the start. It does not necessarily follow that these thoughts are religious thoughts as such; or that a secular society could not share these commitments. Nevertheless, since these commitments were religious at origin, the attempt to separate religion from politics could not be absolute, as the secular consensus would have it.

ALL HUMAN BEINGS ARE CREATED EQUAL

This concept of human equality is the first substantive content given in the Declaration of Independence to the category of self-evident Truth: "We hold these truths to be self-evident, that all men are created equal."

The equality of all human beings, if self-evident, was certainly denied in American history. In the period prior to the Civil War, Senator John C. Calhoun denied that this assertion was true, let alone that it was self-evident. Calhoun stated on the floor of Congress in 1848 that there was "not a word of truth"[118] in the Declaration's claim that all men are created equal. Other supporters of slavery were equally firm in dismissing this basic principle.

The equality principle is foundational to democracy, which treats each citizen as formally equal in political life. The equality principle is now written in the constitutional text, as the Equal Protection Clause of the Fourteenth Amendment. That Amendment, which was not passed until the Civil War settled this matter on the battlefield, prohibits any State from denying to any person in its jurisdiction the "equal protection of the laws." Constitutional democracy is impossible without this principle.

The equality principle roots in the *Old Testament* creation story, in Genesis 1:27: "So God created man in his own image, in the image of God he created him; male and female he created them." All humans are created in the image of God; thus all humans are in principle equal.

Of course we failed as a society to realize the full implications of the equality of all. We Americans practiced racial slavery and oppressed native people. But Genesis declared equality, despite the nineteenth century efforts of Southern apologists for slavery to enlist the *Bible* as support. The nature of biblical equality with regard to women needs particularly to be remembered. Despite its traditional rendering in male dominant language, the *Bible* does not presume that the male, rather than the female, is the image of God. The last part of the verse, stating "male and female he created them" was interpreted by some of the rabbis to mean that the original human form was hermaphroditic. For some Christian thinkers, the text implies that the marital union is the image of God.

I am not suggesting that belief in the equality of humankind requires belief in the *Bible*. Certainly this principle can be understood from other starting points. But Western democracy did learn this principle from the *Bible*. Equality is as religious a principle as is "God created the heavens and the Earth" in Genesis 1:1. Insofar as equality is a principle necessary for democracy, a strict separation between democracy and religion is bound to be unstable.

THE SINFUL NATURE OF HUMANKIND

Although this is not always acknowledged, the concept of sinful humankind is not a Christian concept as opposed to a different *Old Testament* view. Genesis 6:5 describes God's view of human nature prior to the flood: "The Lord saw that the wickedness of man was great in the earth, and that every imagination of the thoughts of his heart was only evil continually." This understanding does not change throughout the *Old* and *New Testaments*.

The framers were familiar with the biblical understanding of human sinfulness. According to Daniel L. Dreisbach, this is the bedrock of the constitutional commitment to checks and balances. Dreisbach summarizes this relationship as follows: "The framers, convinced of man's fallen nature (and of the concept of original sin), eschewed pure majority rule; enshrined individual liberties; and devised a system of civil government committed to the diffusion and separation of powers, checks and balances, and limited, enumerated, and strictly delegated powers only."[119]

Perhaps the fullest statement of the framers' view of the link between the constitutional system and the nature of man is contained in Federalist No. 51:

> It may be a reflection on human nature that such devices should be necessary to control the abuses of government. But what is government itself but the greatest of all reflections on human nature? If men were angels, no government would be necessary. If angels were to govern men, neither external nor internal controls on government would be necessary. In framing a government, which is to be administered by men over men, the great difficulty lies in this: You must first enable the government to control the governed; and in the next place, oblige it to control itself. A dependence on the people is no doubt the primary control on the government; but experience has taught mankind the necessity of auxiliary precautions.

As Madison's reference in Federalist 51 to mankind's "experience" shows, the framers did not look to the *Bible* alone or even in detail for a framework of government. The framers had other models, including of course, their political history on this continent. Nevertheless, the starting point of the Constitution—its political anthropology so to speak—is biblical. As Hanah Arendt observed in *On Revolution*, even though the substance of the American Constitution is Roman in origin, its model of authority is "Hebrew in origin and represented by the divine Commandments of the Decalogue."[120] Indeed Federalist No. 51 sounds just like the famous aphorism by Reinhold Niebuhr: "Man's capacity for justice makes democracy possible; but man's inclination to injustice makes democracy necessary." This link between religious and political thought restates the difficulty, if not impossibility, of pulling them apart.

The view that humans are prone to corruption is as accepted in this culture as is the commitment that all humans are created equal. In the instance of equality, one might say that our fundamental law teaches, indeed requires, this commitment. In the case of sinfulness, however, how does one explain this general agreement? Why should Americans feel that checks and balances are a necessary limitation on government power? The French Revolution, for example, did not proceed from this principle.

Americans have learned about human nature from the *Bible*, either directly or from our societal atmosphere, which itself derives originally from the *Bible*.

Democracy must operate from some sort of understanding of human nature. Our democracy is not rooted in the expectation of human perfectibility, but rather in a biblical realism about man's potential. Richard Neuhaus described the nature of our democracy as follows in *The Naked Public Square*: "Democratic discourse, as Reinhold Niebuhr tirelessly insisted, depends not so much upon our agreement about righteousness as upon our agreement about sin—our own sin, and thus our own fallibility, as well as the sin and fallibility of others. Democratic discourse requires that no party fashion itself as the moral majority in order to imply that others belong to an immoral minority."[121] The anthropology of American democracy is biblical.

The implication of understanding American democracy this way is that this biblical borrowing ties our democracy to a religious understanding of reality. If that is the case, the secular consensus could not account for the American experiment.

"THE WORLD WAS MADE FOR MAN"

This quote is from Daniel Quinn's book, *Ishmael*[122]—Quinn's famous fable about a gorilla who achieves self-consciousness and teaches a student about the alienation humans experienced, and continue to experience, in agricultural-industrial civilization. Yet, the sentiment that the world is made for humans goes well beyond Quinn. That the world is made for man is the foundation not only for American constitutional law, but also for our entire political/economic/social life. Americans and other Westerners are anthropocentric. This is why, when we debate drilling for oil in the Arctic National Wildlife Refuge, we ask whether our economic need for oil outweighs our aesthetic concerns about keeping the wilderness pure for our grandchildren to see and enjoy. We do not ask about the rights of nature.

Sometimes Americans do talk about "protecting the environment." For most of us, however, the natural world has no claim to an existence independent of humans. Protecting the environment means keeping environmental harms from affecting humans, either physically or psychologically. There are some deep environmentalists for whom the natural world is not a resource for humans, but they are a small minority of the American people. Deep environmentalists do not have much democratic influence.

Like equality and human sinfulness, our culture originally learned this lesson of the centrality of the human from the *Bible*. In Genesis 1:28, God says to the male and the female, "Be fruitful and multiply, and fill the earth and subdue it; and have dominion over the fish of the sea and over the birds of the air and over every living thing that moves upon the earth." In other words, nature counts for very little compared to the value of human beings. In addition, the suggestion of "subduing" the earth implies that there is something hostile between humans and "unimproved" nature. Unfortunately, we are finding out that this biblically inspired relationship to nature is very destructive, both for nature and for humans.

The important implication of the religious source of our relationship to the environment is that secularism now also believes that the world was made for man, even though secular thought presumably lacks any understanding of why it thinks so. According to secularism, there is no creator to have given the world to humans as our resource. Without such a justification, it is apparently just tyranny on the part of humans to go on taking from the world and using it without attributing to the world any independent status and protection. Secularism goes on using the world in this way, but without secular justification.

Only a very few voices in American law have called for independent standing for the natural world. C. D. Stone did, in 1974, in a classic book entitled, *Should Trees Have Standing?*[123] Another such voice was the naturalist, Justice William O. Douglas. Nevertheless, even Douglas wrote of standing for nature from man's point of view: "Contemporary public concern for protecting nature's equilibrium should lead to the conferral of standing upon environmental objects to sue for their own preservation."[124] It is very difficult for this culture to sustain any independent concern for nature.

In Daniel Quinn's book, the gorilla teacher tries to help the secularly oriented student to see the power and depth of the cultural assumption that the world was made for man and to see as well how this originally religious understanding has now become a secular/cultural one. It is hard for the student to see this assumption about man and nature as an assumption, because it is so well accepted in the culture as to appear self-evident.

The following exchange from the book shows how religious and secular understandings here are mixed:

"Look, the world wasn't made for jellyfish, was it?"

***

No.
Of course not. The world was made for man
That's right.
Everyone in your culture knows that don't they? Even atheists who swear there is no god know the world was made for man.

***

Think of the consequences of taking that as your premise: If the world was made for you, *then what?*

Okay, I see what you mean. I think. If the world was made for us, then it *belongs* to us and we can do what we damn well please with it."[125]

According to Quinn, humans have been doing what they damn well please with the world for 10,000 years, with consequences we are now beginning to understand and fear. In this exchange, the student sees that atheists too know this originally religious teaching about man and nature, even though they do not believe in God and are not religious.

THE UNITED STATES AS THE LIGHT TO THE WORLD

In a law review article in 2001, James Gordon explained the religious sense of American exceptionalism that motivated Justice John M. Harlan, the elder, in Harlan's nineteenth century constitutionalism:

Civic religion involved the belief that Providence had chosen the United States to be a Christian example to the world, and it promoted confidence in, and love of, all things American. If the United States was not yet perfect, it was working toward perfection under the guidance of Providence. Through the United States, God's plan for humankind was unfolding. In short, Harlan still believed with his Calvinist forebears that America was a city on a hill, intended to be a light to the world.[126]

By using the term "civic religion," Gordon nicely bridges the gap between Christianity per se, that is, the use of Christian imagery in a national context in the nineteenth century, and the more secular use of religious terms that comes later in American political discourse.

Of course, the original biblical people who, like the Americans, were to be a blessing to the world were the Hebrew people, as promised by God to Abram (Abraham) in Genesis 12:2–3:

I will make of you a great nation, and I will bless you, and make your name great, so that you will be a blessing. I will bless those who bless you, and him who curses you, I will curse; and by you all the families of the earth shall be blessed.

Professor Gordon is describing a political and national interpretation of this notion of chosenness, which remains religious, even specifically Judeo-Christian. In Harlan's interpretation, the American system is regarded as the same sort of gift from God to the people of the world as the Hebrew people were.

By the time we get to President George W. Bush's Second Inaugural Address in 2005, the imagery of American chosenness has changed a little, but the message is similar: "So it is the policy of the United States to seek and support the growth of democratic movements and institutions in every nation and culture, with the ultimate goal of ending tyranny in our world ..." and "[a]dvancing these ideals is the mission that created our nation."[127]

It is not unusual for American Presidents to describe American policy as inspired by God. Michael Maddigan wrote in 1993 that "Public acknowledgment of the existence of God has been part of American civil religion from the beginning. Every President has mentioned God in his inaugural address, although none has used sectarian references."[128]

In President Bush's Second Inaugural Address, God seems an absent presence, perhaps directing affairs, perhaps not:

> We go forward with complete confidence in the eventual triumph of freedom. Not because history runs on the wheels of inevitability; it is human choices that move events. Not because we consider ourselves a chosen nation; God moves and chooses as He wills. We have confidence because freedom is the permanent hope of mankind, the hunger in dark places, the longing of the soul. When our Founders declared a new order of the ages; when soldiers died in wave upon wave for a union based on liberty; when citizens marched in peaceful outrage under the banner 'Freedom Now'—they were acting on an ancient hope that is meant to be fulfilled. History has an ebb and flow of justice, but history also has a visible direction, set by liberty and the Author of Liberty.[129]

President Bush's stated theology here is surprising. He does not claim that God is necessarily on America's side in the struggle for freedom. President Bush sounds like Lincoln in President Lincoln's Second Inaugural Address. Both assert that we do not know what God's choices in history are. The difference between them is that Lincoln suggested that we could not be sure whose side God was on between the North and the South. God may be punishing both sides. Thus, Lincoln might have suggested that, though we could not understand it, God could be on the side of the Islamic radicals opposing our policies. It is a little hard to imagine President Bush saying such a thing.

Although uncertain in his choices, God is present in President Bush's Second Inaugural Address. There is unmistakably something beyond us and our own wishes that America encounters in our historical mission. This American belief in an American mission, just as American beliefs in truth, equality, constitutional government, and human use of the world, cannot be understood without regard to religion and religious meaning.

Robert Bellah's well-known chapter nine, "Civil Religion," in his 1970 book, *Beyond Belief*,[130] applied Rousseau's term "civil religion" to American public political rhetoric. Looking back at chapter nine from the vantage point of today, it is surprising just how genuinely and traditionally religious Bellah's understanding of American civil religion was. This is precisely where some later commentators, like Steven Epstein, differ from Bellah, even though they use the term American civil religion. Epstein argues that American civil religion is secular in content, however religious its trappings might seem.[131]

Bellah did not regard references to God on public occasions as secular, or cynical, or meaningless. Expanding a talk he first gave in 1966, Bellah argued that these religious references—he used President Kennedy's inaugural address as his model for civil religion—are understood to mean that man is not the measure of all norms. References to God suggest that even though our political system is based on majority rule:

> [T]he will of the people is not itself the criterion of right and wrong. There is a higher criterion in terms of which this will can be judged; it is possible that the people may be wrong.

This description of American civil religion is genuinely religious, even orthodox. It is not merely vaguely spiritual. Bellah acknowledged this and indeed worried about it. He asked whether America could have an agnostic President. He was asking in effect whether the language of our civil religion is not too religious for such a political event. Bellah's asking that question as early as 1966—a time that Neuhaus would have said was close to the pinnacle of secularism in America—suggests that the whole notion of the naked public square, and the concomitant assumptions of the secular consensus, were never solidly embedded in American political life.

All of the above examples of the religious foundations of important themes in American public life, examples that could be multiplied, suggest part of the reason why no secular consensus could have endured in America. The secular consensus aimed at beginning anew, without the domination of religious modes of understanding reality, especially political reality. To be secular means to have starting points that are independent of religious language and worldview. If, instead, our democracy always depended on principles borrowed from religion, so that one could not say with confidence whether these principles are religious or secular, then the secular consensus had already failed. The subsequent loss of popular support for secularism, though noticeable as the political collapse of the secular consensus, was not that significant. In a sense there never was and never could have been a secular consensus in America in the first place. All we actually had during our most secular period was a ban on certain religious behaviors in certain public settings, like public schools.

We never had a separation of Church and State. We never had a government neutral about religion. Government could not be neutral about the commitments discussed above.

But is this recognition just something unique about America? Americans regard European public life as much more secular than ours. Though this view may no longer be as accurate as Americans have assumed—Europe is subject to some of the same changes that have occurred in American political life—it is nevertheless true that European politics are still basically secular. So the attainment of some form of secularism in politics cannot be impossible. Yet, the American experience suggests that there is something deep in political life that at least lends itself to religious expression. It may be that political life cannot be secular in a fundamental sense.

CHAPTER 5

Religious Elements in Deep Political Life

The secular consensus attempted to promote a political life untainted by religious motivations and worldview. This goal assumed that there is an intelligible distinction between religious reasons for doing things and political reasons—or more generally, that there is a reliable distinction between religion and political life. From the point of view of the secular consensus, it would have to be possible to distinguish religious acts and motives from political acts and motives. The two realms would have to be genuinely separate for secular political life to be possible.

If that is so, if the religious and the political realms are really separable, then the mixing of religious and political life in America, which figured so prominently in the presidential election of 2004, manifests something particular about this society rather than anything general about the relationship of religion and politics. Even if America has not practiced secular democracy, in principle secular democracy could exist elsewhere.

But the assumption that religion and politics are genuinely and fundamentally separate is not necessarily true. The distinction between the political and the religious aspects of life may be ambiguous. Or, there may be no such distinction at all.

The boundary between political and religious life can be viewed in three ways: historically, theologically, and philosophically. Historically, many of the concepts used in politics are basically borrowed from older religious traditions; theologically, politics sometimes serves as the realm where different conceptions of God, and the relation between God and man, are worked out; philosophically, political theory and religious insights can be seen as addressing the same basic questions of human life.

The point of the secular consensus was never to oppose religion as such. The secular consensus did not mean to compete with religion, but to set religion aside. Religion was to be limited to private life, and perhaps eventually to disappear altogether. Politics was not viewed either as an alternative religion or an alternative to religion. So, if deep connections between religion and political life inherently exist, the secular consensus could not have succeeded in its goal of creating a religion-free, political zone.

In terms of historical connections, Carl Schmitt, the controversial German legal and political philosopher, wrote in his book, *Political Theology* that "[a]ll significant concepts of the modern theory of the state are secularized theological concepts . . ."[132] The example he gives to illustrate this historical movement is that "the omnipotent God became the omnipotent lawgiver."

As a simple matter of history, Schmitt's observation would be hard to contest. We can see, for example, the historical roots of political office visually in such things as the elevation and robes of our judges, which are reminiscent of priests. Our President comes to us from the Biblical King (through European monarchical practice). Consent of the governed first occurs at Sinai, when the people proclaim in Exodus 19:8, "All that the Lord has spoken we will do." Many of our political phrases have their source in religious tradition. The first to use the phrase "wall of separation" between Church and State, for example, was not the arguably secular Thomas Jefferson but the unarguably religious Roger Williams, who, in 1644, referred to the "wall of separation between the Garden of the Church and the Wilderness of the World."[133]

These sorts of purely historical connections might be thought to lack any essential continuity of content, however. Judges are not today thought of as priests, nor do we even remember that religious origin. The wall of separation may have had a different meaning for Jefferson than it did for Williams and it is undoubtedly from Jefferson that the modern meaning of the wall of separation comes.

But in other contexts, the historical connections still live. The practice of separation of Church and State did not emerge out of Enlightenment skepticism of, or hostility to, religion. Separation emerged in Puritan New England. John Witte describes the practice this way:

In the New England communities where their views prevailed, the Puritans adopted a variety of safeguards to ensure the basic separation of the institutions of church and state. Church officials were prohibited from holding political office, serving on juries, interfering in governmental affairs, endorsing political candidates, or censuring the official conduct of a statesman. Political officials, in turn, were prohibited from holding ministerial office, interfering in internal ecclesiastical government, performing sacerdotal functions of clergy, or censuring the official conduct of a cleric. To permit any such officiousness on the part of church or state officials, Governor John Winthrop averred, "Would confound[] those Jurisdictions, which Christ hath made distinct."[134]

This separation did not mean for the Puritans a disconnection between Church and State. The two realms were linked and both were understood to be subject to God. Nor did separation imply equal political rights for religious dissidents.

The Puritan separation of Church and State is clearly ours. The Puritan separation of Church and State explains, for example, the established American understanding—an understanding that otherwise seems rather odd given freedom of speech—that ministers, priests, and rabbis are not to endorse political candidates from the pulpit. This limit on ecclesiastical involvement is a continuing consequence of the historical experience of separation by the Puritans.

Freedom of religion also has a clearly religious history. Martin Luther had a radical understanding of freedom from Church authority, premised on the free power of God: "Furthermore, I acknowledge no fixed rules for the interpretation of the Word of God, since the Word of God, which teaches freedom in all other matters, must not be bound."[135] In America, Elisha Williams, rector of Yale University similarly preached in 1744 that the right of conscience in the affairs of religion roots in the power of Christ: *"That a Christian is to receive his Christianity from Christ alone."*[136]

These religious concepts, which could easily be multiplied, were, as Schmitt stated, secularized in a vast movement beginning in the seventeenth century. The secular consensus would say that the process of secularization so changed these religious ideas that their religious derivation is unimportant. George Sabine stated a view like this in his *History of Political Theory* in 1950, which described the seventeenth century as the period in which theology was gradually freed from political theory and classical, rather than biblical, sources became the norm for political thinking. These classical sources themselves were modernized in accordance with naturalism and rationalism. This trend, in combination with the advances in mathematics and science, led to a new view of political life. According to Professor Sabine:

> Social phenomena generally, and political relationships in particular, began to be conceived as natural occurrences, open to study by observation and more especially by logical analysis and deduction, in which revelation or any other supernatural element had no important place.[137]

The secular consensus would suggest that religion was left behind in the intellectual history of the West. But looking more closely, Sabine is not describing secularism. He is describing the absence of revelation and supernaturalism in the proper study of the world. The reason that study can be limited in this way is that revelation and supernaturalism do not affect the world. That view can be understood as a change in theology. So, the movement to empirical political science in the seventeenth century might be understood not as secularization as such, but a movement from one religious viewpoint to another. The change that Sabine was describing was in a sense both a theological and a political change.

This is a theological understanding of political life. For Schmitt, political concepts were secularized theological statements not just historically—that is, not just in strict derivation—but because of their "systematic structure," a "systematic relationship between jurisprudence and theology." This describes theology as a second mode of understanding the relationship of politics and religion.

The political change to what could be considered modernism was a change in the understanding of God and God's relationship to the world. As Schmitt wrote, "The idea of the modern constitutional state triumphed together with deism, a theology, and metaphysics that banished the miracle from the world."[138] The natural sciences could go forward because an understanding developed that God expressed himself through the regular processes of the laws of the natural world. Political thought could go forward in the same way because the sovereign—the substitute for God—did not intervene in a valid legal order. The rule of law in the modern liberal state did not admit of such intervention, in a sense from without. It was not that God did not exist. It was not that sovereignty did not exist. Rather, the rationalism of the Enlightenment conceived of systems proceeding only naturally, with internal logic. Schmitt saw this in the political, as in the physical realm.

Schmitt was no liberal himself. He was criticizing this political theology. But for our purposes, the point is to see the connection between theology and politics. In Schmitt's view, political understandings parallel theological ones.

The self-understanding of the American Constitutional system illustrates Schmitt's point. The Constitution is not an atheistic document, though it makes no reference to God. God was not expected to intervene in the regular processes of governance, except, perhaps, in the vague background concept of Providence. This deistic view, in Schmitt's terms, can be demonstrated by the actual reference to God in the Declaration of Independence. The "separate and equal station" to which the colonists felt entitled was vouchsafed to them by the "Laws of Nature and of Nature's God." This God is the God of deism. Clearly, this is not the God of revelation and miracle but the God behind the laws of Nature. In other words, it is not at all anticipated by the colonists that God will intervene in history in order to free them. They are entitled to independence by virtue of general principles.

The laws of nature do not admit of exceptions. Such an exception would be a miracle. The parallel that Schmitt was drawing in the political realm, which he called "the exception," was to some sort of emergency power that would suspend constitutional government. Schmitt famously wrote, "Sovereign is he who decides on the exception." Liberal constitutionalism has as much conceptual difficulty with this political exception as it does with miracles in the physical universe.

The theology of liberal American constitutionalism became clear at the moment of crisis sparked by 9/11. This crisis led to the first serious judicial discussion of a true emergency power since the *Steel Seizure* case during the Korean War.[139] The context was the government claim of a right to hold American citizens extrajudicially.

In *Hamdi v. Rumsfeld*[140] the government was holding indefinitely an American citizen captured on the battlefield in Afghanistan. The government argued that Hamdi was an enemy combatant, and that, as such, the government had the right to hold him without charge indefinitely. A four-Justice plurality opinion, written by Justice O'Connor, held that while the government did possess statutory authority to hold an enemy combatant, the prisoner nevertheless had the right to a hearing to challenge the assertion that in fact he was an enemy combatant. Justice David Souter's concurrence in which Justice Ruth Ginsburg joined, agreed that Hamdi had a right to a hearing and agreed that Congress could authorize such a detention. Justice Souter disagreed, however, that Congress had in fact statutorily authorized detention in this case. The statutory authorization for detention in this case was not a clear enough statement by Congress.

These six Justices suggested that even in an emergency, the rule of law applies. Thus, the writ of habeas corpus was held to authorize judicial oversight of an executive branch detention of an American citizen. Justice Scalia's opinion, joined by Justice Stevens, sharpened the question presented. Justice Scalia denied that the executive branch, or Congress either, could, as a general matter, authorize indefinite detention of an American citizen. Hamdi therefore had the right to be tried for a crime or released. The only way to hold an American citizen indefinitely, according to Justice Scalia, is by a formal suspension of the writ of habeas corpus by Congress, pursuant to Art. I, Section 9, of the Constitution. Thus, if Hamdi were to be held without trial, Scalia was calling on Congress to invoke, in effect, Schmitt's exception to constitutional government.

The rest of the Court let Justice Scalia's challenge go by without response. But Justice Clarence Thomas, also seeing the stakes in the case, criticized Justice Scalia's opinion for a willingness to countenance unconstitutional governance. The suspension of the writ of habeas corpus cannot be understood to change constitutional requirements and norms. Habeas corpus is merely a remedy. The suspension of the writ denies judicial review of government action, but suspension cannot validate government action that would otherwise be unconstitutional. In Schmitt's terms, Justice Thomas was denying that the exception exists.

The theological import of the Hamdi majority is that the world moves in its regular ways. Carl Schmitt would say that for the majority of the Justices, God does not intervene directly in the world.

The essentially theological nature of political theory is also clear in the writings of John Locke, perhaps the patron saint of the Constitution. Locke envisioned a government in which power would be exercised in the name of a consenting people. This was to lead to limited, as opposed to tyrannical, government. For Locke the purpose of the consent of the governed to limited government was to leave the citizen free to pursue his salvation. Reason was the mechanism through which the individual would find his way to God. It is true that the pursuit of salvation becomes the pursuit of happiness in the Declaration of Independence, but the structural relationships are the same, the political relations are the same, and the role of the individual is the same. Locke's salvation is Jefferson's happiness. I am not referring here to the substitution by Jefferson of happiness for Lockean "estate" (property), but rather the overall view by John Locke of the proper goal of human life. That framework reflects a theological commitment.

Even the theory of religious freedom practiced in America today has a theological content. The theology of freedom of religion concerns the nature of religious belief. The American assumption is not just that religious belief should not be coerced as a normative matter—though that is certainly our view—but that religious belief cannot be coerced as a religious matter. A forced assent to any religious proposition would not be valid. This is not just a political understanding but is a theological one. It assumes that the will of the divine for man is voluntary worship and acceptance.

The secular consensus tried to banish religious associations from these and other political notions. Schmitt's point is that this cannot be done. Political life, at least in the West, has its own theological basis.

The final form of religious-political interaction is the philosophical, which raises the question of the ends or goals of both religion and politics. In *Democracy and Political Theory*, Claude Lefort suggests that religious and political life might be competitors, or even partners, occupying the same social space: "[B]oth the political and the religious bring philosophical thought face-to-face with the symbolic, not in the sense in which the social sciences understand that term, but in the sense that, through their internal articulations, both the political and the religious govern access to the world."[141]

This is the deepest level at which the secular consensus might be thought inevitably to fail in its efforts to seal political life off from religious inquiry and commitment. Lefort describes the philosophical/political task—and the religious task—as the disclosure of Truth:

What philosophical thought strives to preserve is the experience of a difference which goes beyond differences of opinion ... the experience of a
difference which is not at the disposal of human beings, whose advent does
not take place *within* human history, and which cannot be abolished therein;
the experience of a difference which relates human beings to their humanity,
and which means that their humanity cannot be self-contained, that it cannot
set its own limits, and that it cannot absorb its origins and ends into those
limits. Every religion *states* in its own way that human society can only open
onto itself by being held in an opening it did not create. Philosophy says the
same thing, but religion said it first albeit in terms which philosophy cannot
accept.[142]

Lefort has something quite specific in mind in terms of what philosophy
cannot accept from religion. For Lefort, writing in the context of Christian
civilization, the difference between political philosophy and theology is
the nonacceptance by philosophy of the specifically Christian revelation
that "Jesus is the Son of God." Naturally, the exclusion of that Christian
claim alone cannot satisfy the goal of the secular consensus to separate
Church and State. The secular consensus attempts to do more than keep
that specifically Christian claim out of the public sphere.

Religion and philosophy, including deep political philosophy, ask similar and overlapping questions concerning human life. They both ask how
we should live. They both ask how we should live together as a community. There is no coherent way—other than purely arbitrary will—to
distinguish religious answers to those questions from secular ones.

If political life is understood in Lefort's terms, as a quest for the deepest
truths of the meaning of human life and as open to the transcendent, then
political life would seem to be inherently religious. Or, perhaps it would
be better to say that political and religious understandings are looking
at, and dealing with, the same reality. When President Bush asserts in his
Second Inaugural Address that history "has a visible direction," he should
not be accused of offending any secular sensibility. Marxists, who are certainly secular, believe the same thing. Nevertheless, even though most secularists assert the same truth, President Bush's assertion obviously is not
secular. It is an echo of what Walter Brueggemann, the great *Old Testament*
scholar, considers the core biblical understanding of God, in his book, *Theology of the Old Testament*:

The *Old Testament* insists that there is a moral shape to the public process
that curbs the raw exercise of power. It equally insists that there is a hidden cunning in the historical process that is capable of surprise, and that
prevents the absolutizing of any program or power.[143]

If we see things this way—that is, if we believe that history has a moral
shape—what would a truly secular democracy look like? The political arguments that Americans think of as secular, as opposed to religious, look

very different from this perspective. They look like internal "religious" disputes over the right understanding of the moral shape of history. Secularists object not to the idea that history has a moral shape, but to how this moral direction of history is said by religious people to be set. For President Bush, a religious man, the visible direction of history is "set by liberty and the Author of Liberty."[144] Secularists presumably believe it is set in some other way or sense. My point is that the commitment that history has a direction is a religious understanding, notwithstanding how one imagines this takes place.

The believer might say, for example, that God forbids abortion and gay marriage. The liberal nonbeliever would reject the word "God," of course, but more fundamentally would deny that the moral shape of history is against abortion and gay marriage. The nonbeliever would also reject, in principle, the claims by ministers, rabbis, and priests to have some special and reliable access to the moral shape of history. But the nonbeliever, in America at least, usually does not reject the claim that history has a moral shape. If that understanding of history is religious, then our political arguments appear to be religious disputes rather than disputes between religion and secularism.

Actually, the relationship between religious and political life is closer even than this example suggests. For what if President Bush had said the opposite in his Second Inaugural Address? What if he had said that history has no shape, but is always a recurrence of the same? Or, what if he had said that all human concerns are just passing vanities? I can find insights such as these in the *Bible*, as well as in many other religious traditions. In other words, the very subject matter of the meaning of human life is religious. It is not just particular proposed answers to such questions that can be viewed as religious.

The problem for the secular consensus is that politics often deals with fundamental issues of the meaning of human life. And certainly, eventually it always does. At some level these are religious concerns.

It would be arrogant to impose the word "religious" on persons who self-identify as atheists, humanists, or agnostics. There are important differences between loving and obeying God, on the one hand, and rejecting such comportments as meaningless. Believers and nonbelievers are not interchangeable. But, as far as American political life is concerned, those real differences between believers and nonbelievers are not at issue. No one in America is suggesting that the role of political office holders is actually to lead American worship of God. In our actual disputes, there is little difference between religious and political assumptions.

At least no one had suggested such a thing until the *Ten Commandments* cases. In his dissent in one of those cases, *McCreary County v. ACLU*, Justice Scalia, joined by Chief Justice Rehnquist and Justice Thomas, stated that he would uphold government religious expression, including presumably statements by political leaders, on the basis of "the interest of the over-whelming majority of religious believers in being able to give God thanks and supplication *as a people*, and with respect to our national endeavors." This language in *McCreary* seems to come close to envisioning the inau-guration of a President as a worship service. Now, America is not going to end up where Justice Scalia describes, nor is it likely that Justice Scalia really meant the full implications of what he wrote. Invocation of God at ceremonial occasions, no matter how sincere, is not truly religious wor-ship. But this is our direction.

Despite the close connection between politics and religion, Lefort does describe one kind of secular political orientation that he regards as an ex-ception. Lefort writes that "liberal thought" encourages us to regard belief in "the people" as "a sign of pure illusion," a "fiction" and regards "only individuals and coalitions of interests and opinions as real."[145] There is, in other words, in this political understanding no such thing as a common good. Lefort says that this "liberal thought," with its radical absence of community, "den[ies] the very notion of society."[146] All forms of politics are reduced to an instrumental grab for advantage. All shared meaning disappears.

Lefort may be accurately describing the thinking of some political theo-rists. Extreme secularists—someone, for example, like the economist and federal judge, Richard Posner—avoid religious questioning, or anything like it, by adopting a dismissive tone about any attempt to see deeper meaning in human life than a passing utilitarianism or materialism. But such radical individualism need not detain us. For if the separation of Church and State requires this kind of liberal thought, and thus ends up undermining political life itself, then that would be a critique of secular-ism, rather than secularism's goal. Most Americans who argue for limits on religion in public life are not aiming at pure individualism. They do not intend to abolish shared political meaning. Indeed, by restricting re-ligion, secularists aim to make room for political life. Secularists do not have the option of the sort of apolitical, radical individualism that Lefort is describing.

Even avowedly secular political thought, if it is really in touch with political life, sees a connection between political and religious meanings. John Rawls, for example, recognizes that religious, and other comprehen-sive frameworks, form the foundation of political orientation. Rawls wrote in 1997 that "[T]he roots of democratic citizens' allegiance to their political conceptions lie in their respective comprehensive doctrines, both religious and nonreligious."[147]

Yet even if it grants this much to religion, the secular consensus, which Rawls reflects, cannot bring itself to fully allow religion in public dis-course. Rawls added, as a caveat, that such comprehensive doctrines may only come into political debate when reasons for public action are given that "are not given solely by comprehensive doctrines . . ."[148] Thus, secularists, even when they have an inkling of these matters, still object when religious views come forward independently into politics.

But this concession by Rawls in 1997 has the flavor of making the best of a losing position. By 1997, the secular consensus had long-since peaked in terms of political influence. The new line drawn by Rawls with regard to religion in the public square, "thus far, but no farther," will not hold any better than did the old one.

This newer restriction by Rawls actually demonstrates Lefort's point. For Rawls is aware that often, if not always, government policy will be supportable by both "religious" and "secular" arguments. This shows, of course, how interconnected these realms are.

But, the new Rawlsean caveat has nothing to recommend it. It might be prudent for religious believers to add secular justifications to their religious arguments, but there is no reason that they have to. Such a suggestion is just one more assertion by secularists of their imagined right to police the language of the public square.

If there is any validity to the suggestion that religion and politics are closely related, the contested fault line between them would become visible where the distinction is most insisted on. That place in our political system has been constitutional law. If religion and politics are closely related, the job of separating them, which the secular consensus assigned to the Supreme Court, was an unsolvable dilemma. The separation of religion and politics failed in law for the same reasons that it failed as a persuasive political proposition generally. It failed because the distinctions needed for the separation cannot be made.

CHAPTER 6

The Separation of Church and State in Principle

People have different ideas about the meaning and desirability of a separation between Church and State. For example, Justice Scalia recently asserted that the Jews were safer in the United States than in Europe during World War II because of the strict separation of Church and State in Europe: "You will not hear the word 'God' cross the lips of a French premier or an Italian head of state," he said. "But that has never been the American way." "Did it turn out that, by reason of the separation of Church and State, the Jews were safer in Europe than they were in the United States of America? I don't think so."[149]

The response to Justice Scalia's statements was heated. Commentator Thom Hartman, argued that, far from separation, Hitler used the blending of Church and State to accomplish his goals.[150] Hartman referred to various aspects of the Third Reich, including the infamous photo of Catholic Priests giving the Nazi salute at a Catholic youth rally in the Berlin-Neukolln stadium in August 1933; the declaration by Pope Pius XII celebrating Hitler's birthday on April 20; the 1933 investiture of Bishop Ludwig Muller, the official Bishop of the 1000-Years-of-Peace Nazi Reich, and, most generally, the July 14, 1933, Decree concerning the Constitution, which merged the German Protestant Church into the Reich and gave the government the right to ordain priests. Hartman quoted the opening of the German Church's constitution: "At a time in which our German people are experiencing a great historical new era through the grace of God," the new German state church "federates into a solemn league all denominations that stem from the Reformation and stand equally legitimately side by side, and thereby bears witness to: 'One Body and One Spirit, One

Lord, One Faith, One Baptism, One God and Father of All of Us, who is Above All, and Through All, and In All.'"

The Scalia flap illustrates the divergence of meaning and support for the separation of Church and State. We do not always mean the same or similar things by the term separation and, of course, we do not agree in principle about whether separation is a good thing. What is suggested in this chapter is that the real dispute is not separation of Church and State, but separation of religion and political life. The latter separation is not actually possible.

The word "separation" and even the concept of separation—either of Church or religion—from the State and/or political life—is not actually in the text of the American Constitution. The phrase, "wall of separation" enters constitutional history late, borrowed from Thomas Jefferson. The Constitution speaks of religion in other ways.

The most significant religious aspect of the Constitution is its failure to mention God. This omission cannot be considered inadvertent or insignificant. The Constitution of Pennsylvania, for example, also a late eighteenth century document, mentions God in its Preamble: "We the people of the Commonwealth of Pennsylvania, grateful to Almighty God for the blessings of civil and religious liberty, and humbly invoking His guidance, do ordain and establish this Constitution." Conversely, the Federal Constitution opens with man on his own, so to speak: "We the People of the United States, in Order to form a more perfect Union, establish Justice, insure domestic Tranquility, provide for the common defense, promote the general Welfare, and secure the Blessings of Liberty to ourselves and our Posterity, do ordain and establish this Constitution for the United States of America."

The omission of God from the Constitution does not mean that the framers thought that God did not exist. They were not atheists. They did not, however, invoke God's guidance in their political endeavor. They did not treat God as active in the political realm.

A God who does not intervene in the world does lead to a form of separation of religion from the State. But it is a separation only insofar as God chooses not to intervene. This kind of separation is not something that man decides. It lies in the nature of God. Our disputes today about the separation of Church and State do not root there—in theological arguments over whether God intervenes in the world.

The original text of the Constitution—that is, before the addition of the Bill of Rights—did contain one reference to religion. This reference was the prohibition of religious tests for office in Article VI: "but no religious Test shall ever be required as a Qualification to any Office or public Trust under the United States."

There is some dispute about the original purpose of the ban on religious tests. The ban on religious discrimination was not limited to differences within Christianity, but was intended as well to allow Jews to serve in federal office. Part of the context out of which the prohibition on religious tests arose was an imploring letter from Jonas Phillips, a Philadelphia Jew, to the constitutional convention.[151] The ban was probably meant at least to allow any religious person to assume federal office.

The ban may even have been intended to allow atheists to serve in public office, since after the Revolutionary War, a number of states still had religious tests that proscribed atheists from public office. The federal religious test language may well have been meant to prohibit these sorts of religiously oriented restrictions on federal public service.

Whether or not the prohibition on religious tests was intended to protect atheists and agnostics, however, its focus did not lie there. The ban on religious tests was thought of primarily as a way of protecting religious diversity in government and political life in general. Edmund Randolph, for example, defended the federal religious test prohibition at the Virginia convention debating ratification by referring to the importance of such diversity: "I am a friend to a variety of sects, because they keep one another in order. [T]here are so many now in the United States that they will prevent the establishment of any one sect in prejudice to the rest, and will forever oppose all attempts to infringe religious liberty."[152]

Randolph's comment endorses only a certain kind of separation between Church and State. Clearly, he did fear the potential political power of religious organizations. But this was not a fear of the influence of religion itself. He thought that the vitality and presence of a variety of religions was both necessary, and perhaps sufficient, to protect religious liberty. Religious liberty was his goal. There is no sense here of promoting atheism or opposition to religion in government and political discourse.

The Bill of Rights, which was added to the original constitutional text, did contain further religious guarantees. The Bill of Rights guarantees were added because, although the framers did not think a specific listing of rights was needed in the Constitution, the ratifying conventions disagreed.

The religion guarantees in the Bill of Rights were more explicit than the indirect protection of liberty that the religious test prohibition provided. The First Amendment both prohibited the establishment of religion and provided for liberty in the exercise of religion, "Congress shall make no law respecting an establishment of religion, or prohibiting the free exercise thereof . . ."

The language of both the Establishment and Free Exercise Clauses omits any direct reference to something like a separation of Church and State. The prohibition against the establishment of religion was certainly directed as a historical matter against the establishment—that is, the official recognition and public tax support of—some particular Christian denomination. Such establishments had been common in colonial history and indeed several remained at the State level after the Revolutionary War. The prohibition against establishment was thought to protect the freedom of Christians—and other religious believers—to practice their own, different, and minority religious traditions without interference and without having to pay for the religious practices of others.

Defenders of strict separation of Church and State extend this reasoning and historical grounding to include religion itself, rather than just particular denominations, as within the ban on establishment. They argue their case from the First Amendment basically as follows. Just as free exercise of religion in choosing among religious traditions is protected by not establishing any one religion, so free exercise in choosing no religion, which is presumably also protected by the Free Exercise Clause, is protected by not allowing the government to establish religion itself. Thus, the Establishment and Free Exercise guarantees are interpreted to require nonreligious government.

Even within this framework, there are different meanings and emphases in strict separation of Church and State. On a formal and institutional level, the separation of Church and State can be accomplished by formal restrictions against mutual interference by Church and State officials. Thus, for example, barring religious officers from holding political office, as we have seen the Puritans practiced, promotes this sort of separation of Church and State.

The controversy over separation today, however, does not involve purely formal separation of that kind. There is no serious movement in America toward electing ministers and other religious leaders to public office. Even if there were, defenders of separation would admit that such religious participation cannot be banned consistently with the protections of the First Amendment.

The specific legal fights today over separation of Church and State overwhelmingly concern three areas: religious education for children in public schools; public support of private religious schools; and symbolic religious expression, either in public schools or in the public square generally. The first kind of case involves, for example, teaching intelligent design in the public schools. The second kind of case concerns matters like education vouchers. The third kind arises with actions like the placement of the Ten Commandments in public spaces.

We will return in the next chapter to review these disputes as matters of constitutional doctrine. Here we are asking about separation in principle. What is the point of separation of Church and State? What is the goal?

We must discount the particular applications of religion in political life in thinking about separation of Church and State. Obviously, for example, many religious voters oppose abortion. It sometimes follows from this fact that supporters of abortion wish to minimize the influence of religion in politics. They wish to do that to discomfort their political opponents.

That is not what I mean by the principle of the separation of Church and State.

Supporters of separation of Church and State are aiming at two desired ends of political life. First, they feel that our political life together should be a matter of human decision and, thus, of reason. Therefore, they oppose the authority of religion. Religion in public life is felt to substitute the authority of tradition or scripture—and the authority of the men and women who purport to speak for the traditions and for scripture—for the reasoned decision by individuals that political life should embody. Separation of Church and State thus is thought to protect human autonomy.

The second political goal of separation is a liberal State in the modern sense. The State must not choose a particular version of the good life and then attempt to impose that version on individuals. Politics must leave each individual free to select his own version of the good life. Religion, of course, is all about defining the proper end of human life. Thus, while religion in the life of an individual might be a proper path for that person, religious ends cannot be chosen by the government for everyone. Therefore, the separation of Church and State leaves each individual free to live out his or her own understanding of the good life. Each person is free to find that good in a religion or somewhere else. This is another form of human autonomy, which is believed to be protected by the separation of Church and State.

So, for someone like the political philosopher Ronald Dworkin, who endorses both these justifications, the separation of Church and State is necessary to promote human flourishing. None of us would be able to fully develop as human beings if the State were to embody and attempt to impose the authority of religion and the ends of religion.

But this all assumes that some sort of separation is possible in principle. Depending on just what is believed to be separated, that assumption is not necessarily reliable. The separation of Church and State in constitutional principle suffers from the same conceptual problem as does the attempt to separate religion and politics discussed in the last chapter.

We can see the conceptual problem by examining the thinking of the author of the most extreme formulation of the separation of Church and State in our constitutional tradition: Thomas Jefferson's metaphor of the "wall of separation" between Church and State. The metaphor of the wall of separation appeared in a letter by Thomas Jefferson to Nehemiah Dodge and Others, in the Committee of the Danbury Baptist Association in the State of Connecticut, in 1802. In the letter, Jefferson wrote the following:

> Believing with you that religion is a matter which lies solely between man and his God, that he owes account to none other for his faith or his worship, that the legislative powers of government reach actions only, and not opinions, I contemplate with sovereign reverence that act of the whole American

people which declared that their legislature should "make no law respecting an establishment of religion, or prohibiting the free exercise thereof," thus building a wall of separation between Church and State.

The language of the letter does not make Jefferson's meaning entirely clear. He clearly means in part that there should be no law requiring a particular religious practice—somewhat like the prohibition on religious tests for public office. He seems to imply, as well, that religion has nothing to do with the sorts of issues that political life decides upon. Religion is private, whereas government policy concerns "actions only." But if this was his view, he states it as description rather than as prescription. In other words, if Jefferson meant this, he was describing how religion actually works. I doubt Jefferson really believed this, for reasons I will indicate below. In any event, we Americans have certainly established that religion concerns public action. In fact, it is the intense involvement of religion in public issues that has brought the issue of separation of Church and State to the fore.

Jefferson's metaphor of the wall of separation has become an important concept in constitutional understanding. Ironically, considering the use to which the "wall" has since been put, this metaphor was first used by the Supreme Court to describe the reach of the Establishment Clause in a case upholding, rather than striking down, government aid to religious schools. The Court referred to Jefferson's language in *Everson v. Board of Education* in 1947.[153] The Court wrote: "In the words of Jefferson, the clause against establishment of religion by law was intended to erect 'a wall of separation between Church and State.'... The First Amendment has erected a wall between church and state. That wall must be kept high and impregnable. We could not approve the slightest breach. New Jersey has not breached it here." Jefferson's wall metaphor had earlier been cited in *Reynolds v. United States*[154] in 1878, but the issue in Reynolds, and the point for which Jefferson was quoted, was the interpretation of the Free Exercise Clause rather than the Establishment Clause. The use of the "wall" to limit the influence of religion in public life really begins with its citation in *Everson*.

There is a great deal of controversy today concerning whether Jefferson should be considered in interpreting the Establishment Clause, since he was not a framer of the original constitutional text, nor of the First Amendment. Furthermore, it has been argued that Jefferson's views on the subject of Church-State relations were not widely shared. Jefferson was on the secular side of the religious continuum of his time. He was known as a freethinker. Jefferson was even criticized during the election of 1800 for being an atheist. In addition, the criticism has been made that whatever "separation" was contemplated by the First Amendment owes as much or more to Roger Williams' belief that a wall of separation was needed to protect the churches against corruption than to any fear that the churches would dominate political life, assuming that this was Jefferson's fear.

Whether Jefferson's understanding of the relationship of Church and State accurately reflects the original intention and meaning of the Establishment and Free Exercise Clauses, or indeed whether Jefferson's understanding of Church and State can be easily stated, are not our concern here. We are considering whether the human autonomy that separation is thought to promote is possible. The important aspect of Jefferson's metaphor for us is that the wall of separation, whatever it is taken to mean today, did not mean for him a wall of separation between religion and political life and specifically not between God and public life. It was a wall of separation between *Church* and State only.

In making that claim, I am not referring to whether religion is needed to instruct the people in morality and is therefore necessary to a healthy republic. There is dispute about whether Jefferson viewed religion this way, though other figures in the founding generation certainly did. Rather, I am referring to the meaning of the God of history. A God of history is inherently political in any sense of that term. Jefferson believed in such a God.

To see this, consider Jefferson's famous words on the future of slavery contained in the Jefferson memorial in Washington, DC—words that every American schoolchild might once have known:

> Indeed, I tremble for my country when I reflect that God is just, that his justice cannot sleep forever. Commerce between master and slave is despotism. Nothing is more certainly written in the book of fate than these people are to be free.

Why would Jefferson tremble about the consequences of the injustice of slavery? Because, as Jefferson saw it, when liberty, which is the gift of God, is violated by a nation, the result is the wrath of God. Here is a fuller treatment of slavery from the *Notes on the State of Virginia*:

> And can the liberties of a nation be thought secure when we have removed their only firm basis, a conviction in the minds of the people that these liberties are of the gift of God? That they are not to be violated but with his wrath? Indeed I tremble for my country when I reflect that God is just: that his justice cannot sleep for ever: that considering numbers, nature and natural means only, a revolution of the wheel of fortune, an exchange of situation, is among possible events: that it may become probable by supernatural interference! The Almighty has no attribute which can take side with us in such a contest.[155]

This statement by Jefferson describes a moral shape of history. Obviously, however one describes the shape of history—whether as God,

Providence, Destiny, or Fate—it would be ridiculous to speak of a separation of these things from the State or from political life. The position of the United States, in Jefferson's view, in 1787, was much like that of the Pharoah in relation to the Hebrew slaves in the book of *Exodus*. These people—these slaves—were destined to be free. If the nation pursued a public policy to the contrary, civil catastrophe would result.

It does not matter in the end that the believer says that God demands freedom for the slave and that the nonbeliever says that justice demands freedom for the slave. Both the believer and the nonbeliever expect consequences of the direst kind from the perpetration of national injustice. Neither the politician, nor the citizen, can be indifferent to justice, or, if operative in history, to God's will. Human autonomy cannot mean indifference to history.

Was the destruction of slavery in America and around the world an accident? A mere contingency? Can we imagine humankind going back to slavery? Yes, pockets of something like slavery still exist. The slave trade in women for forced prostitution still exists. But these are isolated criminal activities. Nothing like the regime of slavery that humankind practiced for thousands of years exists today.

If the nature of reality is that the choices that men and women make are constrained, and, if, in the end, certain outcomes occur in history almost by necessity, and if those outcomes are morally irresistible as well, then the goal of a religion-free public life is impossible. If it can be said that freedom is written in the book of fate, then the *Bible* is to that extent at least a reliable guide to public affairs. How many in this culture sincerely deny that reality is like this?

This is not a matter of overall human progress. Humans invent new injustices all the time. But when they do so, these new injustices are also then subject to the judgment of history. We can call this judgment, as Jefferson does, the wrath of God. We can call it whatever we like. The point is, it is real. As Jefferson, the author of the metaphor, knew, the wall of separation has no possible application at this level.

This insight says little or nothing about the precise relationship of Church and State that might exist in America or elsewhere. There might be prayer in the public schools, or not. There might be government aid to private schools, or not. Money might carry the message, "In God We Trust," or not. Those matters are the subjects of constitutional doctrine, to which we will return in the next chapter. These doctrinal details are not essential to Jefferson's point about the wrath of God. All nations are subject to that wrath, depending on their conduct.

What then of human autonomy? In terms of the authority of human reason, Jefferson would deny that ecclesiastical authority has a monopoly on understanding the shape of history. A man like Jefferson, who, in *The Jefferson Bible*, essentially rewrote the *New Testament* accounts of Jesus to remove the taint of supernaturalism, would obviously not accede to the authority of Church officials in political life or even in religion.

Yet, even though human reason remains central, not all human reason is equal. For if history has a moral shape and if human reason misunderstands that shape, there are negative consequences. So, if humans have a right to make their own decisions, which of course they must if democracy is to mean anything, those decisions can be wrong. Human autonomy cannot mean that all decisions are equally valid. At least, it cannot mean that if history has a moral shape.

The other aspect of autonomy—that the State should not make decisions based upon a particular view of the good life—is now shown, in light of the moral shape of history, to represent an impossible goal. The issue of slavery, which so frightened Jefferson, and which was ultimately decided in blood, did not have a neutral aspect. The state could not be agnostic in this matter of the good life. Slavery was not a matter for individual decision alone. If a God of history concerned with justice existed, as Jefferson believed, slavery was a *collective* threat to the nation.

Slavery is not unique in this regard. If abortion is murder and if abortion is tolerated by public policy, the consequences might be just as grave. Where is the individual decision here? Is the decision of the woman to have an abortion an individual one? If the fetus is a human being, the decision is only individual in the sense that the decision to own a slave is individual. These are not individual, but social decisions. Neither decision could happen without supporting public policy. Isolated abortions might occur whatever the law, but Jefferson and the *Bible* are not primarily concerned with that kind of individual injustice.

This same relationship of the individual and social life obtains in regard to an unjust economic system. The *Bible* speaks on almost every page against the oppression of the poor by the wealthy and the powerful. God promises to hear their cries against injustice. Capitalism may very well turn out to be the new Egypt. If this is so, America will be punished for its economic decisions.

If Jefferson is right, not just about slavery but about the moral shape of history, the whole notion of the neutral State is incoherent. The separation of Church and State, whatever its manifestation, cannot change the moral shape of history.

But Jefferson might, of course, be wrong. In his famous Terry Lectures, published in 1934 under the title, *A Common Faith*,[156] John Dewey argued against the commitment that "justice is more than a moral ideal." Dewey specifically denied that justice is "embedded in the very make-up of the actually existent world." Dewey thought such a claim pernicious because "physical existence" would not "bear out the assertion." At that point—at the point of disappointment—men would abandon the fight for justice and convert their dreams into metaphysics. "For all endeavor for the better is moved by faith in what is possible, not by adherence to the actual."[157]

Dewey's objection is an odd one. Religious believers have not been indifferent to conditions in the world. The great reform movements in American history were generally the product of religious men and women. Dewey knew the social gospel. He knew this was so.

Dewey's example shows that support for the separation of religion from public life in its deepest sense would have to be premised on a very fundamental claim about the nature of reality. It would have to be the claim that history has no intrinsic meaning, nor truth. Without that commitment, separation at its deepest level is impossible.

Seeing separation of Church and State this way shows that a truly nonreligious public life has to have deep commitments of its own about the nature of reality. Such commitments are either religious in nature themselves, or are essentially antireligious. Either way, the confidence that religion can be left to the private sphere, while public decision-making goes on its own way unaffected, is plainly false.

Looking at the author of the wall of separation in this light is sufficient to reject the deeper implications of separation of Church and State. For either we agree with Jefferson, in which case we reject separation of religion from political life, or we disagree with Jefferson, in which case it ill behooves us to forbid a philosophy of history from public expression just because we disagree with it.

Of course, it follows that Jefferson himself must have rejected the separation of Church and State at its deepest level. Jefferson knew very well that political life and God's will in history could not be separated.

That conclusion, however, does not determine the outcome of specific constitutional cases. Even if we agree with Jefferson about history, we could well believe that politics and institutional religion must be kept strictly apart. Unlike the more fundamental version of separation, such an outcome would not be in principle impossible or improper. Apparently, however, separation in this more formal sense has not proven convincing to the American people. For even here, in the limited sphere of constitutional doctrine, the secular consensus is in retreat today.

CHAPTER 7

The Separation of Church and State in Constitutional Doctrine

Up to this point we have considered the comprehensive shape of the secular consensus. It has been suggested that there is no overall way to distinguish religion and politics. Nevertheless, it certainly is possible to assign different roles in public life to political and religious institutions and personnel. That division of roles is the well-known subject of constitutional separation of Church and State in the United States. Even if no separation is possible in principle, there still could be a strict separation in constitutional doctrine between religious language and life and certain forms of political language and life. As we shall see, the secular consensus is collapsing here as well, in the details of constitutional doctrine.

Constitutional disputes about establishment of religion can be grouped in roughly four categories: government aid to religious institutions; public invocation of God and religious themes; teaching religion in the public schools; and the role of religious organizations in public life and government. In all these fields, constitutional doctrine already has blurred the line of separation between Church and State or is one additional vote away from doing so. Given political realities, the additional Justices needed to restrict the prohibitions of the Establishment Clause are very likely to be appointed to the Court and perhaps already have been appointed. On July 1, 2005, Justice O'Connor announced her retirement. Her replacement, Justice Samuel Alito, is likely to take a more permissive view of mixing Church and State than she did. Chief Justice Rehnquist, who died on September 3, 2005, was a fairly reliable vote for limiting the restrictions of the Establishment Clause. His replacement, Chief Justice John

Roberts, is not expected to be more determined in this direction, but there is no indication that his will be more proseparation either. Justice Stevens is near the end of his tenure on the Court. With his departure, the last strict separationist of our time will leave the Court. Thus, religious democracy will probably lead to more expression of religion in the various forms of American public life.

This kind of judicial handicapping is never certain, of course. Justices who are expected to vote one way in an area sometimes change their minds, either right away or over time. But in the area of Church and State, such change is not likely. For one thing, there is no effective political opposition to the greater expression of religion in the public square. The Democrats may enjoy electoral success in 2006 and 2008, and may retake the Congress and the White House, but by and large, Democrats are not pushing the separation of Church and State. They are not running on a platform to take God out of the Pledge of Allegiance or even against school vouchers. Many Democrats are opposed to a constitutional amendment banning gay marriage, but this opposition is not presented as hostility to religion. For this reason, and because long-term cultural trends don't reverse overnight, the Senate is not likely, during the next few years, to reject Supreme Court nominees because they are too religious or even because they favor the mixing of Church and State. Nor is even a Democratic President likely to appoint a strict separationist to the Court. Further changes in Court membership, therefore, will probably move the Court even further in the direction of mixing Church and State.

On the other hand, there is a fifth arena of Church and State—the free exercise of religion. Here, the apparently anomalous case of *Employment Division v. Smith*[158] has narrowed the protection of the Free Exercise Clause for religious practices. *Smith* allows government to prohibit religious practices that violate generally applicable law, even when the banned religious practice is absolutely central to that religion. *Smith* appears to be a high point of achievement of the secular consensus, though that interpretation is not the only one possible, as we shall see below.

The position of the secular consensus on the above issues is as follows: that there should not be government aid to religious institutions; that neither God nor religion should be invoked on public occasions; that public schools should neither teach, nor encourage, religious practice; and that private religious groups and people should not be permitted to influence public policy in accordance with their religious beliefs. In terms of free exercise of religion, the secular consensus agrees with the holding in *Smith* that government interference with religious practices is constitutional unless the government action is actually aimed at interfering with religion. Judged by these commitments, a short summary of current law in these areas suggests that the secular consensus is fading jurisprudentially in America today.

AID TO RELIGIOUS INSTITUTIONS

The most significant recent aid-to-religious institutions case *is Zelman v. Simmons-Harris*,[159] which upheld the Cleveland school voucher program in a 5–4 vote. Chief Justice Rehnquist wrote the majority opinion, in which Justices O'Connor, Scalia, Anthony, Kennedy, and Thomas joined. Justices Stevens, Souter, Ginsburg, and Stephen Breyer dissented. The relevant aspect of the program is that it provided tuition aid directly to the families of students who attended participating private or public schools of their parents' choosing.

The Cleveland voucher program is a clear example of very substantial, though indirect, aid to religious schools. Though public schools were included in the law, only private schools actually participated in the program. Of these private schools, forty-six out of fifty-six had a religious affiliation. Even more dramatically, 96 percent of the 3,700 students receiving tuition assistance were enrolled in religiously affiliated schools.

Justice Souter's dissent convincingly demonstrated that the Cleveland voucher program was a boon to the Cleveland Catholic school system, which was the recipient of most of the money. According to the dissent, the cap of $2,500 on the amount of tuition that could be charged to low income students "ha[d] the effect of curtailing the participation of nonreligious schools . . ."[160] The result of the cap was that the Cleveland voucher system was "paying for practically the full amount of tuition for thousands of qualifying students" at private religious schools, thus "systematically underwriting religious practice and indoctrination."

The scale of the aid that went to religious schools in the Cleveland system was unprecedented in modern American history. But, for the Court majority, the amount of aid was irrelevant. Chief Justice Rehnquist's majority opinion upheld the Cleveland program because it was neutral: the money in the program went to religious schools only insofar as parents sent their children to religious schools. Since the government did not prevent participation in the voucher program by nonreligious schools, the actual religious outcome of parental choice was constitutionally irrelevant.

Although the majority in *Zelman* strongly emphasized parental choice, the majority's emphasis on neutrality and its disinterest in the amount of public money that religious schools received, suggests a broader rationale in the future. Substantial government provision of services and materials to private schools, including religiously affiliated schools, would seem likely to be the next acceptable step. Indeed, a plurality opinion of the Court in *Mitchell v. Helms*[161] anticipated *Zelman* by upholding government supply of "services, material and equipment" to private schools, including religious schools.

It might be objected that the narrow vote in *Zelman* shows that the Court could change course. That is possible, but unlikely. As Justice Souter noted in his dissent, the Court has been moving unmistakably in the direction of allowing government aid to religious schools under the Establishment Clause since 1968. Given the result of the 2004 election and the prospect of personnel changes on the Court, that trend is more likely to accelerate than reverse.

PUBLIC INVOCATION OF GOD AND RELIGION

While the doctrine of the Establishment Clause in the area of public invocation of God and religion is incoherent, the results are fairly clear. The results are simply that government is increasingly free to acknowledge religion, and even utilize religion, in government expression. Indeed, it could be argued that government now is often obligated to do so.

The Court has rather routinely accepted religious—often specifically Christian or Judeo-Christian—symbols, themes, and language in the public square, by asserting that these religious usages have, through historical legitimation or rote repetition, lost their specifically religious meaning. Thus, in *Marsh v. Chambers*,[162] the Court upheld the practice of prayer in the legislature for reasons of history. In *Lynch v. Donnelly*,[163] the Court upheld a crèche as part of a government-sponsored Christmas display, with Justice O'Connor's swing concurrence describing the many nonreligious, Santa-like aspects of the display. It was in her well-known *Lynch* concurrence that Justice O'Connor wrote of the permissible, nonreligious, use of religious language, to show confidence in the future and to solemnize public occasions:

> [G]overnment acknowledgments of religion serve, in the only ways reasonably possible in our culture, the legitimate secular purposes of solemnizing public occasions, expressing confidence in the future, and encouraging the recognition of what is worthy of appreciation in society.

Justice William Brennan, a critic of the mixing of Church and State, wrote similarly of religious language in his *Lynch* dissent:

> [T]hese references are uniquely suited to serve such wholly secular purposes as solemnizing public occasions, or inspiring commitment to meet some national challenge in a manner that simply could not be fully served in our culture if government were limited to purely nonreligious phrases.... The practices by which the government has long acknowledged religion are therefore probably necessary to serve certain secular functions, and that necessity, coupled with their long history, gives those practices an essentially secular meaning."

The Court's acceptance of religious imagery and its redefinition of this imagery as essentially nonreligious was both reaffirmed and undermined in *County of Allegheny v. ACLU*,[164] which disallowed a manger scene in the Allegheny County courthouse, but permitted a Menorah and a Christmas tree outside a nearby public building. The manger scene was just too identifiably religious.

In the *Allegheny County* case, Justice Kennedy criticized the tendency to call religious language secular. For him, this language and these images are religious, though they are still permissible under the Establishment Clause:

> I fail to see why prayer is the only way to convey these messages; appeals to patriotism, moments of silence, and any number of other approaches would be as effective, were the only purposes at issue the ones described by the *Lynch* concurrence. Nor is it clear to me why 'encouraging the recognition of what is worthy of appreciation in society' can be characterized as a purely secular purpose, if it can be achieved only through religious prayer. No doubt prayer is 'worthy of appreciation,' but that is most assuredly not because it is secular.

Is certain religious language really not religious? In *Elk Grove Unified School District v. Newdow*,[165] the case in which the Court dismissed the challenge to the Pledge of Allegiance without deciding the merits of the case, Justice O'Connor described her acceptance of official references to "God" as justified either by what she calls ceremonial deism or by "an extremely long and unambiguous history." But, as Justice Thomas noted in his concurrence in *Elk Grove*, "[I]t is difficult to see how [the pledge] does not entail an affirmation that God exists." Upholding the Pledge of Allegiance with the words "under God" in it, which the late Chief Justice Rehnquist stated he was ready to do, and which Justices O'Connor and Thomas have stated they are ready to do, and which Justices Kennedy and Scalia probably are ready to do, would allow the government to proclaim that we are a nation under God. Since Justice Alito and Chief Justice Roberts will probably agree with this, the Court seems to be on the verge of directly contradicting the secular consensus by upholding the Pledge.

The *Ten Commandments* cases split on the issue of the permissibility of public display of the Commandments, demonstrating the basic divisions in the Court. In *Van Orden v. Perry*,[166] the Court permitted a six-foot display on the state capital grounds in Texas, along with numerous other historical markers and monuments. In *McCreary County v. ACLU*,[167] the Court struck down the display of the Commandments on the walls of two courthouses. Essentially the lineup in the two cases was the same, with Chief Justice Rehnquist and Justices Scalia, Kennedy, and Thomas voting to uphold displays in both cases and Justices Stevens, O'Connor, Souter, and Ginsburg voting to prohibit displays in both cases. Justice Breyer provided the swing vote, upholding the Texas display as predominantly secular, whereas the legislative history in Kentucky demonstrated a "governmental effort substantially to promote religion."

The upshot of the two cases seems to be that government is free to include religious symbols in displays that emphasize their historical significance and include other, nonreligious symbols. Under this standard, there is very little limit on what a determined, and clever, government can do. Whatever this case law means, it does not reflect the beliefs of the secular consensus.

Even more uniformly pro-religion than the public expression cases have been Court decisions requiring nondiscrimination against private religious expression. From time to time lawsuits are brought against school districts for allegedly not allowing schoolchildren to read from *Bibles* during show and tell or on free time. One such case, *C.H. v. Oliva*,[168] brought then-Judge Alito to public notice for his strong dissent in a case in which a young student's poster of Jesus was removed and his story of biblical heroes was censored. The secular consensus would like to ban even private religious references from public school.

The Court has been clear in a number of cases since 1990 that where private speech is permitted in a public school, or University, or on public property, religious speech may not be discriminated against and that such nondiscrimination does not violate the Establishment Clause. This protection of private religious speech probably will have more effect in nurturing a religious tone in public life than anything else government does. The private attachment of the citizenry to religion will ensure that religion becomes a dominant theme in much of the public square in the future.

TEACHING RELIGION IN THE PUBLIC SCHOOLS

The central question for the future of religion and State in religious democracy is whether government may encourage religious belief, particularly in the public schools. The highest accomplishment of the secular consensus was that public schools could neither offer official prayers[169] nor conduct classroom reading of the *Bible*.[170] *Engel* and *Schempp* established the essential principle of the secular consensus: government could not encourage the citizenry, or at least not schoolchildren, to be religious—to believe in God as revealed in the *Bible* or to pray to God. Or, at least government could not do so directly. That is what government neutrality toward religion meant. In the words of Justice Hugo Black, government may not pass a law that "Aid[s] one religion, aid[s] all religions, or prefer[s] one religion over another." This core secular principle later became embedded in the first part of the *Lemon* test, that government action must have a "secular legislative purpose" in order to satisfy the Establishment Clause.

The difference between religious democracy and the secular consensus concerns most clearly this question of government encouragement of religious belief. The Court has never repudiated the principle from *Engel* and *Schempp* that the government may not encourage schoolchildren or anyone else to be religious. Although the government may accommodate religion, by making Christmas a national holiday, for example, the government may not encourage religious belief. In the words of Justice Robert Jackson, America must be "Free for irreligion."[171]

The late Chief Justice Rehnquist began his challenge to the secular consensus on this central point in 1985, in *Wallace v. Jaffree*,[172] which struck down an Alabama statute essentially adding the words "for . . . voluntary prayer" to an existing period of silence in public schools that had been "for meditation." The Court per Justice Stevens struck down this additional wording under the purpose prong of the *Lemon* test because the State "intended to characterize prayer as a favored practice," which it surely did. *Wallace* is a perfect example of the secular consensus in action.

Chief Justice Rehnquist's dissent argued that government could constitutionally treat prayer as a favored activity: "It would come as much of a shock to those who drafted the Bill of Rights as it will to a large number of thoughtful Americans today to learn that the Constitution . . . prohibits the Alabama Legislature from 'endorsing' prayer."

The current Court seems unlikely to formally abandon the principle that government may not favor religion over irreligion. Even assuming that Justice Alito and Chief Justice Roberts take an Establishment Clause position close to that of the late Chief Justice Rehnquist, there may still be five votes on the Court to prohibit direct government encouragement of religion, depending on the factual context. The principle of government nonpreference for religion was strongly reaffirmed in *Santa Fe Independent School District v. Doe*,[173] in which Justices O'Connor and Kennedy joined with Justices Souter, Ginsburg and Breyer, in an opinion by Justice Stevens, to strike down a school district policy of student election to decide whether and what invocation to deliver at varsity football games. The majority opinion revitalized the "unconstitutional purpose" prong of the *Lemon* test and held that the district policy was "implemented with the purpose of endorsing school prayer."

The *Ten Commandments* cases in general, although not involving public schools, sharpened and clarified the Court's division on the principle of government neutrality in favoring religion over nonreligion. In *McCreary*, Justice Souter's five-Justice majority reaffirmed that the "touchstone" for our analysis is the principle that the "First Amendment mandates governmental neutrality between . . . religion and nonreligion."[174] Justice Scalia's dissent, joined by Chief Justice Rehnquist and Justice Thomas,[175] not only disputed the neutrality principle in general, calling the principle that government cannot favor religion over irreligion "demonstrably false," but specified that when government does favor religion, "the Establishment Clause permits . . . disregard of polytheists and believers in unconcerned deities, just as it permits the disregard of devout atheists. . . . Historical practices . . . demonstrate that there is a distance between the acknowledgment of a single Creator and the establishment of a religion."[176] The three-Justice dissent thus endorsed government encouragement of traditional monotheism.

Despite the majority in *Santa Fe* and portions of the *Ten Commandments* cases, the view of Justice Scalia's dissent in *McCreary* is likely to prevail in the long run. In part, this is simply because of changes in personnel on the Court. In his *McCreary County* dissent, Justice Scalia, joined by chief Justice Rehnquist, and Justices Kennedy and Thomas, wrote that "Even an *exclusive* [government] purpose to foster or assist religious practice is not necessarily invalidating." It seems likely that Chief Justice Roberts and Justice Alito will form a new majority around this ambiguous but potentially expansive language. In addition, the current doctrine actually leaves religious minorities more at the mercy of religious majority practice than would a frank acknowledgement of government endorsement of, and preference for, religion.

Ever since *Lee v. Weisman* invalidated the attempt by a school district to give guidelines for high school graduation invocation prayers that would reflect a kind of nonsectarian, "civic religion,"[177] the practice has emerged for students who are selected to speak for other than religious reasons, themselves to pray to God at their high school graduation ceremonies. I attended a public high school graduation in 2004 in which at least five graduating seniors thanked Jesus Christ for his help and inspiration. Such invocations represent private student speech and are protected by the Free Speech and Free Exercise Clauses.

The Court continued down the road of distinguishing private and public speech in *Santa Fe*. All a school district needs to do to avoid invalidation is to authorize a student body president to speak before football games and to give this student no guidelines at all as to what should be said. The student will eventually figure out that a prayer is expected, and, once prayer is traditional, future elections for student body president will ensure that the majority religion is the one expressed. The Court has not eliminated religion in public high schools. It has only eliminated adult leadership.

Nor is it possible to undo this tendency by looking to a school district's motivation in allowing a student to speak before a football game or at graduation. The possible motivations that the Court has regarded as secular, including solemnizing events, are so indistinguishable from religion that as long as a district does not use the term "prayer," the policy of student speech will be upheld. Justice Stevens attempted to prevent just such future subterfuges in *Santa Fe* by pointing out that "invocations" and solemnizing sound like prayer. But a school district can certainly authorize the student body President to welcome players and families from the other school, thus avoiding any religious purpose.

The insurmountable problem in these cases is precisely the one recognized by the Court in *Santa Fe*: the community wanted public prayer. "We recognize the important role that public worship plays in many communities, as well as the sincere desire to include public prayer as a part of various occasions so as to mark those occasions' significance."[178] Where that social desire is strong and well organized, the Court's decisions will be a mere paper barrier. Unfortunately, those communities are precisely the situations in which school district involvement, which the Court has proscribed, would help protect minority religious interests.

The odd aspect to current doctrine is that the same "civic religion" language that cannot be delivered at high school graduations and football games is likely to be upheld in the Pledge of Allegiance. It can be said that one is prayer and the other is not, but this distinction is not very convincing. If the nation can be said, constitutionally, to be "Under God," it cannot hurt to say so at a football game.

The Court will probably end up just where Chief Justice Rehnquist indicated, and where Justices Scalia and Thomas have suggested—that government may permit and encourage a kind of generic religious expression and belief, even monotheism dependent on a Creator. We will not maintain the distinction that permits government officials to do this around adults, but not around students.

This change in doctrine would not necessarily change the outcomes of the core Establishment Clause cases. It may not prove possible for government to conduct prayer or *Bible* reading in public schools in a way that does not violate the continuing concern of the Court with government preference for a particular religion and with government coercion of religious belief. But those legitimate concerns can be served without requiring government neutrality about religion itself.

FREE EXERCISE OF RELIGION

Though the Court is moving away from the secular consensus in the Establishment Clause cases, the Free Exercise cases, which grant wide latitude to the government's interference with religious practice, even allowing discrimination against religion, invite consideration of alternative explanations of these Establishment cases. Instead of protecting faith, perhaps the Court simply wishes to accord to government greater discretion in its actions. Or, perhaps the Court in the Establishment Clause cases is only protecting majoritarian religion. The Free Exercise cases are troubling.

The important recent case law in the free exercise area consists of four cases. *Employment Division v. Smith*[179] set forth a new understanding of the Free Exercise Clause and this understanding was applied in *Church of Lukumi Babalu Aye, Inc. v. City of Hialeah*[180] and *Locke v. Davey*.[181] Congress unsuccessfully attempted to overturn *Smith* in *City of Boerne v. Flores*.[182]

Smith changed the prevailing constitutional test in free exercise cases when generally applicable government policies substantially burden religious practice. Prior to *Smith*, such cases were governed by strict scrutiny—the compelling state-interest test. Justice Scalia's majority opinion in *Smith* concluded that generally applicable laws would not be subject to such exacting scrutiny, but would apparently be given the normally deferring review applied to government conduct. Government action that was "'aimed at the promotion or restriction of religious beliefs'" would receive a stricter level of review.[183]

The surprising aspect of the *Smith* opinion is its recognition–and seeming approval–that the Court had applied strict scrutiny against generally applicable law in "hybrid" cases, in which not only freedom of religious practice but also freedom of speech or of the press was involved. Thus *Smith* created a hierarchy of rights, in which the Free Exercise Clause was accorded less protection than other First Amendment rights.

The two cases that have applied Smith manifested different degrees of deference to the legislature. In *Lukumi Babalu*, every Justice agreed that the City's ban on ritual animal sacrifice violated the Free Exercise Clause. On the other hand, in *Davey*, where discrimination against the free exercise of religion was express—Washington excluded theology from the State's scholarship program—only Justices Scalia and Thomas dissented from Chief Justice Rehnquist's majority holding that there was no violation of the Free Exercise Clause.

Boerne rejected the attempt by Congress essentially to reverse *Smith* in the Religious Freedom Restoration Act of 1993. Justice O'Connor, joined by Justice Breyer, challenged the historical understanding behind *Smith*, which was defended by Justices Scalia and Stevens. Justice Kennedy's majority opinion rested primarily on the role of the Court as arbiter of the Constitution.

These free exercise cases confound the Establishment Clause conclusions reached above. Justice Stevens, for example, perhaps the staunchest secularist on the Court, strongly supported *Smith*. Yet Justice Scalia, who wrote the majority opinion in *Smith*, generally allows substantial government support for religion. More surprisingly, former Chief Justice Rehnquist, who had been foremost on the Court in protecting religion (in the sense of allowing government preference of religion over irreligion), wrote the majority opinion in *Davey*, which allowed a facial discrimination against religion to stand. On the other hand, Justice Thomas, who is perhaps closest to the late chief justice on Establishment Clause issues, was one of only two dissenters in *Davey*.

The Establishment Clause and the Free Exercise Clause work differently in regard to religion and public life. Limiting the restrictions of the Establishment Clause will presumably lead to more public expression of the majority religion—Christianity—since a majority practice is the religious practice government is more likely to encourage and support. Weakening the Free Exercise Clause, on the other hand, will tend to harm minority religious interests, although that was not true in *Davey* itself.

In any event, since *Smith* allows as much or as little accommodation of religion as democratic political life wishes to grant, the case stands as no serious support for the secular consensus. In fact, Justice Scalia noted in *Smith* that several states grant peyote exemptions from State drug laws. As troubling as they are, the new free exercise cases do not inhibit the development of religious democracy.

RELIGIOUS INVOLVEMENT IN GOVERNMENT

In June 2005, there was a flurry of comment about Texas Governor Rick Perry's plan to sign a parental consent abortion bill at a private Christian academy and to discuss a proposed state constitutional amendment banning gay marriage there as well. Governor Perry was quoted as saying of his choice of location that, "A church is an appropriate place to come together and celebrate a victory for the values of the people of Texas."[184] The story in the *New York Times* also reported that the choice of location "is being praised by conservative Republicans as a major victory."[185]

A similar media event erupted at about the same time over a comment by the Democratic National Committee Chairman, Howard Dean, characterizing the Republican Party as "pretty much a white, Christian party."[186] Dean meant this as a criticism.

These comments and situations reflect the viewpoint of the secular consensus—and, of course, the opposite reaction by critics of the secular consensus—that the mix of religion and political life is unhealthy not just when government involves itself in religion, but also when private religious persons and institutions involve their religious views in public life.

The secular consensus regards such religious intrusions as inherently worse than the expression of the same sorts of views by nonreligious people. For example, Andrew Greeley criticized the impeachment of President Bill Clinton as instigated by a cabal of religious groups:

> The most dangerous intrusion of religion into American politics in the last hundred years was the effort of a largely southern, largely Evangelical, largely Calvinist cabal to cancel the election of an American presidency by

gross intrusion into the private life of that President. . . . The attempt to burn
Bill Clinton did not need a John Winthrop to light the fire.[187]

Why does Greeley think that religious motivation is important in this
context? Some people wanted President Clinton impeached simply because he acted immorally. Others wanted him impeached because he
lied under oath. And some, as Greeley says, wanted him impeached because President Clinton violated God's moral law. But some people simply
wanted to cancel the election and put a Republican in the White House.
Surely that motivation was worse than a religious one. Basically, what difference does the origin of the opposition to President Clinton make?

Greeley uses the word "dangerous" and that is clearly the feeling of
the secular consensus. It is bad enough to be ruled by those with whom
one disagrees because of unfavorable electoral outcomes. It is apparently
far worse to be ruled by religiously motivated people with whom one
disagrees.

The problem cannot be that such actions by religious people are unconstitutional. Obviously, private speech by religiously motivated people
cannot seriously be thought to violate the Constitution. It cannot violate
the Constitution for Governor Perry to sign legislation at a religious institution. Such speech and symbols, with the exception of partisan endorsement of candidates by tax-exempt institutions, is protected by the Constitution.

If a secular citizen is ruled by religious opponents, the citizen may feel
that there is little chance of persuading them of the secular citizen's point
of view. The citizen and the religious opponents may not even share a
common language to discuss a political issue.

But this distinction between religious and nonreligious motivations is
not that significant. Many people have strong opinions about political
issues. Having a strong opinion, even an implacable one, is not related
to religious reasoning. Try persuading a member of the ACLU that free
speech is overrated or the CEO of a coal company that we should have
carbon taxes to fight global warming. Religiously motivated opinions are
no harder and no easier to change than any other. This is the reason that
Rawls does not distinguish religious comprehensive views from nonreligious comprehensive views. Anyway, how could strength of conviction
be thought to disqualify religious voters, or anyone else, from democratic
participation?

Of course, the idea that God prefers one politician to another or even
one party platform to another is theologically suspect, even blasphemous.
But the secular consensus is not genuinely concerned about that, except as
such a criticism might be a convenient political weapon.

Some of the secular criticism of political activity by religious voters
is simply hypocritical. Secularists did not bemoan the opposition by

Catholic Bishops to the death penalty or to the abolition of welfare during the 1990s.

We can see in this question of religious participation in public controversy the fundamental problem of secular democracy. Secular democracy requires that religious believers not participate in politics as believers. This is not because the believers will not be persuasive to other voters. Secular democracy is exclusionary in principle. For this reason alone, it would not really be possible for a political system to be both democratic and secular, at least not in a culture as religious as ours. In addition, secular democracy cannot address the deepest issues of the meaning of political life. Finally, secular democracy cannot achieve stable constitutional doctrine. We do not have secular democracy, nor could we.

What happened in the election of 2004 was, then, to be expected. The influence of religiously motivated voters in the United States came of age with the 2004 election. These voters today dominate American politics. Certainly this situation is subject to change with the next election or the next few elections. But any change is unlikely to put the secular consensus back into the cultural dominance it once seemed to have achieved.

PART II

IS RELIGIOUS DEMOCRACY POSSIBLE?

We now turn from the exhausted and largely impotent secular consensus to the vibrant, but untested, specter of religious democracy itself. The phenomenon of religious democracy in America is new. America has been so busy opposing or supporting religion in public life that we have neglected to ask what religious democracy will be like. Neither its critics nor its proponents have yet had to describe the landscape of religious democracy. Part II asks how religious democracy will function and what its implications are. Once separation is no longer a practical goal, once the government is no longer neutral about religion in any sense, the question remains: how religious will the public square become? These are the questions that religious democracy will be forced to confront. In other words, even religious voters must come to terms with American religious democracy.

There is, however, a prior question. Many secular voters think that the Constitution prohibits religious democracy altogether and they certainly think it will prevent it from going very far. Since the Constitution has not been amended, some of these voters are outraged at the change in constitutional understanding this book has described. They think they should eventually win in the courts.

Will they win? No. But the reason they will not has been obscured and must be explained. The process of constitutional change in America is not a subject that has been forthrightly confronted by our legal and political elites. Lawyers, including judges, like to pretend that they control constitutional interpretation. But constitutional interpretation changes along with changes in public opinion, especially deep changes in that opinion.

CHAPTER 8

How Does Our Constitution Change?

We find ourselves either in the middle of, or on the brink of, a constitutional revolution in the relationship of Church and State. Is this constitutional revolution justified? Answering that question requires an understanding of what judges do when they interpret our Constitution. Most judges would probably say that a change in constitutional doctrine is justified if the judges were "wrong" before in their interpretation and are "right" now. But this is not only a simplistic and misleading description of what judges do, it also ignores the role of democracy in judicial interpretation. Fortunately, the people have a role in constitutional interpretation; in fact, they have the crucial role. The justification for the coming constitutional change in the meaning of the religion clauses of the First Amendment is that the people have, in an organic sense, endorsed it.

To see that this is how constitutional interpretation actually changes, we must first examine the way that most judges and lawyers think about constitutional interpretation. Judges and lawyers believe that the purpose of a written constitution is not to reflect the wishes of the American people but to do the opposite—to restrain an unruly and potentially tyrannical majority. This view is an article of faith, deeply held and revered in just about all American law schools. Both liberals and conservatives believe it. It is referred to by many terms, including the large umbrella phrase, "The rule of law."

But this belief does not reflect reality. This assumed role for the courts, especially the United States Supreme Court, has not been fulfilled in American history, could not have been fulfilled given political realities, and should not be fulfilled, because if it were, the people would be ruled by the courts rather than by themselves.

First, let us consider whether this judicial role has been fulfilled historically. Has the Supreme Court restrained abusive national majorities from doing what they wanted to do? The Court enforced slavery and the fugitive slave laws. In fact, the Court struck down the Missouri Compromise in *Dred Scott v. Sandford*.[188] The Court did not protect the freed slaves from Jim Crow laws, and upheld separate but equal despite the Equal Protection Clause of the Fourteenth Amendment.[189] The Court did not protect dissenters after World War I, most notoriously upholding the conviction of Eugene Debs for violation of the Espionage Act.[190] The Court did not order Japanese Americans freed from relocation camps during World War II.[191] The Court upheld Communist Party member convictions under the Smith Act during the 1950s for the teaching and advocacy of overthrow of the government by force and violence.[192] In all these cases, an aroused majority acted tyrannically. Where was the Court when it was needed and when both constitutional text and history would have supported judicial resistance?

Ironically, the one instance in which the Justices did stand for perhaps the longest time against majority will in our history was not a defense of what would be considered human rights, but against government regulation of the economy and federal protection of workers, women, and children in the early years of the twentieth century. This era, known by the name of one of those cases—*Lochner v. New York*[193] did not come to an end until the mid 1930s. This line of cases, however, is not a shining example of the importance of the rule of law.

The cases where the Court has made a difference have tended to be limited contexts rather than general impediments to majority will. For example, the Warren Court criminal procedure revolution—establishing *Miranda* warnings, the exclusionary rule and the right to counsel—consisted of unquestionably important and unpopular Court decisions. Yet these cases opposed the prevailing practices in the administration of justice rather than policies pursued by majorities in the political realm. Putting restrictions on the police and on prosecutors and providing defense attorneys to indigent defendants are very important actions for a court to take, but they are specialized actions in areas of particular judicial expertise. In other words, the Supreme Court was on especially solid ground in justifying its actions.

Other important constitutional cases, as Judge Michael McConnell pointed out years ago,[194] have involved unpopular laws that might have been repealed had they actually been enforced. The homosexual sodomy law struck down in *Lawrence v. Texas*[195] in 2003 fits that description.

Even the Court's acknowledged finest hour—striking down separate but equal racial segregation in *Brown v. Board of Education*[196] was not a judicial act contrary to a national majority. Official segregation was the law only in a minority of States. The *Brown* decision probably had national majority support right from the start, despite powerful and determined local and regional opposition.

All in all, and obviously without fully canvassing the Supreme Court's role in constitutional cases, it can be said that the Court's reputation of protecting unpopular minorities against unsympathetic majorities is at least questionable. That is not surprising. For how exactly could the Supreme Court thwart a determined national majority? Given the way the Court works, how the Justices are selected and who the Justices are, the Court could not be expected to thwart majority will, at least not for an extended period of time. As a group, Supreme Court Justices are mainstream lawyers whose paper trail sparked no determined political opposition. They tend not to be revolutionaries.

In 1957 and again in 1989 the political scientist Robert Dahl examined this traditionally asserted judicial role and concluded not only that it was probably a mistaken view, if the matter could be measured at all, but that this view of the Supreme Court could not be accurate since the political restrictions on the Court, such as nomination of Justices by the President with approval by the Senate, assure that over time the Court will reflect the prevailing views of politically dominant groups. Over time, in other words, the political majority controls the Court.

Dahl's notion of an organic constitutionalism has little support, however, in either the academy of American law professors or among judges. They want lawyers to control constitutional interpretation and they speak and act as if this were so. But Dahl's insight has been expressed in the Court once, in the dissent by Justice John M. Harlan in *Poe v. Ullman*.[197]

Justice John M. Harlan, usually referred to as "the younger" to distinguish him from his grandfather, who also served on the High Court, was appointed to the Supreme Court in 1955 and served until 1971. Justice Harlan served during the years of the liberal Warren Court and was thought of as a conservative minority voice during those years. Given his reputation as the conservative "Great Dissenter" on the Warren Court, Justice Harlan has emerged in our time as surprisingly influential, particularly in regard to the craft of judicial decision-making. Justices Souter and Breyer are particularly influenced by Justice Harlan, whose influence transcends the ideological divisions on the Court.

In *Poe*, challenges were brought by a married couple, a married woman, and a doctor, against the Connecticut antibirth control statute. The gist of the complaints was that for each of the women, "the best and safest medical treatment which could be prescribed . . . is advice in methods of preventing conception." But neither party was able to obtain such advice and information because the giving of such advice and the use of contraceptive devices were claimed by the prosecuting authority to constitute offenses under Connecticut law. The couple, the woman, and the doctor, sued for declaratory judgments that the Connecticut ban on the use of birth control devices in conjunction with Connecticut's criminal accessory statute deprived them of "life and liberty without due process of law." Thus this challenge to the Connecticut birth control prohibition raised the issue of the reach of the Due Process Clause of the Fourteenth Amendment. The Connecticut Supreme Court in effect upheld the statutes. The United States Supreme Court dismissed the appeals from this decision. A majority of the Justices found that the case was not ripe for decision because of a lack of a credible threat of prosecution.

Justice Harlan's dissent was, as he stated, "of unusual length." Justice Harlan argued that the cases were appropriate for declaratory relief, that the issues were justiciable and that the Connecticut birth control ban, as applied to the plaintiffs, violated the Fourteenth Amendment.

It was in the context of this last point that Justice Harlan found it "desirable at the outset to state the framework in which I think the issues must be judged." It was as part of that framework that Justice Harlan set forth his understanding of the relationship of the Due Process Clause of the Fourteenth Amendment to the democratic life of the people of the United States.

Justice Harlan began this section of his dissent by rejecting two views of due process that had not been accepted by the Court. Due process is not limited to merely procedural guarantees. Nor is due process restricted to the protection of rights enumerated in the Bill of Rights of the United States Constitution.

Having said what due process was not, it then fell to Justice Harlan to describe what it is. Justice Harlan stated that due process "has not been reduced to any formula" because "its content cannot be determined by reference to any code."[198]

> The best that can be said is that through the course of this Court's decisions it has represented the balance which our Nation, built upon postulates of respect for the liberty of the individual, has struck between that liberty and the demands of organized society. If the supplying of content to this Constitutional concept has of necessity been a rational process, it certainly has not been one where judges have felt free to roam where unguided speculation might take them. The balance of which I speak is the balance struck by this country, having regard to what history teaches are the traditions from which it developed as well as the traditions from which it broke. That tradition is a living thing. A decision of this Court which radically departs from it could not long survive, while a decision which builds on what has survived is likely to be sound. No formula could serve as a substitute, in this area, for judgment and restraint.[199]

According to Justice Harlan, due process is not a formula, but a balance. The balance is between the liberty of the individual and the needs of society. Judicial action that supplies content to that balance is a rational process. The balance struck has regard for history—for traditions accepted and for those rejected. The judicial role in relation to this balance roots ultimately in judgment and judicial restraint. We can thus identify two "sources" for constitutional adjudication in *Poe*: rationality and history.

Justice Harlan's dissent in *Poe* is usually regarded as relating to the much discussed issue of the proper "sources" of due process—that is, where a Justice could legitimately look for confirmation that a particular government action violates the Fourteenth Amendment. In recent years, the Justices have argued over the uses of history and text and current values. But Justice Harlan apparently also had in mind what happens to decisions after they are rendered. That is a matter quite different from the usual substantive due process disagreement over the legitimacy of judicial recognition of nontextual rights.

Once the notion of the "reception" of a judicial decision is understood as a part of Justice Harlan's substantive due process methodology, other parts of the quotation from the *Poe* dissent can be understood in their expanded reference as well. Justice Harlan stated that "[O]ur nation" and "this country" strike the balance of due process. Judicial decisions plainly play a part, but they do not seem ultimately to control the due process balance. Something apart from judges and courts is involved.

Justice Harlan's view was that a decision that "radically departs from" tradition "could not long survive." But, how, exactly, was that to happen? What agency could account for this nonsurvival?

According to Justice Harlan, it is tradition that actively supplies the needed restraint on the Court. It is in this sense that the tradition is a living thing. The tradition ensures that radical departures by the Court do not survive. In other words, although the Justices on the Supreme Court represent the Nation in formulating the balance of due process, the tradition to which the Court contributes in this way, is *self*-correcting. When the Court decides in accordance with the trend of historical development, the decisions survive. When the Court departs—radically at least—the decisions do not survive.

Do the Justices themselves do this correcting? In a sense, the Justices must do the correcting because decisions that are out of the tradition can only be overruled or abandoned by the Court.

Yet, it is not the Court that Justice Harlan has in mind. He is not saying that we Justices will correct ourselves. For that would not justify substantive due process review against the charge that the judge is roaming at his or her discretion. The correction must come from outside the judiciary.

Instead of what judges decide, it is "the balance struck by this country" that forms the living tradition that overturns or accepts judicial decisions. It is the people, broadly conceived, who are the key to Justice Harlan's thinking. It is the people who decide the direction of constitutional interpretation, at least in the due process area.

It is not unusual for constitutional decision-making to be described as a "dialogue" between the Court and the people. But Justice Harlan is not here describing a dialogue. In the end, Justice Harlan says, it is the people, and not the Court, that control. It is the constitutional vision of the people that decides the direction of judicial decision-making. The tradition, as a living thing, acts to control the Court.

Who are "the people" who have such power? In using words like "our Nation" and "this country," Justice Harlan does not seem to be referring to Congress or the President. He is not referring to the possibility that Congress will try to overturn a decision of the Supreme Court interpreting the Constitution through ordinary legislation. He seems to have in mind something more organic, of which statutory responses to a judicial decision or judicial nomination struggles in the United States Senate might play a part, but a process that would not be limited to such formal and official actions.

What Justice Harlan seems to have in mind is similar to what Justice Ginsburg meant in regard to changing understandings of gender roles when she wrote that judges "do read the newspapers and are affected . . . by the climate of the era. . . . A sea change in United States society. . . . Their enlightenment was advanced publicly by the briefs filed in Court and privately, I suspect, by the aspirations of the women, particularly the daughters and granddaughters, in their own families and communities."[200]

A "sea change" is something that happens. It is not a matter of convincing someone. It is not a conversation. It is not entirely or necessarily conscious. The Justices do not have to announce that they have been corrected by the people. The Justices do not even have to realize that they have been corrected. In fact, the Justices who issue an opinion outside the tradition may not even be the same Justices who later overrule or abandon it. The evolutionary process works in the long run.

Nor does this process depend upon the willingness of particular Justices to be corrected. It does not depend upon their "theory" of the relationship of law and democracy. It does not depend on their approach to constitutional interpretation. As the popular saying would have it, correction happens.

This suggests that Justice Harlan's language might be regarded as tautological. As a description of what actually happens with regard to judicial decisions, Justice Harlan's words would be difficult to test. Any decision or line of cases that is overturned is likely to have generated serious public opposition. Therefore, any such change by the Court could be described as a vindication of Justice Harlan's insight. On the other hand, any unpopular decision or line of cases that is not overturned or abandoned might be described as having generated insufficient public opposition. To make matters worse, the ultimate standard—departing radically from the tradition—is measured in Justice Harlan's formulation, only by the decision's later abandonment. By definition, a decision that is abandoned was outside the tradition. A decision that is not abandoned was not outside the tradition. But, how would anyone be able to tell what decisions were otherwise outside the tradition in order to test whether such decisions do not survive?

We need not be put off by such methodological objections. Justice Harlan was not a political scientist. He was not attempting to make a testable hypothesis for a model of judicial decision-making. He had something else in mind.

Justice Harlan no doubt believed that he was describing the constitutional tradition accurately. It is significant in that regard that Justice Harlan's grandfather had dissented in *Plessy v. Ferguson*[201] and Justice Harlan lived to see that decision overturned in *Brown v. Board of Education*[202] shortly before he joined the Court. But what Justice Harlan really had in mind was more normative than descriptive.

In a recent article skeptically evaluating the claim that constitutional interpretation is an autonomous undertaking, Yale Law Professor Robert Post uses the term "culture" to refer to "the beliefs and values of nonjudicial actors" and the term "constitutional culture" to refer to the "specific subset of culture that encompasses extrajudicial beliefs about the substance of the Constitution." Professor Post skillfully explores the relationship between constitutional culture and judicial decision-making.[203]

The term "culture" could be used to describe Justice Harlan's process of survival of judicial decisions. Culture is amorphous and general, though powerful. There is a sense in which culture controls judicial decisions.

Nevertheless, "culture" will not quite do for what Justice Harlan is describing. Justice Harlan is making a claim about governance. When the nation—the people—set the balance of due process, or decide concerning any other constitutional realm, the people have the right to rule. We have only one word that adequately describes rule by the people. That word is "democracy." Justice Harlan is describing our democracy.

Justice Harlan is manifesting a different understanding of constitutional law's relationship to democracy than that which is usually presented in judicial opinions. In a recent dissent, Justice Scalia wrote that when the Constitution does not control a particular outcome, we confront "the wonderful reality ... that [the people] govern themselves ..."[204] Justice Harlan is suggesting an even more wonderful reality—though Justice Scalia might not think so—that even when a majority of the Justices on the Supreme Court believe the Constitution applies in a certain way, the people still govern themselves.

What we have in this quotation is a testament by Justice Harlan to democracy. Because we are the sort of people that we are, and because our system operates the way that it does, the Court will be corrected when its decisions are outside the mainstream public understanding of the Constitution. What kind of democracy is this?

Abraham Lincoln had an understanding of democracy parallel to that of Justice Harlan in *Poe*. Lincoln articulated this understanding in the Lincoln-Douglas debates of 1858:

> In this and like communities, public sentiment is everything. With public sentiment, nothing can fail; without it, nothing can succeed. Consequently, he who molds public sentiment goes deeper than he who enacts statutes and pronounces decisions.[205]

In terms of the relationship of law to democracy, Yale Law Professor Bruce Ackerman also describes something close to Justice Harlan's view when he writes of the "considered judgment of a mobilized majority of American citizens" that can give higher lawmaking legitimacy to acts of government.[206] Nevertheless, even Ackerman, though he endorses a less formal and more organic notion of democracy and law than does the usual law professor or judge, still looks to "the elections of 1866 and 1936 [as] decisive events in constitutional history." It was on those occasions that opponents of the popular will came to recognize that "*the People had spoken*" in a way quite different from the normal consequences of normal congressional elections. Normal elections do not in effect amend the Constitution, but those two elections in effect did so.

Professor Ackerman seeks to maintain a distinction between "higher lawmaking" on the one hand and "normal politics" on the other. And the distinction is dramatic, both in terms of what it accomplishes by way of constitutional change and how dramatic the mobilization of higher lawmaking is.

Justice Harlan is describing something different. A judicial decision outside the mainstream of American understanding of the Constitution will be worn away over time. There need be no one moment, like an election, in which one could plausibly say, the people have spoken. There need be no special popular mobilization. We do not need a *Deliberation Day*, as Ackerman suggested in a 2004 book by that title.[207] Even without such formality, in the end there will be the popular "sea change" of which Justice Ginsburg spoke. Suddenly, though perhaps after long incubation, an understanding that was accepted for a long time—let us say separate but equal in race or the dominance of women by men—is simply no longer viable. As a result, decisions expressing the old view do not survive.

This is, of course, a very different way of looking at democracy than our usual formal approaches. There is no requirement of elections or voting. There is only the requirement of the rights of free speech, association, and of the press, so that the weight of public opinion can come to bear.

Aside from the implications of this for law, does America make political decisions in this way? Not always. Obviously, in matters of detail, our elected officials make our decisions. Just as obviously, many important political issues are resolved through elections in which certain party groupings achieve a legislative majority. These are formal democratic and representative outcomes. They are not necessarily matters of consensus.

But if we look at more fundamental matters, they are often "made" in the same sort of soft, consensus way that Justice Harlan is describing. For example, a public decision by consensus was made to wind down the American contribution to the war in Vietnam. Claims about victory and the need for more American troops could no longer be made credibly after the Tet Offensive in 1968. Similarly, sometime between the spring of 2004 and the summer of 2005, the news coming from Iraq was sufficiently bad that the American people changed their position on the war. A decision of some sort was made to leave Iraq. Since then, the only question has been when and how, though resolution has been slow in coming.

Surprisingly, the same consensus movement is propelling the gay rights movement. That may seem a strange comment given the raft of anti-gay marriage constitutional amendments being passed in the States. But even so, the popular acceptance of gay relationships has increased enormously. Gay marriage or its equivalent is simply inevitable.

These observations bring us back to Justice Harlan's understanding of the relationship of law and democracy. Justice Harlan thought of judicial opinions interpreting the Constitution as subject to public consensus. The decisions themselves certainly could change public opinion to a certain extent. In the end, however, the public would decide the sustainability of such opinions. Are there any examples of the sort of judicial-public relationship that Justice Harlan is describing?

What made *Brown v. Board of Education*[208] such a successful decision? Why is *Brown* such an icon of American constitutionalism?

Brown was enormously controversial when it was decided. The extent of the white backlash it sparked in the affected States is widely forgotten today. The decision was not well reasoned, nor was it well grounded in the text or history of the passage of the Fourteenth Amendment. The reliance in the opinion on social science research was not well received. And the opinion was subjected to a celebrated critique by Herbert Wechsler.

Nevertheless, even at the time, there was a rightness about *Brown*. The *New York Times* wrote at that time that the Justices "have felt behind them the solid weight of public opinion."[209] Despite real opposition, the *Brown* decision became a symbol of national resolve to move, belatedly, toward racial justice. And today, it is safe to say that no candidate for federal judicial office could throw the slightest doubt upon *Brown* and still be considered for nomination or confirmation. What Michael McConnell has called "the moral authority of *Brown*"[210] is now the test by which constitutional interpretation is judged. If an understanding of the Constitution is inconsistent with *Brown*, it is that understanding, rather than *Brown*, which is thrown into question.

Brown is an example, from the positive side, of what Justice Harlan was describing. The decision has been adopted by the American people, almost none of whom have ever read it and most of whom know of it only vaguely. What has been adopted is the principle that the Government may not discriminate on the basis of race. It is fair to say that this proposition has now become, in the words of Justice Harlan, a matter settled by this "nation" and not just by the courts.

Brown not only illustrates democratic ratification of a judicial decision on a crucial constitutional matter, but also illustrates the role of leadership in the formation of democratic consensus. The decision was not the first federal governmental blow against legal racial discrimination. Nor was it the first judicial decision to move in the general direction of racial equality. But it was a dramatic announcement of a large-scale challenge to a widespread racial ideology. Without *Brown*, the dismantling of legal apartheid in the United States would not have proceeded as quickly and as surely as it did. Though democratic consensus is obviously a manifestation of popular judgment, there is still the necessity of wise leadership. Such leadership can present the people with the inspiration from which to come to their own decision. The Court, in *Brown*, provided that leadership.

Another significant line of decisions where the effect of public acceptance can be seen is the prohibition of discrimination based on gender. In 1971, in *Reed v. Reed*,[211] a short unassuming opinion by Chief Justice Warren Burger, a unanimous Court decided that a mandatory preference for males over females as administrators of estates when persons were "'equally entitled to administer'" violated equal protection.

A little more than thirty years after *Reed*, there is no one in American public life who would defend the sort of discrimination against women illustrated in that case. It no longer matters whether the framers of the Fourteenth Amendment meant to eliminate discriminations against women— which surely they did not—nor whether the language of equal protection reached gender discrimination in 1868—which surely it did not. Even though the role of women was a hotly debated political/social issue in 1971, no one today would accuse the Court of having entered the "culture wars" to come down on one side of a cultural controversy. Despite remaining taboos on the participation of women in national life—most significantly in military combat—the matter of ordinary, common law discriminations against women is settled. The people have spoken on this matter by full acceptance of this line of cases.

A final example of acceptance by informal but real consensus is the recent treatment of *Miranda v. Arizona*,[212] the case that announced the famous *Miranda* warnings. *Miranda* warnings have generally been regarded by the Court as not required directly by the Constitution, but instead as a prophylactic rule to prevent violation of the constitutionally protected value of the prohibition against self-incrimination. If *Miranda* was a prophylactic device, then presumably Congress should be able to modify or perhaps limit the requirement of *Miranda* warnings.

This supposition was put to the test in *Dickerson v. United States*,[213] in which the Court confronted, inexplicably for the first time, the provision through which Congress had attempted to modify the reach of the *Miranda* decision in 1968. As part of the Crime Control Act of 1968, Congress required that the voluntariness standard be the only method of judging the admissibility of confessions in federal prosecutions. The administration of the *Miranda* warnings was just one of several factors to be considered in making the judgment of voluntariness. In *Dickerson*, the Court found the voluntariness provision—Section 3501—unconstitutional.

Chief Justice Rehnquist's majority opinion argued that, despite all the judicial language to the contrary, the requirement of *Miranda* warnings was a constitutional rule after all, which Congress could not displace by ordinary legislation. Of special importance here is the reason Chief Justice Rehnquist gave for not overruling *Miranda*. Chief Justice Rehnquist concluded that, *Miranda* should not be overruled because the decision "has become embedded in routine police practice to the point where the warnings have become part of our national culture."[214]

Since the people could always reenact the requirements of *Miranda* through legislative action, this does not seem like a compelling reason either to overrule a case or not to do so. Certainly the police are used to *Miranda*. But what difference should it make to the Court that the warnings are a part of "national culture"?

Chief Justice Rehnquist's language is suggestive of the kind of popular acceptance that Justice Harlan was describing. *Miranda* is not just a decision for police and judges to think about. *Miranda* warnings are on television and in movies. *Miranda* is by now part of our national life together and the case and its requirement of warnings is no longer something that the Court could lightly attempt to change. I may say that I anticipated *Dickerson*. It was to this aspect of popular and judicial interaction in the context of State Constitutional law's relation to federal constitutional law that I was referring in a 1999 article about state constitutional interpretation, when I wrote, "To think that the United States Supreme Court 'owns' *Miranda* . . . after all this time and can do with it what it wishes, is to elevate legal positivism to an unrealistic height. Miranda is part of the general culture."[215] This is the effect of popular acceptance of a judicial decision. Similarly, the Court could not now easily overrule *Brown* or *Reed* either.

What about the negative implications of Justice Harlan's language? Justice Harlan was more concerned with opinions outside the tradition that would not survive.

There are some obvious candidates for the sort of process Justice Harlan was describing. The reception of *Roe v. Wade*[216] by the people has been almost the mirror image from that of *Brown*. From the start, *Roe* sparked controversy that has not diminished over time but remains active and divisive. The holding has been chipped away in a series of restrictive decisions. The Court has been invited by the Executive Branch on several occasions to overrule *Roe*. Even *Planned Parenthood of Southeastern Pennsylvania*[217]—the case that upheld aspects of *Roe* by a 5–4 vote— allowed modification of *Roe* and upheld its "essential holding" primarily by reference to *stare decisis* rather than by enthusiastic endorsement.

The public responses to the anniversaries of *Brown* and *Roe* illustrate the differences in public acceptance. The fiftieth anniversary of *Brown* led to celebrations across the country. In contrast, the anniversary of *Roe* each year leads to large outpourings of dissent.

Nor is this difference a mere matter of passage of time. The *Roe* decision is now over thirty years old. By that time, *Brown* and other cases were already enshrined in the constitutional canon.

It cannot be said that *Roe* has been abandoned by the people. The decision is supported by a substantial group in the electorate. It is opposed by a substantial group. Another group lies in the middle, troubled by the rhetoric on both sides of the issue.

But this lack of consensus does not support *Roe*. The obligation of the Court, in Justice Harlan's understanding, is to be where the people are going. In Alexander Bickel's phrase, in terms of such judicial leadership, the Court "labors under the obligation to succeed."[218] In *Roe*, the Court did not succeed.

Part I suggested that America is on the brink of wholesale constitutional change in regard to the relationship of Church and State. This implicitly reflected the Harlan model. We can see since the 2004 presidential election the national influence of religious voters. With the Senate hearings on Chief Justice Roberts and Justice Alito, we see how personnel changes on the Court relate to such political influence. It is very unlikely that a strict separationist could today be confirmed as a Justice on the Supreme Court. This is democratic correction in action.

There is a dark side to Justice Harlan's understanding of the power of popular constitutionalism. The people can force the Court into injustice. Justice Scalia's dissent in *McCreary* asked why the Court sometimes allows government to aid religion despite the Court's formal adherence to the neutrality principle.

> What, then, could be the genuine "good reason" for occasionally ignoring the neutrality principle? I suggest it is the instinct for self-preservation, and the recognition that the Court, which "has no influence over either the sword or the purse," cannot go too far down the road of an enforced neutrality that

contradicts both historical fact and current practice without losing all that sustains it: the willingness of the people to accept its interpretation of the Constitution as definitive, in preference to the contrary interpretation of the democratically elected branches.[219]

In other words, sometimes the Court is intimidated into permitting government action when the Justices would be inclined to challenge popular commitments. Justice Scalia warned the Court majority in similar terms in *Stenberg v. Carhart*,[220] in which the Court struck down a State ban on partial birth abortions:

> [I]f only for the sake of its own preservation, the Court should return this matter to the people—where the Constitution, by its silence on the subject, left it—and let *them* decide, State by State, whether this practice should be allowed.

It is impossible for an outsider, or even a dissenting Justice, to know the extent to which a majority on the Court today is simply afraid to embrace the tenets of the secular consensus.

The Court is not necessarily unjust when it decides a case that is outside our tradition. Our tradition may be unjust instead. The role of the Court in a democracy is not to serve truth, but ultimately to serve our tradition— to be where the people are and/or where they are going. The will of the people is what must be served in a democracy, even when wrong.

Justice Harlan did not assume that the people are uniquely wise. Especially in a particular case, the people may insist on a course that is likely to lead to social disaster. The Justices may sound a warning to the people. The Justices may try to reason with the people. The Justices may even vote to hold the will of the people at bay in order to delay the disaster as long as possible. These are all honorable actions. But in the end, the people rule and their will, will be done.

So, to say that the democratic will of the people is moving the Court toward a greater acceptance of religion in the public square, is not to assert that this path is better in any sense than the constitutional commitment of the secular consensus. It is simply to say that the people have gone in a different direction and that their opinion must, and will, ultimately control constitutional interpretation.

There is in this view of law and democracy a strange echo of the biblical understanding of the role of the people. In the *Old Testament*, action takes place at the level of the people, especially once the period of the Patriarchs is over. It is the people who are enslaved in Egypt. It is the people who are liberated by God. It is the people who accept the covenant at Sinai. It is the people who enter the land. It is the people who struggle to gain that land.

At a climactic moment in the *Book of Samuel*, it is the people who demand a king.

The attitude of the *Old Testament* about kings is clear immediately. The elders of the people desire "a king to govern us like all the nations." This of course is anathema in light of the Covenant of the people with God. Samuel, the old prophet, is "displeased" by the request for a king and prays to God. God tells Samuel to "[h]earken to the voice of the people in all they say to you; for they have not rejected you, but they have rejected me from being king over them."[221]

Although democracy is not a biblical doctrine, there is something of what we can call democracy in all of these aforementioned actions by the people. This is not democracy in the sense of elections or majority rule. It is a more organic democracy. It is something like the kind of democratic consensus that Justice Harlan was suggesting. In the *Bible*, the people decide what their society will do and they decide this by a sort of democratic consensus.

The attitude of the *Bible* toward the people's decisions is generally that the people choose evil, though they can choose life. Specifically in *Samuel*, they choose a king rather than choosing God to be their king. So, the "will" of the people is not a reliable source of judgment, though that does not alter the fact that the people do, and presumably should, have the right to make these decisions.

Nor is this only the attitude of the *Old Testament*. Part of the outcry against Mel Gibson's movie *The Passion* had to do with its portrayal of "the Jews" rejecting Jesus. But we can now see that this motif—that the people act as a whole and that the people reject God—is not a "Christian" condemnation of the "Jews," but rather a recapitulation by the Jewish followers of Jesus of an *Old Testament* theme. The people have rejected God as their king. Only a small, faithful remnant—in the *Book of Samuel*, the prophet himself and in the *New Testament* the followers of Jesus—choose God as their king. The parallel between these two moments of popular decision is strongly suggested when, in John 19: 19, Pontius Pilate writes this title on the cross—"'Jesus of Nazareth, the King of the Jews.'"

The point here is the attitude of both accounts concerning what the people choose. The people do not choose well. They choose evil and rebellion against God. They are a troublesome people, as Moses puts it. This of course is not to say that the Jewish people are evil—that could hardly be the message of the *Old Testament*—but that people are prone to error. Humans choose sin when God offers salvation.

In returning to Justice Harlan's view of law and democracy, the *Bible* is an important corrective and warning against any facile optimism. The *Bible* teaches that the people do rule. They do decide. It is the people and not any smaller group that must determine the basic direction of society. In biblical terms this is justified both by the responsibility of each member of society to choose the good and the right and by the simple fact that God's judgment against evil falls on society as a whole and not on some particular group within society. If everyone is going to be punished for what society does, everyone must have a say in that conduct.

So, in terms of our society, while the Court may have a leadership role in our democracy, ultimately the people must decide on the course of their society. Yet, we cannot conclude from this that the people will be right. They not only might not be right, but we could almost say they are certain to be wrong in what they do.

Justice Harlan did not promise anything different from this. He did not refer to the "good" tradition or the "wise" tradition. He said merely the living tradition. That tradition acts within the consensus of the people.

Of course Justice Harlan was not thinking of the *Book of Samuel* or the *Gospel of John*. What we can deduce from the *Bible* is not a blueprint for governmental structure, but a context in which to understand human governance and its potential. A system of government should be one in which the voice of the people can be heard, even though the voice of the people is not the voice of God. Justice Harlan understood that and thought we had such a system.

The use of this biblical example, even just as suggestive, foreshadows the argument in the rest of Part II of this book. Chapter 8 has shown that religious democracy is possible in the sense that the Constitution does not prevent it. The question then becomes whether religious democracy is possible in a more general sense. Is it workable? Is it coherent? Does it promise social harmony and justice? Just as in the case of secular democracy, the answers are not simple. Religious democracy has challenges of its own. Nevertheless, as the use of the *Bible* suggests, in the end, religious democracy is possible, and desirable. In the end, America will pursue religious democracy in its fullest sense.

CHAPTER 9

The Problems of Religion in Democracy

It would be a mistake to imagine that only secular democracy has conceptual problems. Religious democracy has its own set of difficulties. There really is a question whether religious democracy is possible. Amy Chua, for example, in her 2003 book, *World on Fire*,[222] argues that democracy in a free-market globalizing context unleashes powerful ethnic and other hatreds, including resentment against the United States and Israel, which are expressed in religious terms. Religion is for her close to the antithesis of democracy. We have recently seen in the democratic emergence of Hamas among the Palestinian people, and Hezbollah in Lebanon, events many would say substantiate Chua's point.

Newsweek editor Fareed Zakaria, in *The Future of Freedom*,[223] sounds similar negative warnings about religion's tension with democracy: "Compromise seems impossible; one can bargain on material issues such as housing, hospitals and handouts, but how does one split the difference on a national religion?" Zakaria attributes this religious incompatibility with democracy to the Abrahamic tradition in particular: "Religion, at least the religion of the Abrahamic traditions (Judaism, Christianity, and Islam), stresses moral absolutes. But politics is all about compromise. The result has been a ruthless, winner-take-all attitude toward political life."

Arthur Schlesinger made a similar point in an essay in the *New York Times Book Review* in September 2005. The essay was about "Forgetting Reinhold Niebuhr," who was perhaps the dominant American theologian of the postwar period. Schlesinger quoted Niebuhr to the effect that religion is dangerous to democracy because it imports absolutes into the political realm, which is and should be, a place of relative values.

Writing about Islam in 2002, Notre Dame Professor Lee Travis was pessimistic about religion and democracy: "The core issue is whether a religious democracy is possible."[224] He asked of Islamic religious law, "[a]re rules governing personal and social behavior based on divine revelation and interpreted by the state compatible with the grassroots participatory ideal of a Western democratic state?"[225] When Salman Rushdie wrote in the *New York Times*, shortly after 9/11, that Muslims should confine religion to "the sphere of the personal,"[226] he was asserting that religion and liberal political life cannot mix. Michael Ignatieff reported in the *New York Times Magazine* in July 2005 that Iranians need to learn this separation lesson:

> It became apparent that what I should have been teaching during my visit was the history of the Protestant reformation. It's not just that Islam badly needs a Reformation. It's also that Iranians need to know how the Reformation and the bloody religious wars that followed it taught the West to put God in his place. Democracy arises, I told the students, not just to enthrone the people but also to separate religion and politics, establishing rules of tolerance that allow all religions to enjoy freedom and creating a political system in which religious and secular arguments compete on equal ground ... [These students] found it puzzling, even disappointing, that religion and politics are not actually separate in the United States. I tried to explain that keeping God in his place is work that never ends.[227]

Even Reza Aslan, in his defense of Islam in *No God But God*,[228] wants Islam relegated to the "moral framework" of a liberal Islamic democracy. Separation of Church and State would be observed. And the Bush Administration, so eager for religious democracy at home, seemed to insist at the beginning of the Iraqi occupation that a democratic Iraq must be secular. All these voices seem to answer, "yes" to Jack Nelson-Pallmeyer's question in the provocative title of his book, *Is Religion Killing Us?*[229]

These objections concern the assumed tendency of some or all religions to lead to religious tyranny, where one religion dominates a nation, to the detriment of all nonbelievers, making harmonious political life and normal political compromise difficult. A different but equally significant issue of religiously based political division arises in countries that are literally divided by religion—for example by geography, as in a Christian majority in one part of the country and a Muslim majority somewhere else, like the Philippines and sub-Saharan Africa. Or, the religious communities may be overlapping, as in India, where a religious majority confronts a restive, sizeable, and identifiable minority. In both cases, religious democracy seems unattainable as long as each religious group uses politics to protect itself and preserve its own prerogatives.

The United States does not have religious differences along ethnic lines. We do not even really have religious disputes between religions. Instead, disputatious issues, like abortion and gay rights, tend to involve a certain kind of religious orientation on one side—called the religious right or some such title—versus a more liberal religious outlook and/or a secular attitude, on the other.

But in America too, as in the rest of the world, religious differences have the potential for intense political division. Martha Minow writes, "If religions offer rich resources for envisioning a better world and motivating people to strive for it, they also generate divisions, hatreds, and barriers to communication and a sense of commonality."[230] Justice Breyer argued in his dissent in *Zelman* that an important goal of the separation of Church and State required by the Establishment Clause is to "protect[] the Nation's social fabric from religious conflict . . ." Many people worry that something like religious democracy would threaten to revive and create intense political divisions.

Certainly religion does stir up strong feelings in America, maybe especially among the secular. In May 2005, I received the following e-mail from a national grass roots political group—the "Not in Our Name Statement of Conscience":

> The Bush government seeks to impose a narrow, intolerant, and political form of Christian fundamentalism as government policy. No longer on the margins of power, this extremist movement aims to strip women of their reproductive rights, to stoke hatred of gays and lesbians, and to drive a wedge between spiritual experience and scientific truth. We will not surrender to extremists our right to think . . .[231]

Before concluding, however, that religious democracy is inherently unstable or otherwise unworkable, it must be specified what sort of religious democracy is meant. There are many different possibilities for the evolution of American religious democracy. This Part of the book outlines some of these possibilities. In the end, the question whether religious democracy is sustainable must be left open. Whether religious democracy is possible in the long run will depend on the kind of religion that America practices. It is already true that many citizens in America vote based, in part at least, on religious considerations. Some government policies are changing because of those votes. By itself, this phenomenon need be nothing more than democracy in action. It need not spell a threat to democracy. Yet, the fears that people express about religion in the public realm are not fanciful. There is potential for bitter religious/political division. These dangers should not be understated. Nevertheless, religious voters cannot be disenfranchised just because their views and their efforts are potentially divisive. Although that conclusion should be obvious, the secular consensus in effect aimed precisely at such disenfranchisement. This and the following chapters attempt to begin a serious and open-minded discussion of religious democracy.

The first and fundamental issue is not that a religious orientation tends to prefer certain public policies, but rather religion and public policy itself. Is there something undemocratic about citizens seeking public policy changes for religious reasons? That, after all, is what Barry Lynn was arguing in Chapter 3 when he objected to Christians reading the *Bible* in order to obtain direction as to the proper path for national policies. Many secularists believe there is something wrong with Christians opposing gay marriage on the ground that homosexuality is condemned in the *Bible*. They oppose this in a way they do not oppose secular criticism of gay marriage.

This is the "theocracy" criticism. When Kevin Phillips accuses the religious right of *"American Theocracy,"* the title of his book,[232] he is referring not just to particular policies, but rather to the motivation behind policies. So, for example, Phillips is not so much concerned about a ban on gay marriage as he is on a ban on gay marriage based on God's will. It is religion on the march that frightens Phillips.

This charge of undemocratic theocracy is simply false. As long as policy is being made by the majority, the result is democratic. If the majority wants the *Bible* to be enacted into law, that result is not undemocratic. Such policies might be bad ideas, but they are not an assault on democracy. They are not theocracy.

Is there a democratic objection to religious voters seeking to impose their will by banning abortion and gay marriage? Of course, this question assumes that there are no countervailing constitutional rights at stake, which, in the case of abortion, is obviously not currently the law. No American government can legitimately violate constitutional rights, of course. But, whether abortion and gay marriage involve constitutional rights is itself a contested question. In any event, it is not a fair criticism of religious democracy that the policy changes it seeks threaten constitutional rights. That is a circular objection. Religious voters sincerely believe that abortion and gay marriage, properly considered, are not constitutional rights and they are prepared to make legal arguments to show that they are not constitutional rights. They may be wrong about that, but their religious motivation by itself cannot prove they are mistaken. Their religious motivation can no more undermine their constitutional theory than could the religious motivation of Martin Luther King rule out his understanding of equal protection.

Assuming, for the sake of argument, that the policy changes sought by religious democracy do not violate constitutional rights, is religious motivation and argument in the policy realm in and of itself a threat to democracy? Justice Stevens has argued that the desire to protect fetal life is simply a religious belief—a theological position. Such a belief, in his view, is entitled to no judicial support because it is inherently religious.[233] Perhaps it should follow that such a view should not be expressed in our democracy. One could say the same things about religious opposition to gay marriage.

Let us assume for argument sake that the pro-life and anti-gay movements are purely and solely religious. Is it fundamentally undemocratic for citizens to demand government action based upon an understanding of revelation? This is essentially the question Lee Travis was asking about the enforcement of Shari'ah in Islamic countries.

But the antidemocratic problem in Travis' example of religious domination lies either in the assumed denial of human rights to some citizens—women for instance—or in the fact that religious courts will interpret religious requirements in a way that removes lawmaking from the democratic process. Suppose a government decides to cut off the hands of thieves as punishment for theft because that is what a certain school of Islamic jurisprudence requires. One could object to this policy either because the punishment is a violation of universal norms protecting human dignity, or because the decision was not being made democratically. But if we conclude that no human right is violated by this punishment and that the majority in the particular country favors this punishment, what precisely is the democratic objection when the majority sentiment is grounded in religion? Why would a religiously grounded majority's will be any less democratic than a secular majority's will?

To put this matter another way, some might say that American support for the death penalty is based on religion since the *Bible* teaches an eye for an eye. Imposing the death penalty might then be criticized as a religious, and therefore undemocratic, action.

But, what if the population turns against the death penalty because the *Bible* also says, "You shall not kill"? What if the death penalty is then abolished? Would that repeal also be undemocratic?

Many decisions in public life are based on substantive moral judgments. There are many issues, from prostitution to drug use, concerning which the harm principle of John Stuart Mill might not be thought to justify government prohibition. These prohibitions are not "liberal" in the classical sense that limits government restrictions to activities that harm others. Yet such prohibitions are common in American democracy.

The imposition of majoritarian morality by recourse to government coercion is a serious problem in political theory, but it is not a problem uniquely associated with religious arguments. The believer might say that prostitution violates God's law while the nonbeliever might say that prostitution is immoral or tends to demean women. Both positions raise comparable issues in terms of democracy and public argument. Neither position is inherently undemocratic, or both are.

Supposing that religious motivation does not necessarily threaten democracy, are there certain religious policy proposals that do so? There are two kinds of issues that especially concern religious voters. The first type of issue is the receipt of public resources by religious organizations, specifically vouchers for education and government money for the provisions of public services. The second type of issue concerns a series of social controversies, especially abortion and gay rights, and the related view by religious voters that the powers of judges to make policy should be curbed.

In the first instance—receipt of public money—there does seem to be something improper about religious voters supporting candidates who pledge, as President Bush did in the 2000 campaign, to funnel public money to religious institutions in the form of "faith-based initiatives." Voting to line one's own pocket must surely undermine democracy.

But this just goes to show that democracy can be unseemly, because voters vote their self-interest in this way all the time. In recent years, in a series of cases, the Supreme Court has declared unconstitutional much of the traditional spoils system.[234] Prior to those cases, a major reason to support a candidate or a Party was the hope that the voter, or the voter's group, would receive government jobs. Some voters still vote their own direct economic interests. Some rich people voted for President Bush because he promised to repeal the Estate Tax. This behavior does not threaten democracy. Self-interest is not per se undemocratic. Nor do these matters always involve mere self-interest. No doubt some rich people believe that repealing the Estate Tax will, in the end, benefit everyone.

Similarly, many religious voters believe both that policies of public support for religious institutions are in their own best interest and also that they are in the common interest. Many religious people believe quite sincerely that religious efforts directed to reducing drug use or improving education work much better than do parallel secular efforts. Such persons are not just lining their pockets.

But, of course, the major policy changes that religious voters are seeking are the second sort of issue—matters like bans on abortion and gay marriage. Do these proposed religious public policy initiatives threaten to undermine democracy?

There is a degree of disingenuousness in accusing religious democracy of antidemocratic tendencies, particularly with reference to religious opposition to abortion and gay rights. Both abortion and gay marriage arose as tendentious public policy matters as a result not primarily of democratic legislative action, but of judicial action. Abortion was more or less removed from regular electoral politics because of *Roe v. Wade* in 1973.

Prior to *Roe*, a general liberalization of abortion laws was occurring very widely in the nation. Before *Roe*, there wasn't an organized, national pro-life movement or anything like it.

In the same way, gay marriage first achieved political visibility in the Hawaii Supreme Court and then in the courts of Vermont and Massachusetts. Prior to the Hawaii case in 1993—the first case to suggest that a ban on gay marriage might be unconstitutional—state laws regulating homosexuality had also been gradually liberalizing. No one thought of enacting a constitutional amendment either at the federal or state level before these cases. When President Bush announced in June 2006 his support of the federal anti-gay marriage amendment, he criticized "activist judges."

In other words, who exactly is antidemocratic in these fields? Is the religious voter who wants these issues decided in the legislature, albeit of course only in a certain direction, antidemocratic, or is the secular voter seeking change in the courts, the antidemocrat?

Admittedly, religious language in the public square is always something of a problem. It is difficult to argue religious premises in a democratic policy dispute. This difficulty does represent a problem inherent in religious democracy. Yet, it is even harder to argue against judicial decisions in a democratic policy dispute. In the abortion and gay marriage contexts, it is not religious democracy that is antidemocratic, but judicial policymaking. Yet secularists do not complain that resort to the courts threatens democracy.

It is true that the current push by opponents of gay marriage to seek State constitutional amendments banning such marriages is antidemocratic, since such amendments thwart ordinary majority rule. Yet this effort cannot be understood except as a reaction against potential, feared, court decisions, which would take the issue out of the hands of voters. Such State constitutional amendments are undemocratic to be sure, but they are fending off potential judicial action, which is even more undemocratic. No movement to pass such an amendment made political headway before judicial decisions legalizing gay marriage.

As a practical matter, the compatibility of democracy and religious policymaking has been demonstrated by America's own recent political experience. As one example, the *Lawrence* decision striking down criminal sanctions for voluntary homosexual sexual conduct was certainly opposed by many religious voters. Nevertheless, that case did not become a rallying point in the 2004 presidential campaign. Nor has there been any substantial political support since the election for the reimposition of criminal sanctions against homosexual conduct. This is so despite the fact that such conduct violates the precepts of traditional religion in America. Gay marriage is a political flash point in America, but imprisonment of homosexuals is not.

What the *Lawrence* episode suggests is that religious democracy does not abolish the give and take of political life. Nor does it seek, at least in America, to impose all the tenets of religious belief and practice on unwilling citizens through the use of government sanctions.

American religious democracy is rarely, if ever, solely religious. Religious voters have sought changes in policy that many nonreligious Americans also favor. And they have done so without relying exclusively on religious arguments or biblical language. In most situations in which religious democracy in America has sought to change government policy, secular justifications have not only been offered, they have been sincerely held, in addition to genuine religious feelings. This is obviously so in the case of abortion and probably so even in the case of gay marriage.

Religious voters have been perfectly willing to debate issues of morality in the public square, even though their religious orientation can make such debate problematical. I admit that it is frustrating to debate gay marriage with people who simply point to the *Bible* as justification for prohibiting it. But I find it much more frustrating to debate the Iraqi invasion with people who simply point to the events of 9/11—events in which Iraq did not participate—as justification for the invasion of Iraq. In practice, religion has not been an instance of particularly undemocratic policymaking or argument in America.

This short excursion at least raises a question concerning any supposed antidemocratic tendencies in religious voters seeking to change government policy. The next question is whether the deeper goals of religious democracy might undermine democratic life.

Religious democracy is not, after all, just a matter of who wins elections or what policies are followed. Some religious voting is a protest against larger trends in the culture—trends that are difficult for people to find ways to oppose. These religious protest votes may ultimately prove ineffectual because the cultural trends at issue are unstoppable. The question, however, is not effectiveness, but whether these religious protest votes tend to undermine democracy.

These sorts of cultural trends go beyond the culture wars. For one thing, trends in culture are broader than policy issues. For example, the legality of gay marriage is a policy issue. But the social acceptance of gay relationships is a cultural trend. Also, many cultural trends have no specific policy referent. For example, many people find makeover shows on television to be destructive of human flourishing. Such shows teach us that we are not acceptable as we are and that our value as people is directly related to unrealistic physical norms. These shows probably harm young women in particular. But no policy proposal is being offered and debated today to deal with these shows. Even beyond the First Amendment issues, there is a feeling that people ought to be able to watch trash if they want to. Finally, cultural trends may have many and overlapping policy implications and consequences without being reducible to a single issue. The materialism of American culture, for example, has unfortunate economic, moral, and environmental consequences, but there is no one issue in political life that seeks to address this.

Undoubtedly, some of the votes supporting President Bush in the 2004 election represented a feeling by voters that unhealthy cultural trends are harming America. These voters might not have thought that a reelected President Bush could actually do anything about such cultural trends. Nevertheless, they might have felt that it was worth voting for President Bush simply as a protest. Does such voting, to the extent it was happening, threaten democracy?

Thomas Nagel has suggested that it is a violation of Rawlsian political justice for a political community, based on commitment to a particular "contested idea of the ends of life" to attempt to move its members "in that direction by coercion, education, the exclusion of other options, and control of the cultural environment."[235] The pattern of religious voting as cultural protest could be viewed as a violation of this sense of liberal politics. Many religious voters would no doubt like to control the cultural environment in order to change the feel and tone of the country.

But Nagel calls the principle Rawls is rejecting, "perfectionism." That does not seem an accurate description of the generalized feeling that American culture is becoming coarse and that society is, therefore, diminished in various ways that are difficult to specify. The feeling by some voters that without basic civility social life is impossible is not an improper basis for political action. The deterioration of American social life can occur from a kind of looseness in morality—more foul language in public, more petty crime, more available pornography, and so forth. But this sort of laxness is not really an alternative conception of the good life that a new religious majority is attempting to prohibit. Religious democracy may object to all these trends in a very particular way, but many nonreligious voters also object to these trends, and for comparable reasons. There is no religious threat to democracy here.

What about the religious claim to know the good? Is that a threat to democracy? Rawls objects to the participation in democracy by holders of religious, comprehensive doctrines to the extent that acceptance by religious communities of equal rights for nonbelievers may be a mere "modus vivendi."[236] Rawls argues that to participate in democratic life legitimately, religious groups must accept equal rights for nonbelievers in principle and not simply as a strategy to employ until the religious group has enough political power to dominate the political system, at which time it would hope to impose its conception of the good life upon the unwilling minority of nonbelievers or minority believers. Religious democracy can, of course, be accused of just this sort of political opportunism.

Although this is a legitimate criticism, there is another side to religious thought about other communities. The Abrahamic religions have a strand of theoretical toleration of what is nevertheless considered wrongful conduct. Islam states that there is to be no compulsion in religious matters. The Nigerian peace activist M. Ozonnia Ojielo has written, "In effect, even Mohammed himself recognized and granted freedom of religion to all the citizens of Medina. This practice of the prophet was supported by the *Holy Qur'an*, which states thus 'Lakun Dinikun, Wali Y Adinii,' meaning, for you, your religion, and for me, my religion. By implication, Prophet Mohammed accepted that there is no compulsion in religion."[237]

In similar fashion, in the *New Testament*, Jesus rejects Satan's offer of secular power, presumably meaning an attempt to bring the advent of the Kingdom of God immediately through political coercion.[238] Jesus did not force his message on people.

As these examples suggest, religious democracy may not be, or at least may not always be, practicing opportunism and subterfuge in its participation in communal democratic life. Perhaps religious democracy can accept in principle majority rule and minority rights as the proper foundation of democracy.

Even if religion does sometimes threaten to impose its conception of the good life, the undemocratic aspect of total worldviews may not be a problem just for religion. Aside from whether our religions genuinely practice tolerance, it is questionable whether liberal political life itself avoids imposition of comprehensive views or dogmas on dissenters. The most contested political issues in our society are inevitably based on fundamental morality. Abortion certainly is a basic moral issue. There is no neutral way to decide whether a fetus is a member of the political community or not.

In the case of gay marriage, one can say "Live and Let Live," only if it is already established that the acceptance of gay marriage will not harm society. But that is a question rather than an answer.

What about the insufferable smugness of some religious people—their assumption that they are godly and their opponents are agents of evil? How can democracy flourish in such an atmosphere? Some religious voters may suffer from such smugness. But religious voters are not any more subject to smugness than the Chicago School of Economics or my fellow workers in the field of global warming.

One final potential political problem with religious democracy is that a fellow religionist may receive votes because of the religious link itself— as a sort of identity politics—rather than because of the policies that the candidate will carry out. Some critics believe that President Bush received some votes from religious voters despite his policies, simply because he self-identified as a religious Christian. As stated above, this criticism is mistaken, at least as a general matter. To religious voters for whom abortion and gay marriage were a serious concern, President Bush presented a clear political alternative to Senator John Kerry. This is not antidemocratic. It is democracy.

The conclusion here is only that religious democracy need not pose a threat to democratic life. But it remains to look at the possible constitutional theories of religious democracy in America. It may be that religious democracy is incapable of any kind of convincing interpretation of the Establishment Clause. If that is so, then religious democracy, although it may have a majority of the votes, will never really be legitimate in America. The secular consensus has always assumed that religion and public life is an all-or-nothing proposition. Either the State is strictly neutral toward religion, or America ends up a theocracy. Religious voters and thinkers were therefore spared any serious thinking about the actual relationship of Church and State as long as they were opposing governmental neutrality in the realm of Church and State. Now that religious democracy is close to victory over the secular consensus, if in fact not already victorious, the time has come to spell out just how religious the public square is going to be in religious democracy.

CHAPTER 10

The Constitutional Doctrines of Religious Democracy

The lines of thought in this chapter have not yet appeared in American constitutional theory about religion. Our attention to the Constitution remains fixated on certain outcomes, such as the chances of overruling *Roe v. Wade*. Serious thought has not yet been given to what an openly and expressly religious constitution would be like. Our constitutional understanding is still secular, in the sense of separation of Church and State and government neutrality toward religion. Religious thinking opposes this understanding and separation and neutrality now usually lose in actual judicial decisions. It has not yet been necessary as a practical matter for religious thinkers to come up with an alternative constitutional understanding of religion and political life.

Before reflecting on the possibility of a new constitutional understanding, we must return to the concept of a religious voter. Who are these religious voters and why are they particularly important to constitutional thought? Part I acknowledged omitting liberal religious voters from the category of religious democracy. Liberal religious voters are not part of the category of religious voters. That omission can be justified by reference to current political usage. But it is not the main reason.

There is a religious divide in America over the constitutional understanding of the role of religion in public life. Many liberal religious voters—the Presbyterian who belongs to the ACLU, the Catholic Priest who testifies against the crèche in a public place, the Jew who contributes money to COEJL, the Coalition on the Environment and Jewish Life—do not need a new constitutional understanding about the role of religion.

These voters accept, often enthusiastically, the tenets of the secular consensus. They believe in the separation of Church and State. They agree that religion per se has no place in public life. For these voters, religion is certainly a motivating force behind political commitments, as in the case of concern for the environment and social justice. But these liberal religious voters express their political commitments only in secular terms once they enter the public square.

This distinction between private religious beliefs and public expression in politics was part of Richard John Neuhaus's criticism of the mainline Protestant Churches in his book *The Naked Public Square*. He wrote of mainline Protestantism that "it is embarrassed to make any religious statement that does not possess redeeming social merit."[239] Or, to put the matter another way, many liberal religious voters do not support any positions in politics that liberal secular voters do not also support. It follows that these liberal religious voters and liberal secular voters share the same constitutional commitments.

Of course, this is painting with a broad brush. Part III will return to the issue of attempting to ground a distinctively liberal religious vision for public policy. This attempt is going on today and was attempted more aggressively during the Clinton Administration. Representative of that effort was Michael Lerner's 1997 book, *The Politics of Meaning*.[240] The effort goes on today in work such as *God's Politics*,[241] by Jim Wallis. These efforts, however, have not yet had a significant political impact in America.

The point here is that for the most part, liberal religious voters emphasize pluralism and ecumenicism in the public realm. Therefore, they do not require a constitutional dogma for religion other than separation of Church and State and government neutrality toward religion.

None of this is the case with regard to those denominated religious voters here—those who, broadly speaking, are part of the Republican Party coalition. Their political commitments put them in conflict with existing constitutional doctrine. Up to now, their constitutional understanding has only concerned particular desired outcomes. Religious voters want a freer hand for government symbolic religious expression and religious teaching. Religious voters want *Roe v. Wade* overturned and want to prevent the constitutional recognition of gay marriage. They also want education vouchers for parents in private religious schools.

These desired outcomes have masked, rather than expressed, a constitutional theory about religion and government. In terms of symbolic speech, for example, "more expression" of religion does not explain how much religious expression is to be allowed in the public square or how "religious" such expression is allowed to be. Basically, religious democracy must explain whether, when, and how the government may use and teach religion. What is the Establishment Clause theory that religious voters are promoting?

The same omission of constitutional theory occurs with regard to the opposition of these religious voters to abortion and gay rights. On what grounds is *Roe v. Wade* to be overturned? On what grounds are gay relationships excluded from the protections of the Equal Protection Clause? Religious voters may eventually come to see that their current reliance on conservative constitutional theory, which is what religious thinkers today endorse, is in tension with their religious commitments.

This book is not the first to suggest that the prior constitutional understandings of neutrality and separation are no longer accepted doctrines on the Supreme Court, but that no new doctrinal synthesis has yet emerged. Noah Feldman, for example, intended to offer just such a new synthesis in his recent book, *Divided by God*. His suggestion was to "offer greater latitude for public religious discourse and religious symbolism, and at the same time insist on a stricter ban on state funding of religious institutions and activities."[242] This latter prohibition, Feldman makes clear, is to prohibit most school vouchers systems.

This is not a book about constitutional doctrine, so this is not the place to debate Feldman's particulars. Nevertheless, it does seem that vouchers solve the problem of public support for religious schools because vouchers go to parents to fulfill a requirement of law. Mandatory school attendance is the State's doing and, therefore, vouchers pay for something the secular voter, as well as everyone else, wants on secular grounds: an educated citizenry. Vouchers do not seem to even raise the problem of government support of religious institutions that Feldman fears.

In any event, Feldman recognizes that we are going to have a religious public square in America. What he does not answer is, how much latitude for religion in American public life there should be in what he calls "greater latitude."

There are many specific constitutional doctrines involved in that question. But I want to concentrate on two fundamental constitutional issues. The first is the question of truth. Current constitutional theory, especially conservative constitutional theory, denies the reality and applicability of truth in constitutional interpretation. This denial has particular implications for abortion and gay rights. The second issue is government religious neutrality. Once that norm is rejected, as it has been or soon will be, what replaces neutrality and separation?

In terms of truth, there is an unholy alliance of religious democracy with conservative constitutional theory. Simply put, for someone like Justice Scalia, the reason that a woman does not have a right to an abortion is that constitutional language and history do not have anything to say about abortion. There is nothing to suggest that any language in the Constitution as originally understood could pertain to a limit on the government's power to prohibit abortions. That historical inquiry is believed by people of Scalia's view to preclude consideration of the abortion issue in constitutional terms. The Constitution is not a "living" one that changes with changes in society. The reason Scalia opposes a living Constitution is that there is no guiding principle that would then inform constitutional interpretation. This would leave interpretation open to the personal, subjective preference of judges. To avoid that, Justice Scalia says he grounds his constitutional understanding on more objective foundations, on textualism and to a lesser extent on original intention. Similarly, gays are not protected under the Equal Protection Clause because they were not thought of when the constitutional language of equality was written. This description puts complex matters in too simple a form, but this is Justice Scalia's basic position.

Religious voters have not had to contest the view that truth has no application in the public realm of constitutional interpretation because Justice Scalia, and conservative constitutional thinking as a whole, agree with religious voters that abortion and gay marriage are not constitutionally protected. But, once *Roe* is overturned, new issues will arise. Once *Roe* no longer protects abortion, legislatures in pro-choice States will pass statutes freely allowing abortion. Those statutes will be challenged in court. The question will then be whether unborn life is protected by the Constitution.

When that happens, the jurisprudential tables will turn. It will be the pro-choice advocates who argue that the word "life" in the Fourteenth Amendment must be interpreted as it was understood at the time of its adoption—when it was not thought to apply prior to live birth. Then it will be the religious advocates who argue against such legal positivism, attempting to gain for unborn life a new status as members of the body politic. The fundamental right of all human life to the protections of the fundamental law will be argued by these religious advocates as a matter of truth. Justice Scalia's jurisprudence, whatever his personal views may be about abortion, will stand directly against this religious effort. Indeed he has already written, in his dissent in *Casey*, that States are free to allow abortion on demand.

Today, religious voters applaud when President Bush claims to nominate a "strict constructionist" to the United States Supreme Court. But soon, there will be a new constitutional context and religious voters may come to regret their support. At that point, a new constitutional jurisprudence will emerge from religious democracy. This new jurisprudence will have to depend on something like natural law principles. Justice Thomas once embraced natural law, but he claimed at the beginning of his Supreme Court nomination hearings that he did not in fact follow a natural law approach to constitutional interpretation.

At the moment, there is no natural law advocate on the Supreme Court. But religious democracy will soon have to develop a new jurisprudential starting point.

Aside from the question of truth in interpretation, the other fundamental constitutional issue with which religious democracy must engage is religious neutrality and religious symbolic expression. One aspect of that issue is religious expression in the public square by private citizens. Religious democracy insists that private citizens have a constitutional right to participate in public life as believers.

This constitutional argument, which was never formally opposed by the secular consensus as a constitutional theory, has prevailed. Religious democracy has already altered the tone of the public square. The point that Richard John Neuhaus was making in 1984 was that the *language* of belief was, at that time, absent from the public square. That has certainly now changed. Even if believers still wish to claim that their perspective is discriminated against, their protests sound hollow given their electoral successes.

The objection to religious expression by citizens in the public square was that religion is a conversation stopper. In 1999, Richard Rorty explained the need to privatize religion as arising from the fact that religion stops public debate as far as nonmembers of the religious community are concerned.[243] Allowing religious language in political debate threatens democracy because political debate then becomes impossible. Since religion is a matter of subjective belief, of taste in other words, nothing can be said when religious believers claim that society should act in a certain way because God demands it. As Professor Steven Gey put this in a 2004 law review article, referring to the thought of John Rawls, "[A]ll arguments regarding policy should ... be cast in terms of public reason, which means they should be defended on terms that are perceived as reasonable even to people whose worldviews are based on irreconcilable ultimate beliefs."[244]

This preference for secular expression in the public square was never put in terms of actual censorship. No coherent constitutional theory ever supported literal suppression of voters' religious political speech. All Rorty said was that it should be thought in "bad taste" to speak religious language in public debate. While not actually coercive in the sense of banning religious language, secularists have engaged in loose talk to the effect that religious expression violates the separation of Church and State. Anyway, today the language of religious believers in the public square is accepted, even dominant. There is no longer a significant political argument for its inappropriateness.

Nor has the public square suffered from this change in tone. Our current political experience demonstrates that religion does not function as a conversation stopper. In our most contentious political/legal issue—abortion—there are clearly strong religious views, probably on both sides, but certainly expressed as specifically religious in the pro-life position. Nevertheless, rarely does anyone argue in the public square that abortion should be outlawed only because God says so. Pro-life religious voters and leaders do argue that abortion kills a human being. While the belief in a soul may make it easier to believe that a fetus is fully human, many Americans believe that the fetus should be protected as human without a commitment to the concept of a soul. Abortion can be opposed on the ground of the distinctive DNA of the developing embryo.

Gay marriage is a better example of a contentious, substantially religious debate. Many people oppose gay marriage basically because the *Bible* condemns homosexuality. Nevertheless, much more political opposition to gay marriage could be called simply social conservatism. Many people just do not like the idea of homosexuality. That attitude is as divisive, undebatable, and uncompromising as religious opposition is said to be, yet, obviously, nothing can be done in a constitutional sense about such "reasons" for banning gay marriage.

Religious democracy has not restricted political debate. It is true that political debates now invoke the name of God without hesitance, and that national leaders do the same on ceremonial occasions, perhaps more often than ever before. All this makes the believer more comfortable in the public square and the nonbeliever presumably less so. But there is nothing here that threatens democratic exchange. Whatever political leaders may mean by references to God, they do not mean that the nonbeliever is outside the political community in any practical sense. Religious language does not, and is not meant to, substitute for ordinary politics. Indeed, the language of God may be invoked by religious leaders in order to gain ordinary political support.

The constitutional difficulty concerning symbolic religious expression is not private expression of religious arguments, however, but formal government symbolism. There have been efforts, for example, to declare that America is a religious nation. Edward Foley refers to efforts in the 1950s and the 1960s to amend the preamble of the Constitution to include the words, "'devoutly recognizing the authority and law of Jesus Christ the Savior and King of Nations'" after "We the People of the United States."[245] The insertion of "under God" in the Pledge of Allegiance in 1954 was this kind of religious identity claim. Indeed, most religion cases concern some form or other of government religious expression—from the Ten Commandments in public places, to crèches on public property, to communal prayer in the public schools.

This sort of government religious symbolism is now constrained by the Establishment Clause. The constitutional questions for the future are: What doctrine might replace government neutrality with regard to religion? How much government sponsorship of religion can there be without violation of the Establishment Clause? Will there be any role for the Supreme Court in this area in the future?

The problem, even for religious sympathizers, is demonstrated in two comments by Justice Scalia in dissenting opinions. In *Lee v. Weisman*, the case that banned prayer at public school graduations, Justice Scalia, joined by Chief Justice Rehnquist, and Justices White and Thomas, complained at the sole focus by the majority of the Court on the rights of the plaintiffs:

> The reader has been told much in this case about the personal interest of Mr. Weisman and his daughter, and very little about the personal interests on the other side. They are not inconsequential. Church and state would not be such a difficult subject if religion were, as the Court apparently thinks it to be, some purely personal avocation that can be indulged entirely in secret, like pornography, in the privacy of one's room. For most believers it is *not* that, and has never been.

> Religious men and women of almost all denominations have felt it necessary to acknowledge and beseech the blesssing of God as a people, and not just as individuals, because they believe in the "protection of divine Providence," as the Declaration of Independence put it, not just for individuals but for societies . . .[246]

Justice Scalia does not claim to have solved this problem of balance— only to have stated it. While a dissenting minority—whether secularist or minority religious believers—clearly has a right against the establishment of the majority's religion, the majority has a right as well to express its belief in a God of history in a fully public way. God affects the world. Justice Scalia is here relying implicitly on Jefferson's view and Lincoln's view that God's will is inevitably a political matter because God affects the world. It is not obvious how, or whether, the conflicting rights of the minority and majority can be harmonized.

The *Ten Commandments* display cases did not need to sharpen this problem, because the Ten Commandments are not, after all, a prayer. But Justice Scalia's dissent in *McCreary*, joined on this point by Chief Justice Rehnquist and Justice Thomas, saw the *Ten Commandments* issue as presenting the same problem as did the graduation prayer in *Lee*. Again, Justice Scalia insists that "*competing* interests" must be acknowledged—on the one hand the interest of the "minority in not feeling 'excluded'"—certainly a weak formulation of the minority's interest—and on the other "the interest of the overwhelming majority of religious believers in being able to give God thanks and supplication *as a people*, and with respect to our national endeavors."

The question of public religious expression has been avoided by religious constitutional thinkers—and the Court—through two unsatisfactory evasions of the real issue. The first evasion is the proposal that we should allow as much religion in the public square as there has been in the past. This is a form of constitutional positivism, like any other form of original intent jurisprudence. For example, it might be said that we can have public prayer today, because President George Washington said prayers in public. The problem with this approach is that it does not tell us what to do with any new religious expression. In other words, it works to allow the Ten Commandments, but says nothing about public display of the *Qur'an*.

The second evasion is the claim that religious expression is not really religious. Again this has worked for certain venerable American practices, like the cry, "God save this Court" to open a Supreme Court session or the slogan "In God We Trust" on our money. But these claims are not really true. Religious believers want religious expressions in the public square because they are in fact religious expressions.

A claim related to that of the absence of religious meaning was the Court's suggestion in *Marsh*, the legislative prayer case, that invoking divine guidance "is simply a tolerable acknowledgment of beliefs widely held among the people of this country." The problem with calling public religious expression mere acknowledgment is that the belief really widely held among the people of this country is that Christ is Lord. The Court probably did not mean to embrace an understanding of the Establishment Clause that would allow public acknowledgement of Christ.

Most religious voters, even among themselves, have not yet decided what the Establishment Clause forbids. Since the 2004 election, the religious coalition that helped reelect President Bush has not pressed to have Jesus Christ recognized as a national symbol, nor that America be declared a Christian nation. Part of the reason for that hesitance is that Jews are an important part—or potential part—of the Republic coalition. For another, even in religious democracy religious pluralism is a favored American commitment. The serious political push has been for public recognition of the less divisive term, "God," in the public square, rather than any more sectarian term.

The claim that the word "God" is nonsectarian is, of course, contested. The Ninth Circuit opinion in the Pledge of Allegiance case was right as a matter of logic that the word God is not a generic term that can be plugged into any religion. The circuit court stated: "A profession that we are a nation 'under God' is identical, for Establishment Clause purposes, to a profession that we are a nation 'under Jesus,' a nation 'under Vishnu,' a nation 'under Zeus,' or a nation 'under no god,' because none of these professions can be neutral with respect to religion."[247] Indeed, Justice O'Connor, at the Supreme Court level, referred to a Buddhist amicus brief making just that point about Buddhism not embracing any form of monotheism, though she still viewed the Pledge of Allegiance as not endorsing religion.

The question of public, symbolic, religious expression is going to become a more pressing constitutional issue under religious democracy. Chapter 7 argued that the Court is likely to allow Government encouragement of religion as a part of the development of religious democracy. But this victory is not without price. Once it is accepted that government may truly encourage, indeed practice, religion, as Justice Scalia seems to argue in supporting genuinely public prayer, then the rights of nonbelievers and those of minority believers must be addressed. Those interests cannot simply be dismissed.

Part III will take up the issue of the nonbeliever. For most secular Americans, the concept of God will not prove ultimately an insurmountable issue. The current religious problem in American political life is based on a lack of theological sophistication by secularists and their hostility to religious hierarchy. Simply put, many secularists are actually believers who do not want clergy to tell them what to do. Such voters may come to see that they are not really threatened by public acknowledgement of God. There are atheists in America. But there are not many.

Much more difficult than the nonbeliever is the place of the minority religious believer in the public square of religious democracy. Justice Scalia finally began to address this issue in his dissent in *McCreary*. If the Ten Commandments are permissible because "the overwhelming majority of religious believers" must be able "to give God thanks and supplication *as a people*" what about the seven million nonmonotheist believers and what about publicly acknowledging Jesus Christ? In other words, when government is permitted to go beyond "a simple reference to a generic 'God,'" where will we go?

Justice Scalia's response is his typical historical positivism. He states, "[O]ur national tradition has resolved that conflict in favor of the majority." By tradition, he claims, the nonmonotheist believer is out of luck. Genuine monotheism is just plain permitted by our Constitution. American Government may acknowledge the Creator God. But, also by tradition, he implies, the majority is not permitted to publicly pray to Jesus Christ.

Justice Scalia displays a breathtaking historical dumbness here. His idea of history is what is called "lawyer's history," which means history from which all ambiguity has been removed in order to give a seemingly clear answer to issues that do not have clear answers. It is not true that one can just look at American history and see that there is a tradition of expression in favor of God, but not in favor of Christ, and that this tradition does not extend to nonmonotheistic traditions. This is an example of a lawyer inappropriately imposing the terms of our current debates upon the past.

Aside from weak history, the worse problem with Justice Scalia's formulation is that it is simple *ipse dixit*—because I said so. It is no response at all. If the nonmonotheist is out of luck today, Jews and the Muslims may be out of luck tomorrow, when Christians decide to praise Christ. Justice Scalia would no doubt vote against such expression. But he has no grounds for doing so. After all, America has not just been religious. We have always been Christian. Why not then express our Christian heritage? That is the problem with using tradition as the sole basis of judicial interpretation of the Constitution.

There was an available route to a similar result of permitting public prayer. Justice Scalia could have contested the claim that our religions are fundamentally divided on the concept of God. Granted, the Ten Commandments are a very specific Judeo-Christian expression. Because they are so particularly associated with one religious tradition, the Ten Commandments did not actually require consideration of the place of God in the public square. The acceptance of the Ten Commandments under the Establishment Clause could be justified without regard to God—by their special place in Western legal history, for example, as Chief Justice Rehnquist suggested in his plurality opinion in *Van Orden*.

But we are now moving into a new era of Establishment Clause jurisprudence—one in which the place of God in the public square must be addressed. Our new questions cannot be determined by tradition. The issue for the future of religious democracy is not neutrality of any kind, but, as Justice Scalia puts it, public expressions of thanks and supplication to God. Given this new context, Justice Scalia is much too cavalier in dismissing the concerns of religions other than Judaism, Christianity, and Islam. It is not true that these "other" religions are outside Establishment Clause protection with regard to public religious expression. Rather, we may come to see that all of "our religions," even those traditionally regarded as nonmonotheist, share a core comportment toward reality that can be the basis of political community. According to Huston Smith, the great and well-known teacher of the worlds' religions, this commitment can be expressed through the language of God:

> Making due allowance not only for differences in terminology but for differences in nuances, in East Asia we find Confucianism's *shang ti*, the supreme ancestor, and beyond him *Tien*, or Heaven. In Taoism, there is the Tao that transcends speech.
>
> In South Asia, Hinduism presents us with *sanguna Brahman*—God with attributes or qualities, among which *sat, chit,* and *Amanda* (infinite being, awareness, and bliss) are primary—and *Nirguna Brahman*, the *neti, neti* (not this, not this) of the Brahman who is beyond all qualities. Buddhism presents a special case because of its ambiguous stance toward God, but though the personal God is absent in early Buddhism, it could not be excluded indefinitely and came pouring in through the *Mahayana.*... The transpersonal God is, of course, solidly ensconced in Buddhism's *sunyata*—emptiness—and *Nirvana*.[248]

In other words, the terms monotheism and polytheism are not as distinct as we usually think. A good example of the ambiguous relationships between monotheism and polytheism is the history of Shinto, the native religion of Japan, in Hawaii. In 1984, James Whitehurst visited Shinto

Bishop Kazoe Kawasacki, head priest of the Daijingu Shrine in Honolulu. Whitehurst reported his encounter in *Christian Century* magazine. He described Shinto as a religion of nature, with numerous deities, known as kami, who are personifications of natural forces such as rivers, fire, mountains, and others. Such a religion would be regarded as polytheistic. But when Whitehurst met with Bishop Kawasacki, he discovered

> a decidedly monotheistic emphasis, which undoubtedly communicates better to a Western-educated audience. One Creator God, Hitori Gami, is shown as the source of all lesser kami manifestations.[249]

For the Shinto priest, "the divine is at the heart of all matter."[250]

The Supreme Court has not always been insensitive to these universal possibilities. The problem has been the issue of government involvement. Justice Kennedy expressed a universal religious theme in his opinion for a 5–4 majority in *Lee v. Weisman*:

> We are asked to recognize the existence of a practice of nonsectarian prayer, prayer within the embrace of what is known as the Judeo-Christian tradition, prayer which is more acceptable than one which, for example, makes explicit references to the God of Israel, or to Jesus Christ, or to a patron saint. There may be some support, as an empirical observation . . . that there has emerged in this country a civic religion, one which is tolerated when sectarian exercises are not. . . . If common ground can be defined which permits once conflicting faiths to express the shared conviction that there is an ethic and a morality which transcend human invention, the sense of community and purpose sought by all decent societies might be advanced. But though the First Amendment does not allow the government to stifle prayers which aspire to these ends, neither does it permit the government to undertake that task for itself.[251]

Justice Kennedy here recognizes the potential importance of communal prayer expressing "the shared conviction" of transcendent norms. He recognizes the bedrock commitment in all our religions that Justice Scalia failed to acknowledge in the *Ten Commandments* cases.

The reason that Justice Kennedy cannot develop this insight into a genuine religious jurisprudence of the Establishment Clause is his wooden understanding of what "government" is and his inability to conceive of civil society apart from government. The parents of graduating seniors, most of whom want prayer at a graduation ceremony, are not the government. They should be allowed to create a prayer for this public occasion. Justice Kennedy says that the First Amendment does not allow the government to stifle prayer. But by destroying all opportunity for communal religious expression, which is the sort of common expression of praise and thanks that Justice Scalia describes, the Supreme Court *is* stifling prayer and inhibiting the experimentation that leads to religious common ground. This is the same problem the Court had in the *Santa Fe* case discussed in Chapter 7. When the community wants prayer at public occasions, the Court is going to have to get out of the way.

Of course the idea of common religious ground can become a caricature. Our religions are not all one thing. It really does matter whether I say the Sh'ma, or worship Jesus Christ, or pass under a torii arch. Nor would all or most believers agree with Huston Smith, or with James Whithurst, that monotheistic beliefs occur in all religions. That sort of comparative religion is an insult to serious religious believers.

But we are not dealing with religion in itself or even our religions in themselves. We are dealing here with political community and its capacity for transcendent expression. The Supreme Court should not readily assume that minority believers are excluded by monotheistic religious expression at that level. All religions express gratitude and practice prayer. It is at least not clear that any religious believer is harmed or excluded when general expressions of thanks and supplication are offered publicly in the language of other religious traditions. That is why America should be able to find public, transcendent expressions that do not divide religious believers. The language of God may turn out to be that expression. The defenders of religion on the Court should have held out this possibility in the *Ten Commandments* cases.

The conclusion here can only be that religious democracy has constitutional challenges to face. But this discussion has so far only dealt with the external issue for religious democracy. The issue of public, communal prayer concerns the relationship of the religious outsider to the majority's religious expression. What is just as significant, however, is the internal meaning of religious democracy. That is a theological matter. Whether religious democracy is possible also depends on the answer to the question, how is America conceptualized in religious democracy? Do believers feel that they represent the nation as a whole or do they see themselves merely as a dissenting segment of the nation, a saving remnant? What can democracy mean, in the end, to a religious community when many fellow citizens remain nonbelievers or minority believers? That is the theological/political issue for religious democracy. Different answers to this question are possible. The answer that American religious democracy ultimately gives may determine the future of democracy itself.

CHAPTER 11

The Theology of Religious Democracy

Religious voters face the question in every election, "who are these other voters and what can be expected from them?" In other words, American religious democracy requires religious voters to conceptualize their relationship to nonreligious voters. In shorthand, we can call all self-identified believers in any of the religious traditions, "the community of faith" and the specifically Christian believers, "the Church." Everyone else—the self-identified nonbelievers—we can call "the world." The relationship of religion and democracy then turns on how America is regarded by the community of faith. Is America to be treated as entirely encompassed by the Church? Entirely encompassed by the community of faith? Or is America the world? Or, is America some combination of these?

In September 2006, Villanova Law School held a conference entitled "From John Paul II to Benedict XVI: Continuing the New Evangelization of Law, Politics and Culture." Think about how that could sound to the old Protestant suspicions. It could sound like the Catholics trying to take over America. And, during the 2004 election, wasn't the Catholic Church trying to tell American Catholic politicians how to vote on abortion by threatening to deny certain politicians communion? These are the kinds of issues religious democracy must face across the board.

There are three possible religious orientations that religious democracy can take in its relationship to the general society. If America is conceptualized as the Church, then some parts of the community have fallen away from Christianity and these people need to be returned to the fold. Perhaps these people should be forced, for their own salvation, at least to live up to the minimal standards of the Church. If, on the other hand, America is composed of different communities of faith, all of whom share a religious orientation toward reality and a certain ecumenical spirit, then with sufficient give and take, it ought to be possible to develop public policies of a decent society more or less acceptable to everybody. Finally, if America is thought of as the world, then the Church might attempt to convert it, or redeem it, or withdraw from it. All these categories can also be mixed.

As a nonbeliever, which is a complex status I will return to in Part III, I am not asking these questions for the sake of the community of faith and its faithfulness. Naturally there is a specter of theological harm that may beset the Church from the mixing of Church and State. That is referred to as the danger of Constantinianism, which involves the confusion of Christian community with the power of the State. That is the danger that Jefferson Powell was referring to in Chapter 1. But the threat of Constantinianism cannot be the concern here for two reasons. For one thing, only believers can address a potential theological harm threatening the community of faith. So, those who are not members of the community of faith—and in particular not members of the Church—cannot know whether this latest form of Constantinianism is to be avoided or not. Certainly nonbelievers cannot preach to the Church about its mission. Believers, such as Stanley Hauerwas and Randall Balmer, have raised this issue, but they are in a proper position to do so.

Second, the concern that "secular" and political uses of religious symbols will be harmful to the Church sounds insincere when spoken by someone who is outside the community and who perhaps has an agenda the community does not share. So, for example, when Justice Brennan pointed in his *Lynch* dissent to the "insult[]" that commercial use of a crèche in a Christmas display causes to believers, the believer may legitimately ask whether Justice Brennan, who wanted a separation of Church and State anyway, can possibly be the right person to protect the theological integrity of the Church. Someone like Justice Brennan inevitably provokes skepticism in such a context. This is not to speak of Justice Brennan's personal piety, but his official role as a Supreme Court Justice committed to the separation of Church and State.

The question of orientation can also not be asked out of an unrealistic insistence that voters ignore their religion completely when voting or otherwise participating in democratic life. Thomas Nagel asks whether the insistence by John Rawls on certain limits in liberal political discourse is psychologically possible for the believer: "To base political values on something less than our most comprehensive transcendental values can seem both morally wrong and psychologically incoherent."[252] Without resolving whether that is the case, it is certainly psychologically impossible for the believer to vote as if he or she were not a believer. This is especially true in the case of the Abrahamic religions, which believe that all societies are subject to God's judgment. The *Old Testament* is very clear, for example, that the sins of Nineveh described in the book of *Jonah* promised destruction for that pagan city. It did not matter that the inhabitants were not Hebrews.

It is also the case that every nation will be judged as a whole. This means that the believer cannot be indifferent to the conduct of the nonbelieving others in his or her society. Not only are all citizens members of the human family, and thus capable of gaining salvation, but everyone will also suffer from God's wrath, including the believers though they are themselves obedient.

Abraham Lincoln adopted this universal perspective in his Second Inaugural Address, in which God was portrayed as working out the divine purpose through the American Civil War. In Lincoln's understanding, there is no political actor who is not a part of the divine plan. The notion of a purely secular political life is alien to Lincoln in this address. That does not mean that clerics should have political power, or that there should no distinction between Church and State. But it does mean that God's will must be taken into account in every public decision, since that will is dispositive of the outcome. There is, therefore, for Lincoln, no fundamental, nonreligious, political decision.

Thus, in the issue of abortion, one cannot expect any believer to be indifferent to the killing of human life, which is how the matter is seen by many religious voters. Since the unborn child is generally not taken into account, the believer cannot say that this is a matter for personal conscience. To insist that the believer keep out of it would be to commit the error of Jonah, who thought that the sin of nonbelievers did not matter.

But, in the case of gay marriage, and even more so in the case of the civil rights of gay unions, the hostility of believers raises the question of what role the Church is to play in a pluralist political entity. Inescapably, for the believer that is a question of theology, of the proper role of the Church, given its mission.

The two extreme approaches—that religion should not enter political life for theological reasons, on the one hand, and that voters must ignore their religion in all cases, on the other hand—are the extremes. There is room between them for clarification of the attitude of the community of faith, and in particular the attitude of the Church, toward America.

AMERICA AS THE COMMUNITY OF FAITH—AS THE CHURCH

One model for religious democracy is to treat political life as if America were the Church and therefore subject to all biblical and other religious injunctions. In this way of thinking, America is either a Christian nation or at least a nation uniquely under God.

Treating America as the Church is different from asserting that all nations are under God because all people are subject to God's will. That is a different kind of religious political thinking, one that does not treat America as if it, uniquely of all nations, were the Church.

When religious voters try to banish wrongdoing from America, they may be acting as if there were no difference between what believers inside the Church are obligated to do and what citizen in America must do. They may be treating America as identical to the Church. In this perspective, America is in a special relationship with God.

In principle, in this special relationship, America might be especially blessed or especially cursed under God's judgment. But in practice, America has been regarded by most of the religious voters who make up the Republican Party coalition, as especially good, at least in the sense of the intentions of its leaders. President Bush, and most Americans, are regarded as good and the people who behave wrongly are enemies of God who are to be defeated and then brought back to God. From this perspective, all public policy engages in this struggle as either moving toward victory or away from it. This is what Bob Jones was saying when he wrote to President Bush, as quoted in Chapter 1: "You owe the liberals nothing. They despise you because they despise your Christ."

This whole mindset has led to criticism from within the Church. Richard Parker, for example, remarked critically that "Ronald Reagan persisted in calling John Winthrop's 'city on a hill' a 'shining city on a hill.'"[253] In other words, it is an error to confuse Church and State. Nevertheless, for good or ill, this identification of America by believers as the embodiment of the Church has not been unusual in American history.

When America is viewed as in a special relationship with God, sin in America cannot simply be tolerated as something one would expect from nonbelievers. If America is the Church, then sin must be prohibited by government just as sin is prohibited within all the communities of faith. For instance, gay marriage cannot just be regarded as something that gays do in America that has nothing really to do with the Church. In this way of thinking, there is no conceptual space for the sin of nonbelievers.

Religious countries must look at themselves in this way. Saudi Arabia looks at itself this way. Iran looks at itself this way, which makes the problem of minority religious communities in Iran so difficult. Israel looks at itself this way, which again is why the internal problem of the non-Jewish Israeli Arabs has been intractable. And American religious democracy sometimes looks at itself this way.

It generally follows (in the perspective that America is the Church) that America has an obligation to the world, much as the Church has the obligation in the *New Testament* to convert the world—the resurrected Christ says to His disciples in Matt. 28:19, "Go therefore and make disciples of all nations"—much as Israel was to be a blessing to the nations. President Bush's desire to bring freedom and democracy to the world fits very well into this way of thinking. One can easily see why he thinks he is doing God's will in the expansion of democracy.

It does not necessarily follow that America has the same obligation as does the Church to actually spread Christianity. America might just be God's instrument to bring justice to the world. But some religious voters plainly do think that America should spread Christianity and they act accordingly. This attitude complicates the American effort in Iraq. *Time* magazine ran a story on June 30, 2003, asking the question on its cover "Should Christians Convert Muslims?" The story described the tensions that conversion was causing in Iraq. Earlier American opposition to the presence of Islam in any new Iraqi constitution also fueled the suspicion in the Islamic world that, rather than simply fighting terrorism, America was engaged in Iraq in a new competition between Christianity and Islam. President Bush's reference to our presence in Iraq, and the war against terrorism generally, as a "crusade," contributed to this Muslim perception. He was once quoted as saying, "This crusade, this war on terrorism, is going to take a while" and this quote was widely disseminated in the Muslim world.

The perspective that America has a special, religious obligation to the world—that this is America's destiny—can lead to all sorts of imperial projects. As Amitai Etzioni, the principal figure in the communitarian movement, writes, such a view implies "that the United States has been ordained by a power greater than that of any person or a combination thereof, to undertake a mission."[254] Etzioni does not approve of the implications of such a view: "The notion that the United States has been sent by God to do whatever it chooses to do is dangerous." But Etzioni is not describing the internal perspective of religious people when he writes that. Religious people do not think of themselves as sent to do what they choose. They are trying to be faithful to God's will.

At one extreme of this understanding of America's role in the world, a conflation can occur of the *Gospel* with the particular political/economic/legal system that is championed by the United States. Such a conflation can suggest that our system is the ultimate and last word in human governance. Unfortunately, this is sometimes America's understanding. Rumu Sarkar, the General Counsel for the Overseas Basing Commission, wrote critically, but accurately, in 2005:

> Modernization theory is based on the assumption that development is the inevitable, evolutionary result of a gradual progression led by the nation-state that results in the creation (and ascendancy) of Western-styled economic, political, and cultural institutions. These institutions rest on three pillars: a free market capitalist system, liberal democratic institutions, and the Rule of Law.[255]

This conflation implies that judicial review, market economics, and representative democracy are the way that God intends people to live for all time. In 1992, Francis Fukuyama called this the "end of history."[256]

This notion of the "end of history," or eschatology, is originally a Judeo-Christian concept now put into the service of an expansionist American foreign policy. In this parallel, what we could call the American system is the end of history and America's job is to spread this *Gospel* all over the world.

Fukuyama is now busy trying to distance himself from the Iraq War and the overconfidence of President Bush's foreign policy, an overconfidence Fukuyama bears some responsibility for. But even in a sort of apology for neoconservatism that Fukuyama wrote in the *New York Times* in February 2006, he still treated modernity as without major flaw and something for which there is an underlying universal human longing.[257] In other words, Fukuyama has learned nothing.

The parallel between regarding the American system as utopia and salvation history can be heard in descriptions of millennialist biblical doctrines. G. Edward White's describes such doctrines as "portray[ing] the course of history as taking place across a distinctive time continuum, one in which eventually God's truth would be revealed, sin would disappear, the fall of man would be redeemed, and the 'end of history' would be achieved in a millennial state of grace."[258]

At its extreme domestic end, this view of America as the Church can tend to abolish any distinction between religion and politics and fuses government with the Church. In law, this tendency identifies government officials with biblical roles, as Michael Perry does when he identifies judges with the prophets of the *Old Testament*. Perry wrote in 1982 that judicial review "represents the institutionalization of prophecy. The function of noninterpretivist review in human rights cases is prophetic: it is to call the American people—actually the government, the representatives of the people—to provisional judgment."[259] In this absurdly inflated view, secular law should always be controlled by natural right and revealed truth. Earl Warren plays the role of Moses.

Richard John Neuhaus, who is critical of this tendency, tries to draw a distinction in *The Naked Public Square* between a "theonomous culture" and a "theocracy." A theonomous culture is one that "acknowledges accountability to transcendent truth" and "one in which religious and cultural aspirations toward the transcendent are given public expression."[260] Neuhaus believes the United States should be theonomous. A theocracy, on the other hand, is "a false theonomy" one "in which an institution, namely organized religion, claims to embody and authoritatively articulate absolute truth." Theocracy is "an act of historical closure, and therefore a form of idolatry."[261]

As I stated above, as long as democracy is practiced, a political system is not literally a theocracy. But it can happen that the *Bible*, or one interpretation of the *Bible*, is regarded as absolute truth by a voting majority that controls a society's political system. It is not clear whether Neuhaus regards that situation, which might be our situation in America today, as a theocracy.

The theological objections to this sort of mixing of Church and State are beyond my scope. But, Neuhaus is articulating democratic objections as well as theological ones. Obviously there is no room for democracy in an actual theocracy. But even where the forms of democracy remain, the identification of society with the Church threatens legitimate democratic pluralism. So we may take Neuhaus as stating the democratic objection to the total identification of the State with the Church.

This tendency to identify America with the community of faith has been, for obvious reasons, a temptation only for Christians. Generally, non-Christians have not seen America as representing their community of faith.

Surprisingly, this relationship between non-Christian believers and America has recently been changing. As religious democracy has become more established in the United States, there has been a growing tendency to view all religions and all believers as united in a struggle against secularism. This surprising change is why the term "Judeo-Christian" now so readily comes to the lips of politicians and religious leaders. If the tradition is Judeo-Christian, then Jews can also begin to view America as embodying their community of faith.

This expansion of the solidarity of the community of faith was manifested in constitutional law in the *Allegheny County* Christmas crèche case in 1989, in which a Jewish menorah was included in the "holiday" symbols at issue in the case. Justice Blackmun's lead opinion contained a rather full description and explanation of the Menorah and of the Jewish holiday of Chanukah, noting the participation of Chabad, an orthodox Jewish group, in the erection of the Menorah. Since the time *Allegheny County* was decided, there has been even more support in the Jewish community for communal religious expression. Some American Jews now identify with religious democracy in the United States despite its overwhelmingly Christian associations.

This change does not seem to have much affected American Muslims yet, no doubt because of the special circumstances of American involvement in the Middle East and the war on terror in general. But, eventually, there is likely to be in the United States a larger forging of links among believers of all kinds. Religious democracy will then begin to see America as representing religious faith in general rather than as representing basically the Church.

The tendency by religious voters to see America as the Church is associated with the conservative spectrum of politics today. But the identification of America with the community of faith is not just a conservative tendency. Michael Perry, mentioned above, is a liberal. The mainline Protestant churches and the Conference of American Bishops pushing liberal domestic economic policies sometimes seem to be acting from a similar view. In 2000, for example, the National Council of Churches issued its "covenant to overcome poverty," which suggests the same identification of the nation with the community of faith.

Another example of a left-wing conflation of gospel and politics is Jim Wallis' book, *God's Politics*,[262] which is, on the surface, precisely a progressive call to America to be faithful to the Gospel's understanding of social life. A final judgment on Wallis's view is difficult to make, however, because the book can also be understood as an appeal to the evangelical community itself to take a more nuanced approach when it is in the world influencing government policy. Wallis could then be taking the situation as it already exists rather than as normative. The Church is already in the world influencing political life and Wallis might just be reacting to that.

Finally, the identification of America with the community of faith is not only a function of traditionally religious orientations. The Humanist Manifesto of 1933, which was a statement of belief by progressive religious and secular leaders, saw itself as addressing America as a whole and converting America to a new religious or quasi-religious understanding of reality—religious humanism. John Dewey, one of the signers of the Manifesto and perhaps America's leading thinker of the time, did not see any more reason for a separation of politics from first principles than does any member of the religious right today. Dewey's biographer, Steven Rockefeller, describes Dewey's integration of the religious and the political as follows: "Dewey found that as his moral faith in unifying social ideals matured, his personal adjustment in relation to his world deepened and his life gained in religious quality."[263] All the same kinds of messianism and intolerance can arise from the identification of America with a secularized "religion." This end of history can be understood to be as irresistible as God's will ever was.

This has been a short survey of one possible way of looking at the place of America in the theology of religious democracy. The threat to democracy from this perspective is straightforward. Acting from the point of view that America is the community of faith, the Church may attempt to take society over, as if everyone were already a member of the Church, imposing obligations and responsibilities on everyone that are only appropriate for those who really are members of the Church. Religious democracy may lead the Church to attempt this kind of social and political takeover.

But there is another possible theology for religious democracy, one in which the community of faith is a minority and does not represent the entire community. Under this view, America is understood as the world, potentially an alienating and alienated presence.

AMERICA AS THE WORLD

The main difference between America as the world and America as the Church is the acknowledgment that, at least for the time being, America and the community of faith are separate. The community of faith is a minority in the larger society. The standards of conduct for believers are separate and different from those for members of the society as a whole. There is no attempt to treat nonbelievers as identical with believers. In the words of Khaled Abou El Fadl, law professor and Commissioner to the U.S. Commission on International Religious Freedom: "[D]emocracy is an appropriate system for Islam because it denies the State the pretense of divinity. Moral educators have a serious role to play because they must be vigilant in urging society to approximate God, but not even the will of the majority can come to embody the full majesty of God."[264] The moral educator here does not think of the nation as God's representative, but only that all people are ultimately subject to God's will. The community of faith confronts in various ways a nonbelieving society. Once this perspective is accepted, the community of faith must decide what its relationship should be with the rest of society, that is, with the world.

In America, non-Christian religions have usually adopted this perspective automatically. After all, no Muslim or Jew can believe that America is literally a part of the Islamic or Jewish world. America is obviously the world to the non-Christian, rather than the community of faith. As suggested above, this may be changing, but for the moment most Jews, Muslims, Hindus, Buddhists, and others see themselves as minorities and must decide what their relationship is to be with the rest of America, as must those Christians who do not see America as the Church.

There are four basic orientations the community of faith that sees itself as separate can take with regard to America. The community can serve in different roles: as influence, witness, converter, and as nonparticipant. The community can take all or some of these orientations at different times. Religious democracy is compatible with some of these orientations, but not with all of them.

Probably the most common attitude for the separate community of faith to take with regard to America is to attempt to influence America in what the community views as a positive direction. M. A. Muqtedar Khan writes, for example, that "the mission of Islam and Muslims in the West can be to become the moral conscience of free societies."[265] This can be the role of the moral educator. Many religious voters probably are of this view. They may not think of America as the community of faith itself, but they are willing to join with other voters—religious believers or not—to help create or maintain a decent society in the United States.

Religious voting of this kind can contribute to, and eventually merge into, a kind of religious democracy. Whether that occurs, and it seems to have done so in the United States, depends mostly on the percentage of religious voters in the electorate. When a lot of particular communities of faith all vote in a certain direction, electoral politics will be affected. The current change in American political life to religious democracy is somewhere between this kind of change and the tendency of believers, described above, to merge America with the Church.

The difference between this sort of coordinated religious voting and voting as a religious bloc, which views America as the community of faith itself, is that when different religious groups vote in the same direction, their political power is diffused. They never lose the sense that, although they may be in a coalition, they are still a minority. So, Khan is quick to add that "religious minorities in America are becoming extremely nervous about the relations between the Christian Right and the Republican establishment . . ." Thus, constitutional separation of Church and State may be a high priority for these religious communities even when religious voting is, in general, effective at changing the direction of government policy.

The other models of interrelationship between the community of faith and the larger society—the world—presuppose a less optimistic outlook. They are not consistent with the religious democracy that America has become.

In the second model, that of witness, the community of faith observes and proclaims the breakdown of the larger society. This may be what some religious groups were doing in the United States in the 1960s and 1970s, before despair and outrage led to a more organized and participatory political response. In this model, the community of faith sees the breakdown in the life of the larger society and attests to that breakdown as the inevitable consequence of the refusal of the larger society to embrace its truth.

In the third model, that of conversion, the community of faith is not involved with the concerns of the larger society. The community instead concentrates on the task of conversion. This was the view reported in a sermon by Jerry Falwell in 1965, criticizing ministers who were actively involved in the Civil Rights movement: "'Preachers are not called to be politicians, but to be soul winners. . . .'"[266] Paul takes something of this view in his letters in the *New Testament*. Paul is not terribly interested in how the Roman Empire is doing. He does not attempt to influence it, as in the first model. Nor does he take much notice of its cruelty and violence, as in the second model. His attitude toward the corruptions of earth is mostly implied. Paul goes about his task of bringing the good news to everyone. This view is not necessarily one of indifference to social life, but can reflect, as it does in Paul, the certainty that what society in general thinks is important, is ephemeral. The community's truth is what is moving history.

There is a temptation, especially among secularists, to regard the conversion model of interaction as nonpolitical or personal, but that frame of reference is false with regard to Paul in particular and Christianity in general. Christ is not an apolitical event for Paul. Christ simply does not fit into any available political category in the Roman world.

N. T. Wright's recent book, *Paul*,[267] reminds us again of the mix of politics and theology involved in Paul's essentially Jewish critique of pagan empire. On the one hand, the Emperor is not Lord—Kyrios—though he claims to be; Jesus is Lord. This is obviously a highly political claim in the first century. On the other hand, this does not call the community to immediate political/military revolt—the authorities instituted by God are to be obeyed, for now. Both claims are political and both are theological. On essentially similar grounds—that God is Lord, not Caesar—the Jewish revolt of 66 C.E. against Roman occupation would be launched just a few years later.

For some Christians today, Christ may be felt to fall outside our politics and has little to do with it. Christ is a different kind of politics. Such people may be very socially engaged, but quite nonpartisan in politics. On the other hand, there probably are communities of faith in which conversion is seen as displacing political life altogether, by meditation or mysticism or in some other way. In any event, this third model is not consistent with the religious democracy I have been describing.

Finally, there is the model of the community of faith in withdrawal from the larger society. This stance of nonparticipation is further removed from the affairs of society than is even the model of conversion. The community of faith that is not participating may be self-contained, as many monks are.

The stance of nonparticipation can take two different forms. In the pure form, there might be no participation in the larger society's political life. For example, the community of faith might never vote. In a more mixed form, the community might participate in politics to the extent its own interests are involved. In America that might mean ensuring that limits—constitutional or otherwise—on majority power are kept in place. That could lead to strong support for the separation of Church and State and for free exercise of religion.

There are probably no examples of a complete and consistent division between the view of America as the Church and the view of America as the world. America's current political-religious context is a mixture of various forms of these two perspectives.

AMERICA AS BOTH CHURCH AND WORLD

There is an odd disconnect in American political life in which certain matters are thought to pertain to America as the Church and others are said to concern solely the Church or community of faith itself. The distinctions can appear to be inconsistent.

In the case of some liberal religious voters, large-scale economic arrangements are viewed as directly governed, in principle, by the standards of the *Torah* and the *Gospel*. Thus, poverty, business regulation, capital punishment, and the role of the market are matters of public religious concern. They are to be addressed through collective action and are a proper subject of political activity. They are subject to religious democracy. To that extent, America may be thought of as the Church.

Yet, in matters pertaining to sexual behavior—birth control, abortion, and gay marriage—the liberal religious voter is inclined to say, with Governor Mario Cuomo, "[M]y own religion ... required me to accept the restraints it imposed in my own life, but it did not require that I seek to impose all of them on all New Yorkers."[268] At this point, the community of faith is conceptualized as separate from the larger society. The larger society here is to be free to go its own way.

The converse situation obtains in the case of many conservative religious voters. According to them, matters such as abortion, gay marriage, stem cell research, and the right to die should be governed by the standards of the *Torah* and the *Gospel*. These matters are to be constrained by public law and are the proper subject of political action. Here religious democracy is properly at work. In this realm, America is the Church.

Yet, when it comes to the economic life of the larger society, collective action, religious or otherwise, is to be resisted and matters left to private arrangement. Government action in the economic realm is a threat to personal autonomy. The Church is certainly concerned with poverty, for example, but asserts that the way to approach poverty is by activity within the Church—a food bank, a clothing drive, and so forth. Here, in the economic realm, America is not the Church but is separate from the community of faith. In this realm, America is the World.

These distinctions—America as Church versus America as World—inevitably break down at the hands of authentic theology, especially Christian theology. The theologian Karl Barth, in a remarkable talk to Swiss trade unionists in 1911 confronted exactly this question of God and social life.[269] At the time, some Christians felt that religion had nothing to do with matters such as socialism and that those issues improperly brought the Church into politics. On the other hand, some Christians felt that a Christian had to vote socialist in order to keep faith with Christ.

Barth was referring to these distinctions when he described "the inherent connection between Jesus and socialism," cautioning that what he had to say "has nothing to do with your attitude toward the church." In this talk, Barth more or less obliterates the categories of Church and world. Barth makes it clear that even though the concerns of the trade unionist—that is, of the socialist—are "in line with the concerns of Jesus" because they aim to create solidarity among the poor and vulnerable, the methods of the trade union movement for social justice will be unable to further these aims:

> [A]mong us the greatest part is program, whereas for Jesus program and performance were one. Therefore, Jesus says to you quite simply that

you should carry out your program, that you should *enact* what you *want....* Then you will be true socialists.[270]

If I may attempt a translation from Barth into the terms used here, religious democracy as I have been describing it could never be authentically religious, no matter what issues it pursues in the public square, for *Torah* and the *Gospel* are different from a political program to be enacted by the government as a result of a process of voting. While that might sound like the urging of political passivity, Barth understood his counsel as the deepest political radicalism. We are to be *Torah/Gospel*, not just individually, but as alternative social realities. If we look with Barth, through the lens of *Torah* and *Gospel*, it will not be easy to say, as religious democracy thinks it can, who is the Church and who is the World.

CHAPTER 12

The Political Theory and Policies of Religious Democracy

Religious democracy could prove unsustainable if there are important policy issues that it is unable to address. Religious democracy might be unable to address certain issues because of its sectarian divisions. Alternatively, religious democracy might be unable to do so because it cannot consider all political matters in a reasonable and fair way. It may even be that religious democracy will founder on its inability to come to its own terms with modernity, unable to decide between acceptance and resistance.

In order to consider these possible objections, I will divide some of the important issues facing America into four groups, with special attention to those issues that might especially trouble American religious democracy: religion and modernity, religion and individual liberty, religion and electoral competition, and religion and international cooperation. I cannot do full justice to any of these themes, but I can at least outline the questions that religious democracy faces.

I am dealing here with religious democracy as a general concept. There are many kinds of religion, and, therefore, many kinds of religious democracy. Many religious voters have attitudes about particular issues that some secular voters might find narrow-minded and intolerant. That is not really the focus here. If religious democracy is possible in principle, the attitudes of believers on particular issues will simply become the subject of electoral competition. Those attitudes are not a legitimate objection to religious democracy itself. We are asking here whether there are any fundamental incompatibilities between religion and democracy.

RELIGION AND MODERNITY: SCIENCE, TECHNOLOGY, CAPITALISM, AND THE ENVIRONMENT

Ever since Galileo was condemned by the Catholic Church's Inquisition in Rome as "vehemently suspected of heresy" and forced to recant, there has been a concern that religious authorities are opposed to scientific investigation. The efforts that are going on in the name of religion to undermine the teaching of evolution in public schools further that concern, as does the resistance by believers to the teaching of the age of the earth in geology. On November 8, 2005, Kansas became the fifth State to adopt science standards that cast doubt on the theory of evolution. In terms of geology, a 1961 book, called *The Genesis Flood*, by John C. Whitcomb and Henry Morris,[271] became a major catalyst for the modern creationism movement by attributing geological evidence of the age of the earth to Noah's flood and denying the continuity of geological changes in history. While not as widespread as the debate over intelligent design, the challenge to mainstream geology may gain strength in future years.

If it were the case that religion is inherently obscurantist, there might be reason to oppose religious democracy. Most of us would resist if told that science must be subject to Church authority. But this is a pseudo-issue.

The suggestion that there is an inherent tension between religion and science, as opposed to criticisms by some believers of some aspects of science, is simply false. The western scientific tradition was created by churchmen. Copernicus, for example, was a Polish Monk. There was not always Church censorship of even drastically revolutionary scientific thought. Nor do all communities of faith object to most scientific investigation today. Karl Barth himself, obviously quite an orthodox Christian voice, wrote in the *Church Dogmatics* that Genesis should not be thought of as promoting a particular cosmology:

> It is no doubt true that human faith has always expressed itself in a particular conception, and human witness in a particular presentation, of the Word of God, and in so doing they have attached themselves to certain cosmologies.... The fact that this has continually happened does not mean, however, that the Word of God itself ... contains a specific cosmology....[272]

The Catholic Church, for another example, has come to terms with modern astronomy, biology, and geology. In 1992, Pope John Paul II declared that the denunciation of Galileo was an error. In 1996, the Pope issued a statement calling evolution "more than a hypothesis,"[273] which strengthened the Roman Catholic Church's acceptance of evolutionary theory. There has been some dispute about the significance of that statement, but in November 2005, Monsignor Gianfranco Basti, director of the Vatican Project Science, Theology, and Ontological Quest, reaffirmed Pope John

Paul's statement. "There is 'proof' of evolution," he said. At the same news conference, Cardinal Paul Popard, head of the Pontifical Council for Culture, warned against ignoring scientific reason:

> We know where scientific reason can end up by itself: the atomic bomb and the possibility of cloning human beings.... But we also know the dangers of a religion that severs its links with reason and becomes prey to fundamentalism.[274]

The important thing, Cardinal Popard said, is that the universe did not make itself, but has a creator.

As Cardinal Popard's statement shows, there may be an essential resistance in Judeo-Christian thinking to certain kinds of technological applications of science, but not opposition to the scientific enterprise itself. The stem cell debate, for example, does not concern investigation of the natural world but the method by which that investigation might go forward. The dispute is over the status of a human embryo. It is true that religion as a whole relativizes scientific discovery and subjects it to other norms, ethical and otherwise. But just as all civilized people condemned Nazi "scientific" experimentation with human subjects, holding science to other norms is not opposition to science itself.

The fear that technological civilization is destroying our essential humanity is not confined to religious believers. One of the most popular statements of this theme is Bill McKibben's 2003 book, *Enough*.[275] McKibben's book is not religious or secular, but transcends the religious/secular divide. Similarly, when Pope John Paul II condemned the "culture of death" in the West, he was not raising a purely religious concern.

This is the case as well with the Catholic Church's critical stance toward capitalism. Antonio Perez describes the history of this resistance as follows:

> Perhaps the strongest formulation of the Roman Catholic Church's position—rejecting not capitalism but rather rejecting treating capitalism as an all-encompassing ideology—is found in the Papal encyclical on the concept of development for the post-colonial era. Pope Paul VI, after noting the rise of industrial society, observed that "it is unfortunate that on these new conditions of society a system has been constructed which considers profit as the key motive for economic progress, competition as the supreme law of economics, and private ownership of the means of production as an absolute right that has no limits and carries no corresponding social obligation."[276]

The condemnation of materialism in western culture has been a consistent theme in Church teaching in recent years. There are many secular

Americans who are also deeply worried about the penetration of a certain kind of economic thinking into America's moral foundations. Such people welcome the Catholic Church's resistance to the market even if they disagree with the Church on most other matters.

There is an irony here. While the Catholic Church may be associated with opposition to the extremes of technology and the market, it is easy to see that religious voters in America, including Catholics, are not opposed to either. Churchgoers in America are, plainly, among the vast consuming public. Materialism should be a consistent religious concern, particularly among Jews and Christians, but it is not. The "What Would Jesus Drive" campaign is a notable, but limited, exception.

The Judeo-Christian opposition to materialism also ought to be a basis upon which to address the modern human threat to the environment. Again, the record of Judaism and Christianity on this issue is mixed at best. As discussed above, there is a certain tendency in biblical religion to regard nature as mere backdrop to man.

Yet, religion is also one of the potential foundations of the acceptance of limits to human growth, without which no environmental improvement is ultimately likely. The Jewish sage, Maimonides, taught that the beings of this world are not to be regarded as existing just for the sake of man. Karl Barth wrote of nature "in its otherness, of equal dignity" with man, of the nonhuman creatures "with their own dignity and right, and enveloped in the secret of their own relation to their Creator."[277] These statements are not isolated or idiosyncratic. The support that Pope Benedict XVI received from animal rights groups at the time of his election as Pope, because of his stand on the rights of animals, was widely reported in the media. There is no inherent opposition in religious democracy to the health of the natural world.

It is true that the Catholic Church's opposition to artificial birth control, which Pope John Paul II called "intrinsically evil," is certainly a potential practical impediment to environmental improvement. But this is not a conceptual opposition. The Church is not pressing for unlimited human growth. That stance, as the Club of Rome knew well, is exclusively a secular one. The well-known 1972 report, *The Limits to Growth*,[278] presciently set forth many of the elements of the environmental crisis humankind now faces, and identified economics and technology as the basis of the threat, not religion.

RELIGION AND LIBERALISM: INDIVIDUAL LIBERTY AND THE RIGHTS OF WOMEN

Can religious democracy respect individuals' liberty, especially the rights of women? This question should be divided into three viewpoints:

the internal administration of the Church, the establishment and free exercise of religion, and the practice of other rights in society.

The Church is not internally a liberal democracy. As the forced resignation of Reverend Thomas Reese from the magazine *America* in May 2005, shows, the Catholic Church enforces a form of orthodoxy in its internal speech. Additionally, women are not permitted to become Catholic priests. This is not just true of the Catholic Church. Every community of faith practices limits that the wider society does not share.

But the communities of faith generally do not seek to apply such purely internal restrictions directly to the larger society. This is an instance of the issue of Church and world. Religious democracy need not treat America as if it were subject to all of the requirements of the internal discipline practiced by communities of faith. Perhaps there is a tendency by communities of faith to forget the legitimate distinction between the community of faith and the larger society, but that is usually an error from the perspective of the community of faith's own beliefs. That sort of error constitutes the threat of theocracy. That tendency in religious democracy may represent a potential threat to democratic life, but it is not a mistake that religious democracy must inevitably commit.

The situation is quite different with regard to the rights of religion itself, that is, the establishment and free exercise of religion. There, religious democracy must plainly insist on religion's uniqueness in society. Religious democracy in principle is inconsistent with a strictly secular interpretation of the Establishment Clause. Religious democracy, in any form, sends a message that society favors the practice of religion. Nonbelievers, if they are realistic, must see themselves in a minority position in religious democracy. Indeed, after the presidential election of 2004, nonbelievers in America must already suspect that it will be difficult for the Democratic Party to win a national election without at least defusing the religious issue and softening the image of the Party as hostile to faith. This is already a form of political coercion and censorship. This pressure is not undemocratic, indeed the response is adopted to win elections, but it does alter the relationship of Church and State.

This is a bedrock dispute in the theory of democracy. If liberal democracy must be secular, as Rawls maintained in *A Theory of Justice*, then religious democracy cannot survive. Over time, it must become, first, not liberal and later, not democratic. I do not believe that Rawls is right, but only history will judge.

The reach of the Free Exercise Clause, in contrast to establishment-of-religion issues, should expand under religious democracy. The restrictions that the *Smith* case placed on the Free Exercise Clause cannot be ascribed to the wishes of any American community of faith. Indeed, the opposition of religious communities to *Smith* has been practically unanimous.

Even politically powerful religious groups, such as the National Association of Evangelicals, have condemned *Smith*, even though *Smith* is more of a threat to religious minorities than to mainstream groups. It is to be hoped that one accomplishment of religious democracy, and one litmus test President Bush will legitimately and openly apply to any future nominee to the Supreme Court, will be a commitment to overturn *Smith*. Unfortunately, since *Smith* was not an issue in the Roberts and Alito nomination hearings, no one can say what their positions will turn out to be. On the Third Circuit Court of Appeals, on at least two occasions, Judge Alito used highly restrictive techniques of interpretation to limit the reach of *Smith* and may favor overturning it.

In terms of other rights, religious democracy is always likely to oppose a certain nihilistic and degraded tone in society, as well as the denigration of cherished religious symbols. Thus religious democracy poses some risk, at least in theory, of exercising censorship and reimposing sanctions against blasphemy. More practically, religious democracy in the United States has consistently opposed particular exercises of human autonomy, either because they are said to harm others, as in the case of abortion, or because they are said to threaten what it means to be human, as in the case of the right to die.

In assessing these concerns, distinctions among rights should be made. In general, communities of faith in the United States seem to have accepted the radical freedom of speech that America practices. Of course it helps that such freedom of speech often inures to the benefit of religious believers. On the other hand, believers have objected to public support for works of art that are felt to be insulting. A photograph by artist Andres Serrano depicting the figure of Christ on a cross in a pool of urine, once so inflamed Senator Jesse Helms that he denounced it on the Senate floor and started a crusade against the National Endowment for the Arts. Such objections are likely to increase under religious democracy. But the test of liberal political life is not the practice of public subsidies for dissenters, but the absence of jail time. The fact that government is less likely to fund objectionable art is not a threat to individual liberty.

Religious democracy is often viewed in American political terms as hostile in general to the concept of fundamental human rights enforceable by the courts. That could be a threat to individual liberty. This appearance of hostility to judicial review, however, may be misleading. It may be a result of unsophisticated jurisprudence by American religious thinkers. The antijudicial tendency results from opposition to particular judicial decisions, most notably *Roe v. Wade*. The historical reality, however, is that substantive due process in *Pierce v. Soc'y of Sisters*[279] protected the rights of Catholic parents to educate their children in the Church, away from the assimilationist pressures of the public schools. Thus, while the ascent of religious democracy may entail restrictions on certain forms of autonomous decision-making, it would not suggest an across-the-board reduction of freedom in America.

In terms of the rights of groups, the two groups that might feel threatened by the success of religious democracy are gays and women. In terms of gay rights, opposition to gay marriage helped fuel Republican victories in 2004. In terms of the rights of women, President Bush seems to be committed to do all he can to overturn *Roe v. Wade*. No one really knows the views of Chief Justice Roberts on *Roe*, but there is no reason to doubt that Justice Alito is genuinely opposed to a constitutional right to choose.

Certainly the prospects of gay marriage received a setback in the 2004 election and in a recent string of State judicial decisions rejecting various challenges to State prohibitions on gay marriage. No doubt as well the momentum toward the acceptance of gay rights within the Church has been reversed with the current threatened split within the American Episcopal Church over the issue of the ordination of a gay Bishop, and the removal by the highest court of the United Methodist Church of a lesbian minister in October 2005.

But, as in the case of rights generally, a distinction can be made between rights in society and rights in the Church. In principle, communities of faith should not oppose the rights of homosexuals in society. They should not oppose government ordinances prohibiting discrimination against gays, for example. And indeed, the Catholic Church and other communities of faith do not uniformly oppose such legislation. For that matter, communities of faith should not necessarily oppose secular gay marriage, even if scripture condemns homosexuality. After all, practitioners of gay marriage are, presumably, not members of these communities of faith. Religious opposition to liberal divorce laws, which is another example of a social practice that violates religious norms, certainly has diminished. In part this lessening of opposition has been in response to the recognition that nonmembers of the community should not be bound by the norms of the community of faith. While the distinction between members and nonmembers has been ignored by the communities of faith in regard to the rights of gay people, in principle religious democracy need not pursue discriminatory policies in this field. It is to be hoped this will eventually prove to be the case with regard to gay marriage, but such a change will take a long time.

Unlike gay rights, the situation for women may well improve in religious democracy compared to the current status of women in American society. Whether this turns out to be the case will depend on whether the right to an abortion, which is plainly at risk from religious democracy, is a sine qua non for women's rights. That is obviously not for me to say, but there are many women in America who do not view abortion in that way.

Religion has a mixed record in terms of the rights of women. In the Arab world, for example, women are clearly not equal citizens and religious authorities support this subservient status. In the Netherlands, Ayaan Hirsi Ali has waged a struggle to liberate Muslim women from a religious tutelage that even liberal Western society has been unable to penetrate. Religion enforces many unjust restrictions on women. As Donna Sullivan writes, "[M]any gender specific human rights violations are grounded in cultural and religious practices."[280]

On the other hand, religion can also serve as a protest against secular oppression. In Turkey, for example, some women are donning headscarves despite a ban on the practice, in protest against the government.

In America, the rights of women have been undermined, not by religion, but by the demands of the dominant capitalist model. American economic life is sexist, in practice, if not in law. The desire of women to have children, let alone the desire of men and women to care for their children, are relentlessly punished in economic terms. Equal rights for women are not possible when the market's insatiable appetite for unlimited work is not curbed by public policy and declining average wages force many women with young children into the market. Nor are equal rights for women possible when men divorce their wives and, based on the unequal economic evaluation of their contributions, women and children lose wealth and income thereby, while men gain. And these are only the economic aspects of the rights of women in America. The constant advertising barrage promoting the sexual image of women is so unhealthy that the self-esteem of younger women is constantly at risk. Pornography and pornographic images have become almost a norm in America in recent years. As mentioned above, Ariel Levy's new book, *Female Chauvinist Pigs*[281] and Pamela Paul's new book, *How Pornography is Transforming Our Lives, Our Relationships and Our Families*[282] document how widespread, and how damaging, pornographic female images have become in American culture. Religious democracy can serve as a way to address and challenge all these inequities and harms.

The relationship of religion, pornography, and women's rights is a sensitive matter in this society, for there is a widespread fear of religious coercion. A story in the *Pittsburgh Post-Gazette* on October 12, 2005, described the rise of "raunch culture"—very sexually explicit public behavior by young women.[283] The story suggested that "feminists are torn" over this trend, which some think of as a liberation of women's sexuality. That seems ridiculous. The behavior by young women described in the story was not liberation, but an adolescent boy's dream. Yet, Ariel Levy, who was quoted in the story ridiculing such "liberation," felt she had to add, "People think I'm trying to lead women back into the burka ... I'm just trying to start a discussion here."[284] So great is the fear that religion will curb freedom that some secularists prefer the enslavement offered by this culture to the real liberation that religion can bring.

The concern that religious democracy will undermine individual rights is based in part on the consistent religious criticism of the individualism of American society. But this religious critique is not destructive of human rights. Indeed, this religious critique of excessive individualism supports the criticism by the political left against the dominance in America of the market, and the diminution in this society of any notion of social solidarity. Hyperindividualism has not proved to be a sound foundation of liberal democracy, but a threat to it. The emphasis by religious democracy on community may represent a change in American political life, but not one for the worse, and not one that threatens freedom.

RELIGIOUS DEMOCRACY AND ELECTORAL COMPETITION: CONSTITUTION AND DEMOCRACY

When religious groups participate in democratic life, nonbelievers may fear that the believers lack commitment to democracy. Their participation in democratic politics may be regarded by outsiders as a temporary expedient to be jettisoned once the religious group attains power.

Insofar as religious democracy looks to a norm outside democracy for legitimacy, which of course every religion does, it can be argued that religion cannot participate fully in democratic life. Many have suggested, for example, that Islam cannot recognize democracy as fundamentally legitimate. Francis Fukuyama has made this claim repeatedly, calling Islam "particularly resistant to modernity."[285]

This tendency to relativize democracy is not limited to Islam. Rabbi Eliezer in the *Talmud* famously states, "Be not concerned about your voting" when the rabbis vote, in good majoritarian fashion, on a matter that Eliezer believes should be controlled by tradition and reason.[286] In the United States, there is a Christian movement working to impose the *Bible*, rather than any secular, constitutional governing framework, as the frame of government. Along these lines, Professor David Dow, has objected to religious democracy as inconsistent with the democratic norm that the people must be able to enact any law they want.[287] The people cannot be bound to certain preexisting religious codes or even the will of God. Religion can never accept these concepts. In religious democracy, majority will cannot be absolute.

But these concerns are grossly exaggerated and excessively theoretical in terms of the American political context. Constitutional democracy itself limits the power of majority rule and religious democracy here, whatever may be true elsewhere, has proceeded entirely by majoritarian methods. Indeed, it is the opponents of religious democracy who have resorted to the courts, in part because of the democratic success of politicians who appeal to the religious leanings of voters.

The tendency of the Democratic Party to denigrate religion—or at least to be perceived as doing so—has been the actual antidemocratic problem in America. Conversely, religious groups have been content to play the electoral game. In fact they have played the electoral game extremely well.

The surprising ability of religious groups to work together to further the reelection effort for President Bush in 2004 is the best evidence that religious democracy works. The main members of the religious portion of the Republican Party coalition—Catholics and Protestants—have certainly opposed each other politically in the past. All of that was subsumed in the 2004 electoral effort. Even funding for Catholic schools, traditionally a source of conflict, has been supported by the new religious coalition. An effort was even made during the campaign to reach out to Jews, by toning down specifically Christian rhetoric. All this suggests that religious democracy is neither inherently divisive nor undemocratic.

The impeachment and attempted removal of President Clinton is an exception to the general willingness of religious groups to use purely electoral methods to gain and maintain power. The tendency to demonize political opponents, which was exemplified by some religious people in regard to Clinton, is, admittedly, an undemocratic tendency potentially present in religious democracy. When voters believe that their political party especially serves God, they may end up believing as well that their opponents especially do not serve God.

This tendency to demonize opponents is a potential threat to democracy that religious democracy may or may not be able to resist. We do not know whether religious democracy can curb such tendencies. If it cannot, religious democracy will not be able to sustain itself.

RELIGIOUS DEMOCRACY AND PEACE AMONG THE NATIONS

Religious democracy may not be able to quiet international competition between countries with different religions. Not only do religious differences exacerbate international tensions, but they can also spill over into domestic religious unrest. An example of this tension is the relationship between India and Pakistan. The movement called political Hinduism embodies opposition to Pakistan internationally and hostility to Indian Muslims domestically.

Along this same line, there is deep, international, Muslim suspicion of American foreign policy intentions. A poll was taken in the fall of 2003 testing public opinion in Indonesia about the United States. In a story reporting the results, the *New York Times* wrote: "The majority of Indonesians, who are moderate Muslims, view the campaign against terrorism as a war on Islam, and the war in Iraq has fueled those views."[288]

The suspicion of America in the Muslim world has only grown since 2003. In June 2006, *The Pew Global Attitudes Project* published a study of

Muslim and non-Muslim attitudes in thirteen nations.[289] In one amazing, but unfortunately representative result, there was not a majority of Muslims in any country polled who believed that Arabs carried out the 9/11 attacks. This probably means that a majority of Muslims in the world believe that those attacks were carried out by America or Israel or some shadowy agency.

Domestically, the exception to the religious harmony present in the 2004 Republican Party coalition was the American Muslim community. The CNN 2004 presidential election exit poll did not list a category for Islam in the "vote by religion"[290] question, listing only Protestant, Catholic, and Jewish, and for every other voter who identified with a religion, "Other." This "Other" religious group, which represented 7 percent of the voters, supported Senator Kerry with 74 percent. This is not necessarily a Muslim vote, but it is likely that Muslim voters made up a substantial portion of this group.

The reason that Muslims were by and large not part of the Republican coalition was not any theological dispute between Christians and Muslims per se. Instead, the problem presumably was American Muslim opposition to American foreign policy under President Bush, specifically the feeling that the war against terrorism is really against Islam.

Most Americans, of course, would vehemently deny that the war against terrorism is a war against Islam. On the political right, the war is said to be for morality, as William Bennett wrote in his 2003 book, *Why We Fight: Moral Clarity and the War on Terrorism*.[291] On the left, the fight is said to be for democracy, as in George Packer's collection of essays, *The Fight is for Democracy*, also published in 2003.[292] Recently, the sides have begun to merge. Some on the right now say that the war is for democracy, most notably that the war in Iraq is creating the potential for democracy in the Middle East. Some on the left now say the war is for morality, to liberate women from the patriarchy of traditional societies. Support on the left for the war in Iraq on these terms has waned, but mostly because President Bush's announced goal of liberating Middle East society is not succeeding in Iraq. The important point, though, is that all of these goals can be heard by Muslims as code words that suggest that Islam may be the real target. Islam may be understood as the implied force that opposes democracy and the liberation of women.

Americans believe we are sincere when our government denies that we oppose Islam. We say to ourselves that America permits free exercise of Islam, just like we treat every other religion. We don't ban headscarves in public schools, like the French do. We are not militantly secular, like Turkey. So, this widespread feeling that we oppose Islam must be mistaken—a horrible and serious misunderstanding.

But the impression of American hostility to Islam has some basis in fact. For one thing, the Bush Administration, from the beginning of the war in

Iraq, sought to exclude Islam from any new Iraqi constitution. The original Bush Administration plan, as outlined by L. Paul Bremer in the *Washington Post*, had been that a new Iraqi Constitution would be drafted by an appointed body, leading to a process of eventual elections and transfer of sovereignty. This plan was scrapped because of Iraqi, mostly Shiite, objections. In March 2004, an interim Iraqi Constitution was adopted that was to expire once a government was elected under a permanent Constitution.

Comments by Bush Administration officials in the fall of 2003 about the role of Islam under an Iraqi Constitution revealed the American hostility to Islam. *Time Magazine* reported on November 24, 2003, concerning the Bush Administration's acceptance of the idea that a permanent Iraqi Constitution had to be drafted by elected representatives. In the article, Michael Elliott wrote that the change meant that Washington would not "achieve its larger goals. For the idealists in the Administration, one purpose of the adventure in Iraq was to create in the Middle East a democratic, pluralistic state with protections for the rights of minorities and women."[293] The article suggested that the Administration's hope had been to limit the role of Islam in Iraq but that the Administration was now ready to give in to Iraqi political realities. Two unnamed officials were quoted in the article as follows, "'Islam's going to be in [the constitution], no matter what.... We don't have to make Iraq look like the U.S. If we get [a stable country] that's more Islamic than we would like, that's O.K.'"

For all the rhetoric about "radical Islam" or "Islam-fascism," there was no form of Islamic belief that the Bush Administration was really comfortable with. The effort was made to keep any form of Islam marginalized in Iraq, which turned out to be a futile effort. This Bush Administration hostility to Islam is complicated. Certainly the Administration is not antireligion, at least as Americans see religion. Nor, despite the issue of conversion, was the Bush Administration pushing Christianity on Iraq.

Part of the opposition to Islam may have stemmed from a deeply felt revulsion at the excesses of Islamic law. During summer 2006, reports from Aceh, Indonesia, where police have begun to enforce the Shari'ah by publicly caning men and women for drinking alcohol or gambling, reminded Americans that we are united in our opposition to such practices. As elsewhere in the Muslim world, the punishments in Aceh have fallen most heavily on women.

Yet, the Bush Administration is closely allied with Saudi Arabia, where the Shari'ah is also strictly enforced. This suggests that Islam in Iraq was viewed as especially inimical to particular Bush Administration goals. Probably it was felt, for understandable reasons, that Islam in Iraq would provide a rallying point for anti-Israel, anti-American and pro-Iran popular sentiment.

This view, however, raises serious issues beyond the scope of this book. Any religion that suggests a critique of modernity will pose a threat to American interests in the world. America greatly benefits from today's status quo in terms of economics and power, so any form of religious protest could oppose American policy. Given the radical nature of the *Bible*, the potential for protest against American interests should be as strong in Judaism and Christianity as in Islam.

Perhaps Christianity and Judaism have come to terms with modernity in a way that Islam has not. Perhaps this, rather than support for terrorism, is the fundamental basis for American-Islamic tension in the world. It may be that opposition to the West is a continuum in Islam, in which violence is the extreme part. These issues, however, take us too far afield from the point here, which is American opposition to Islam.

Another indication of American hostility to Islam is the issue of conversion. In the June 30, 2003 issue, *Time Magazine* ran this question on its cover: "Should Christians Convert Muslims?" The story described efforts of some Christian groups in Iraq to convert Muslims to Christianity. The story also gave the background of Christian missions around the world, including Afghanistan, in which the same issue of conversion has come up. Mainstream Christian aid groups do not engage in conversion, but newer groups do. While conversion efforts have waned since 2003, the underlying support for conversion has not abated.

This willingness to try to convert Muslims to Christianity reveals an attitude by some Christians that there is no salvation outside the Church. This may be an understandable attitude for Christians to take, but, for practitioners of other religions, it certainly suggests hostility.

This impression of hostility was reinforced when General William Boykin, our Deputy Under Secretary of Defense for Intelligence, was quoted concerning a fire fight against a Muslim warlord he had fought in Somalia: "I knew ... that my God was bigger than his. I knew that my God was a real god, and his was an idol."[294] In May 2004, there were reports linking Boykin to the abuses at Abu Ghraib, which reinforced the point about hostility to Islam. The editor of *Middle East Report*, Chris Toensing, said at the time of Boykin's possible involvement, "This will be taken as proof that what happened at Abu Ghraib is evidence of a broader culture of dehumanizing Arabs and Muslims, based on the American understanding of the innate superiority of Christendom."[295]

Is this disharmony and international religious competition an inherent aspect of religious democracy? Must religious democracy in America mean Christianity on the march? Will religious democracy promote international tension and even war?

These are serious questions. Unlike religious democracy at home, we do not have a model of peaceful international cooperation despite religious differences. Thus, televangelist John Hagee gathered 3,500 evangelical Christians in Washington to praise Israel's 2006 incursion into Lebanon as a "war of good versus evil." On the issue of intrareligious peace, with Christian, Jewish, and Muslim tensions so high, we can only hope and pray that religious peace is possible when religion dominates public life.

PART III

THE RELIGIOUS VOID IN AMERICAN POLITICAL LIFE

Void? How can anyone suggest that there is a religious void in American political life? Religion is now a pervasive fact of American political life. To secular people, the suggestion that there needs to be more religion in politics will sound like a cruel joke. They would agree with the literary critic Harold Bloom, who after describing Spinoza in a New York Times Book Review as an "Epicurean materialist," added, "A transfusion of Spinoza into our religion-mad nation could only be a good thing."[296] Many of these voters supported Howard Dean, whose candidacy for President came to public attention with a wildly popular speech to the California Democratic Party in March 2003. That speech included these fateful words: "I want my country back . . . I don't want to listen to the fundamentalist preachers anymore."[297]

We do have a lot of religion in America, but not enough of a certain type. Sometimes we divide politics into religious believers on one side and nonbelievers on the other. In theory, this need not be a threat to political life. America has many political divisions. We have blue States and red States. Division is the stuff of political life.

Religious division, however, is deeper than other divisions. People may change their minds about tax cuts and the war in Iraq, but never about religion itself. So, if believers tend to be on one political side, in our case the Republican Party, that fact threatens to overwhelm all other political realities in America. We need religion that can overcome this division.

The second reason we must have more religion is even more significant. All politics needs religion because religion is the source of both social and personal meaning. Religion is not something a political party can do without. It is not something a people can do without.

CHAPTER 13

The Current Political Imbalance in American Religious Democracy

Despite electoral reality and democratic possibility, religious democracy is opposed, even loathed, by millions of Americans. The depth of the opposition to religion in politics should not be underestimated. In May 2005, Chris Hedges wrote an antireligious-right article for Harper's Magazine that included what amounted to a prediction of civil war. Hedges' story ended with a warning from his ethics professor at Harvard Divinity School: "[He] told us that when we were his age, and he was then close to eighty, we would all be fighting the 'Christian fascists'.... Homosexuals and lesbians ... would be the first 'deviants' singled out by the Christian right. We would be next."[298]

The opposition to religion is not always manifested as hostility. Sometimes it manifests in unbridgeable distance, as in a *Harpers Magazine* column about the Reverend William Sloane Coffin, Jr., who died on April 12, 2006.[299] Coffin was an influential Protestant voice for peace and justice for many years. Lewis Lapham, the crusty columnist for the secular left, attended a memorial service for Coffin and wrote about it in *Harper's Magazine*. Lapham's column distinguished between Coffin's courage and effectiveness in the past and the moribund quality of the left in general and the Democratic Party in particular, today.

There was no doubt in Lapham's column about at least one aspect of this decline. Coffin's religious grounding gave him enormous power. Lapham even repeated a story about Coffin that if you spent enough time with him, you would almost become a Christian.

"Almost become a Christian" could be the political mantra of our age. The secular left has lost the American people. Voters who might once have followed a William Jennings Bryan or a William Sloane Coffin into progressive religious politics, now tend to follow Jerry Falwell, or Pat Robertson, or James Dobson, in a quite different direction.

Yet, as obvious as this is, nothing much can be done about it. The historical forces that created a William Sloane Coffin don't exist anymore. Those forces now tend to create secular social critiques. There is no point in simply urging people to return to Christianity. For many, that just cannot happen.

What accounts for this pervasive distance, and sometimes hostility, to religious democracy? For that matter, what accounts for the politically conservative orientation of religious democracy? Those two questions are probably related. There is indeed a political/religious problem in America. But the problem is not religious democracy itself. The problem is that many voters are cut off from the possibility of participation in religion in the political realm. The reality that only some voters participate in religious democracy has had very negative political consequences. It has led to smugness in believers, who imagine their political coalition is righteous, and to unbecoming disdain of religion by nonbelievers, who imagine only narrow-minded fools could believe all that stuff. This chapter suggests how this political imbalance might be changed.

What follows is a proposal for secular American political life. But the proposal is not new. As early as 1961, in *Torasco v. Watkins*,[300] the Supreme Court described "religions in this country which do not teach what would generally be considered a belief in the existence of God . . ." Later, in *United States v. Seeger*,[301] the Court granted conscientious objector status based on a belief that "occupies a place in the life of its possessor parallel to that filled by the orthodox belief in God . . ." If the voters looked at religion in similar terms today, we would not so readily speak of "religious voters" and "secular voters." We would conclude instead that most Americans are religious, in the sense of openness to the transcendent realm, and that neither party has a monopoly, nor even a competitive advantage, in religion.

There are people today making similar suggestions for reaching out to secular voters in religious terms. These are voices that argue for a "spiritual left" or a "politics of meaning." *Tikkun* magazine is a good example of such an attempt by Jewish progressives. The problem with such attempts is that they tend either to be ideologically self-serving or mainly humanist/psychological. They are ideological in that the political positions taken are indistinguishable from what liberal secularists already hold. The political determinant, therefore, is not religion in any sense, but secular thinking. The humanist/psychological perspective is the assumption that man is the central issue and measure for political life and that psychology—personal religious experience—is the path to Godhead.

In contrast, this book suggests that history and the trans-human, rather than psychological experience and humanism, are the proper religious ingredients for a nonreligious age. The God of history does not lead to reassuring liberal political outcomes and might lead to American self-criticism, which is greatly needed. History is not ideological, as a certain kind of politicized religion tends to be, on both the left and the right.

The limits of left-leaning politicized religion can be seen in a 2005 article by Michael Lerner, in *Tikkun*, entitled "After the Fall: Why America Needs a Spiritual Left."[302] Lerner felt he had to reassure the skeptical, secular left that he was not proposing that "people on the Left should all become religious or spiritual."[303] This sort of apology often takes place in political, liberal religion. *Tikkun* and similar voices cannot be too religious and still be credible to secularists. They cannot insist that religion is the answer to our current deep problems. They cannot mount fundamental religious critique but are only allowed to say what their secular allies say already. In contrast to this sort of pallid religion, we need more religion and deeper religion. We need religion that speaks plainly, without self-consciousness. Change of that magnitude, however, away from secularism to some form of meaningful belief, can occur, if at all, only with a candid assessment of our current political/religious context.

Our current context is generally separation of liberal politics from religion with a dash of religion as long as its critique is not taken seriously. This context can lead to political amnesia and blindness. Secularists tend to overlook the importance of religion and its historical role in American public life. Peter Beinart, editor at large for *The New Republic*, has been writing about the possibility of renewing American liberalism. His 2004 essay, "A Fighting Faith: An Argument for a New Liberalism," was widely discussed.[304] His new book, *The Good Fight: Why Liberals—and Only Liberals—Can Win the War on Terror and Make America Great Again*,[305] expands the argument he made in that essay. Beinart wants to recapture the greatness of American postwar liberalism, which he describes as a willingness to use military force to confront tyranny abroad, an investment in worldwide economic development, an insistence on American humility and a commitment to economic and social justice at home.

One of the heroes of Beinart's account is the theologian Reinhold Niebuhr. In the essay, the book, and even more in an April 2006 *New York Times Magazine* article, "The Rehabilitation of the Cold-War Liberal,"[306] Beinart suggests Niebuhr as the "model" for liberals today.

The most important qualities that Niebuhr exemplifies for Beinart, and ones America so lacks today, are humility and an appreciation of moral ambiguity. Beinart fears that America has become morally arrogant. In the book, in powerful language, Beinart criticizes President Bush for denying America's capacity for evil, a capacity that America has unfortunately demonstrated in the war on terror.

But, the word evil roots in religion, specifically in something like the biblical fall of man. You cannot have a Niebuhr without the Protestant

tradition that created him. Both the willingness and generosity to engage the world, and the moral strength to accept limits on power, root
in the biblical tradition. Beinart just assumes that these qualities can be
reasserted without their original, religious foundations. It does not occur
to him that liberalism cannot shed its religious history and grounding and
maintain the very qualities he so admires. Beinart does not see this because secularism cannot appreciate religion.

The insensibility to religion in the Democratic Party, exemplified by
Beinart, is only one side of the strange American political imbalance regarding religion. In addition to Democratic Party secularism, religious
democracy has served to cement the Republican Party in power. With the
exception of ethnic groups that traditionally vote Democratic, like Jews
and African Americans, voters who self-identify as practitioners of religion are likely to vote Republican.

Republican domination of religious voters has been the case even
though the policies pursued by that Party have not been what one might
expect of a Christian-oriented political organization. Obviously, that is a
matter of judgment. Just for starters, though, Jesus praised the peacemak-
ers, while President Bush has felt obliged to wage continuous war since
9/11. Jesus was hostile to the rich while President Bush cuts their taxes.
Both of these policies—the War on Terrorism and reducing our tax system's progressive quality—may be necessary and even beneficial. But they
are not the policies one would expect from religious democracy.

This Republican Party dominance has two political consequences. First,
given the simple numbers, a pro-God political party in America is going to
have continued political success over a perceived anti-God political party.
That does not mean that the pro-God party will win every time. But it will
usually win.

That by itself is not a problem for democracy. It is not a flaw in religious
democracy that it favors one political party, anymore than voting rights
for women is questionable because women tend to vote for the Democratic Party in larger numbers than do men. The CNN exit poll in the
2004 presidential election showed a significant gender gap between the
candidates.[307] Among men, President Bush won, 55 percent to 44 percent
for Senator Kerry. But among women, President Bush lost, 48 percent to
51 percent. Yet, that does not constitute an argument against women voting any more than it is an argument against voting by men.

The second consequence of Republican Party support by religious voters is that no broad, politically progressive coalition can be maintained in
America today. Such a coalition cannot be sustained by self-identified secular voters. Not only are there not enough of them, but the concerns of
poverty and peace are inherently religious themes. Historically, progressive American political causes—from slavery abolition to the eight-hour
day—were supported by religious voters. As E. J. Dionne has written,

"How strange it is that American liberalism, nourished by faith and inspired by the scriptures from the days of abolitionism, is now defined—by its enemies but occasionally by its friends—as implacably hostile to religion."[308] Secularism has proven too thin a political diet to nourish fundamental concerns. This is disastrous for progressive political causes.

There are deeply pious and authentically religious people doing important political work in America today. This work does not consist in reaching out to secularists on secular terms or scoring political points. These true saints are simply practicing their religions. Every religious tradition in America has its progressive political side. A number of Catholics are, in fact, radically left-wing. Thomas Merton's life and writings, and Cardinal Joseph Bernardin's seamless garment understanding of "life" issues, have greatly enriched political dialogue in this country. Nor are Catholics alone. Jim Wallis is just one example of progressive politics in the evangelical community. The National Council of Churches has always championed the rights of workers and other progressive causes. Rabbi Michael Lerner, editor of *Tikkun* magazine, mentioned above, courageously promotes a program of peace and reconciliation in America and the Middle East. Other examples of what could be called "left wing" religion abound in America.

Because these efforts are not religion reaching out to the secular political world, but are, instead, religion being true to itself in the secular political world, these efforts are impressive and powerful. An example of this work is the current "Torture is a Moral Issue" campaign. On Wednesday, June 14, 2006, an ad for this campaign was published in the *New York Times*. Among the signatories were people with enormous religious credibility, who are not usually involved in political issues, such as Elie Wiesel, Stanley Hauerwas, Archbishop Theodore McCarrick, and Archbishop Demetrios.

Eventually, torture may undermine President Bush's standing with Christians. Indeed, that could have happened already, but the Democratic Party has been incapable of pressing torture as a moral issue. This inability may be part of the Democratic Party's hostility to religion in any form, even when there is partisan advantage to be gained. It is as if Democrats are afraid to say that torture is wrong for fear that someone might respond, and so is abortion.

Genuinely religious people such as these must be part of any renewal of the American Left. But this book is not an attempt to reinvigorate left-wing religion. That kind of religion exists in American Judaism and in both Catholic and Protestant Christianity and will remain important despite recent gains by the religious right. The Catholic Church in particular is now offering perhaps the most creative and fundamental critique of modernity that can be found anywhere. So there is a sense in which the future of progressive religion is bright.

But even a renewal of the tradition of left-wing religion will not heal American politics. While this renewal of the Left has to include religious voices, it must also include secularists. The growth of progressive religion would still leave many millions of secularists outside. Without these secularists, no large-scale progressive movement is possible in America. So, this book is, in part, an attempt to speak to secularists.

In addition, though left wing religion in America is impressive, it has not had very much political influence. Unless there is a change in the political context, that will remain the case.

One important reason for this lack of influence is institutional. In American politics, a cause generally needs a political Party to support and promote it. Usually this means one of the two major parties. Progressive religion has not gotten a hearing in recent years in the Democratic Party. This has meant in practice that it has not received much of a hearing in a political sense at all. So one political problem for left-wing religion is the resistance of the Democratic Party to religion.

The perception of hostility in the Democratic Party to religion, and to believers, is perhaps the crucial element in American political life today. It blocks the formation of a coalition within the Party of progressive religious and nonreligious elements. Such a coalition is necessary for its numbers. Even more fundamentally, however, a liberalism that distrusts religion will never gain the trust of the American people and will never form the basis of truly popular politics.

Is it really true that the Democratic Party is antireligious? The comment by Howard Dean, alluded to above, characterizing the Republican Party as "pretty much a white, Christian party" certainly suggests that it is. The perception of the Democratic Party as antireligion, however, goes much deeper than an isolated comment. Howard Fineman and Tamara Lipper wrote about that comment in *Newsweek*:

> But Dean's real problem may not be his mouth but his mind-set. He and his aides seemed genuinely mystified at the idea that his characterization of the GOP was a political mistake. But by labeling the other party a bastion of Christianity, he implied that his own was something else—something determinedly secular—at a time when Dean's stated aim is to win the hearts of middle-class white Southerners, many of whom are evangelicals. In a slideshow presentation at the DNC conference last weekend, polltaker Cornell Belcher focused on why those voters aren't responding to the Democrats' economic message. One reason, he said, is that too many of them see the Democrats as "antireligion". And why was that? No one asked Dean, who wasn't taking questions from the press.[309]

The difficulty in building a Christian left in the Democratic Party was illustrated in the *Pittsburgh Post-Gazette* in November 2004, when, in response to a question by a columnist—"Where's the Christian Left?"—a sympathetic reader wrote the following:

> My guess is that 'the Christian left' resides in the Democratic Party. Unfortunately, the Democratic Party aggressively supports abortion and stem-cell research requiring the destruction of human embryos. These, of course, are antithetical to Christianity, and therefore many Christians have abandoned the Democratic Party. While these Christians might like to go "left" on economic justice issues, they are compelled to go "right" on the life issues. Economic justice means nothing if you haven't made it out of the womb.[310]

Another example of public belief in the Democratic Party's antireligious bent appeared in the June 12, 2005, *Pittsburgh Post-Gazette*. Reverend N. Graham Standish wrote an article arguing that no political party can claim to embody God's Will.[311] In the course of the article, Reverend Standish revealed that he left the Republican Party in 1992 because the political attack style of the Republicans conflicted with his notion of the teachings of the Gospel. He then added, in a devastating, though offhand observation, "For a time, I considered joining the Democratic Party, but they seemed to have little interest in people of faith . . ." [312]

Dr. Standish clearly had no anti-Democratic Party axe to grind. If someone like Dr. Standish received this impression, it can only be that this is the reception people of faith tend to receive from the Democratic Party. So, when Howard Dean criticizes the Republican Party for being "pretty much a white, Christian party" it does not occur to him or to many other Democrats that he is treating the category "Christian" as if it were an insult.

Democrats now know that this impression of religious hostility is a formula for political disaster. The Party has received a great deal of counsel to open itself up to religion and to speak the "language of values." There is a lot of talk today that Democrats face a "religion gap" and criticism that the Party cannot speak the language of religion. In their 2006 book, *Take it Back*, political strategists James Carville and Paul Begala complain that many Democrats refuse to speak in religious terms: "Democrats need to hit voters where they live—or, rather, where they pray."[313]

The Party is attempting to follow this advice. In the 2005 election cycle, Virginia Lt. Governor Tim Kaine, a Democrat, was elected Governor in a campaign aimed at religious voters. Kaine's first ad was aired on a Christian radio station. His first TV ad highlighted his experiences with Catholic missionaries. And when his opponent attacked him for his opposition to the death penalty, Kaine used the opportunity to emphasize his religious beliefs. He responded to the attack, "I'm not going to change my religious beliefs for one vote."[314]

Kaine was elected mostly for local reasons, as is true in many elections. In terms of religious appeal, however, Kaine took positions that would be difficult for national Democratic candidates to take. Kaine opposed gay marriage and civil unions. He opposed partial-birth abortion and never had to deal with *Roe* itself—he said he would enforce abortion rights as they stand. In addition, his opponent, Jerry Kilgore, inexplicably refused to say in a debate that he would sign antiabortion legislation if *Roe* were overturned. Kaine also criticized courts for declaring the "under God" language in the Pledge of Allegiance to be unconstitutional.

During June 2006, an evangelical group led by Jim Wallis organized a conference in Washington DC to lobby Congress on behalf of the poor. Six hundred clergy and their followers heard speeches from both sides of the isle and reportedly gave standing ovations to Howard Dean and Senators Hillary Clinton and Barack Obama. The DNC confirmed that the Democratic Party was making a conscious effort to reach out to religious voters.

Despite this one apparent success, in what must be considered an overwhelmingly favorable context, the religious outreach effort has not worked. The Democratic Party has been unable nationally to comply with advice to speak the language of faith. Partly this is because of a clash of issues. Women's rights groups and gay rights groups are important members of the Democratic Party coalition. Insofar as religious progressives might challenge abortion and gay rights, it is hard for the Party to open up to these voters. That was why, despite the embarrassment to the Party, pro-life Pennsylvania Democratic Governor Bob Casey was not permitted to address the 1992 Democratic Party National Convention. That is the nature and limit of coalition building in a political organization. The Republican Party has its own, similar, fissures.

But issue conflict is not the major reason that the Democratic Party fails to welcome people of faith. Many religious progressives, after all, support both the right of women to choose and gay rights. The main problem is something else. The hostility to religion among secularists in the Democratic Party is a real phenomenon. It will not go away because of an election victory in Virginia or advice from political consultants. The fundamental problem, as James Traub put it in writing about Carville and Begala's book in the *New York Times Magazine* in March, 2006, "is that many Democrats don't pray and even the more religious among them tend to inhabit a world in which moral and political principles are understood to have secular foundations."[315]

A person I know reacted almost angrily to Senator Obama's speech to the Jim Wallis group. Why, she wanted to know, does religion have to be spoken of at all? Who are these religious voters who might vote for Democrats if only they talked religiously? Why not just serve the poor, as Jesus would have done, without talking about religion?

Many secular people, and some liberal religious people, would prefer that Democratic leaders and candidates not speak the language of faith in the public square. Even if Party leaders can convince people who feel this way that religious talk is an electoral necessity, they will remain skeptical and suspicious until religious language expresses something meaningful and appropriate for them.

There are secularists in America who are still working hard on secular foundations in order to divorce politics and government from traditional religious sources. Alan Dershowitz' new book, is entitled *Rights From Wrongs: A Secular Theory of the Origin of Rights*.[316] That book is part of an overall attempt to develop a fully secular politics. A similar attempt with regard to constitutional law is represented by Isaac Kramnick and R. Laurence Moore's 1995 book, *The Godless Constitution*.

There are also attempts to develop a fully secular inner and moral life. The publisher calls Sam Harris's new book, *The End of Faith*, a "truly modern foundation for ethics and spirituality that is both secular and humanistic." All of this can be attributed to the continuing work of the heirs to the secular consensus discussed in Part I.

Why is this work continuing in the face of political failure, indeed political catastrophe? At the risk of oversimplifying, much of the determined hostility against religion among secular voters lies in the fact that religious training for many Americans ends at the grammar school level. As Huston Smith puts it, "Your standard criticisms of religion sound so much like satires of third-grade Sunday school teachings that they make me want to ask when you last read a theological treatise and what its title was."[317] Secularists tend to think of God as fundamentalists portray God. They think of the *Bible* as a rule book. They regard religion as oppression and therefore they oppose it. They reject supernaturalism and miracles and think that this is a rejection of religion.

In other words, the change in the Democratic Party, and among secular voters generally, which will break the monopoly that Republicans have on religion, that gives the Republican Party an important electoral advantage, is a change in theology. It is not a matter of political accommodation, so that religious language is more welcome in the public square. It is not a matter of constitutional interpretation, so that "under God" in the Pledge of Allegiance is not contested. Those issues are symptoms of discomfort with religion. They don't go to the heart of the matter.

The main change, when it comes, will be to think about religion in a different way. What does it mean, after all, to be a nation "under God"? It could mean to be "under a transcendent being" who gave clear direction in the *Bible* to oppose abortion and gay marriage. It might mean nothing at all, just medieval mumbo jumbo designed to promote huckster preachers and politicians from Idaho. But it might mean that there is a trend in history against oppression and that the military and economic power of the United States stands under judgment.

Most secularists do not know that there are many ways to understand the religion of the *Bible*. They are unaware that the great Jewish thinker, Maimonides, sought to explain biblical wonders, as far as possible, in accordance with the laws of nature. They have never heard of Dietrich Bonhoeffer's condemnation of a "positivism of revelation," or of his call for religionless Christianity in *Letters and Papers from Prison*.[318] They do not know that Rabbi Mordecai Kaplan rejected supernaturalism and the chosenness of Israel. They never read H. Richard Niebuhr's reference to God as "the structure in things"[319] or, in Cardinal Francis George's formulation, "Paul Tillich's understanding of a God above the God of theism, a totally immanent God, a God as Ground of Being, rather than God as Someone who is able to enter into our history, the God to whom we pray and to whom we go when we die."[320] This description of Tillich may have been negative for Cardinal George, but it is perfect for the secularist. Most secularists know nothing of any of this. Ill-trained in, and ignorant of, religious matters, people call themselves secular as a well-intentioned, but quite unnecessary, act of self-defense. They do not know that they are warding off only one kind of religion.

Prior to the short-lived success of the separation of religion from political life, Americans we now would call secular were actively pursuing the meaning of God in a nonsupernatural context. Evidence of this can be seen in the surprisingly religious Humanist Manifesto of 1933 and in John Dewey's 1934 book, *A Common Faith*. Dewey said that he would give the name God to the "*active* relation between ideal and actual." While he absolutely rejected the notion of a supernatural being or of personal immortality, Dewey, despite criticism, continued to use God language. He did this because he thought atheism lacked "natural piety," which he also thought organized religion sometimes lacked. Dewey did not think of man as isolated in the universe, but as at home and that the word God might "protect man from a sense of isolation . . ."[321]

As long as religious ignorance continues to influence secular voters to oppose religion in political life, to "keep God in his place,", as Michael Ignatieff put it in Chapter 9, the political harms we are experiencing will continue. The political harm from religious democracy in America is not the baleful influence of religion on the public, but the fallout from the fact that only a little more than half of the population participates in religious democracy. I am referring in the word "half" to the close divide between the Republican and Democratic Party coalitions. This religious divide between the parties is just enough to ensure political power for the Republican Party, but not enough to develop authentic religious democracy. An authentic religious democracy would challenge prevailing religious assumptions in the public square. America will not have that kind of religious democracy until those who mistakenly regard themselves as secular are able to take a new look at religion and develop original rather than second-hand insight into what religion means.

The current religious/political stalemate pits those who pray in public, which Jesus criticized, against those who seek to live without prayer. Neither option contributes to a healthy political realm. America faces a situation today not unlike that facing John Dewey and others in 1933. Their response was an attempt to help modern men and women who felt cut off from traditional religious forms to experience vibrant religious life. That response led to the Humanist Manifesto. It also led to Dewey's book, *A Common Faith*.

In hindsight, we have to say that their effort failed. Dewey and the others were trying to find a space between fundamentalist or traditional religion, which Dewey regarded as unacceptably supernatural, and a militant atheism, which Dewey also rejected. But even though they failed, the need to fill that space has not vanished in our day. We must be willing to begin again where the drafters of the Humanist Manifesto left off.

In principle, a religious renewal in America would not require resuscitation of the biblical tradition. People could look elsewhere for religious foundations. They could look to Wicca, or indigenousness traditions, or Buddhism.

In practice, however, a rebirth of religious orientation in America can only be based on the *Bible*. The *Bible* and the *Bible*'s story of God are the foundation of the American tradition, political and otherwise. Rediscovery of religion here has to begin with the *Bible*.

Is this suggestion an unholy use of religion for mere political gain? A rebirth of religion in America is surely a more serious matter than a hoped-for partisan change in voting patterns.

That criticism is part of the misunderstanding of the religion of the *Bible*. The *Bible* concerns exactly the sorts of things Americans vote about. The *Bible* is politics. As N. T. Wright says of the biblical tradition, "to be nonpolitical is to be irrelevant."[322] A political rebirth of biblical religion is just what the *Bible* has in mind.

What can be done about the current political/religious divide? Secularists need to take another look at religion, not traditional religion but the promise of our religions. What is secularism after all? What does it accept and what does it deny? What does it mean not to believe in God? These deep and important questions are not being asked today among secularists. Perhaps the answers suggested in the next chapters will help some secularists rediscover religion—the transcendent realm that the *Bible* describes. Properly understood, most secularists would be entirely open to this realm. In the end, they must be. For without hope of the transcendent, no politics that matters is possible.

CHAPTER 14

Biblical Religion and Secular Believers

The goal here is a simple one. This chapter tries to convince secular voters that they are in fact religious in their orientation to reality. Therefore, they have no need, nor justification, for hostility against religion in political life. From their own, secular, perspective, the *Bible* is a wonderful, popularly persuasive teaching for political life. Who are these secular voters who I claim are religious?

Some would say that as far as the *Bible* is concerned, the question of who is a believer is easy to answer. To be a Jew is to believe in God and to follow the commandments of the *Torah*. To be a Christian is to believe in Jesus Christ as the Son of God and to obey God's will as revealed in the *Old* and *New Testaments*. For example, because both the *Old Testament* and the *New Testament* condemn homosexuality, a believer cannot accept gay marriage even as a secular government policy. We could come up with similar definitions for any other organized religion.

It is not just fundamentalists, or right-wing believers, who think in these terms. Even liberal religious believers tend to regard the *Bible* as a sort of answer-in-the-back-of-the-book. When liberal believers within the biblical tradition embrace something condemned in the *Bible* (such as gay rights), there often is an air of guilt and defensiveness around the effort. This is the feeling one gets reading Michael Perry on the subject of the *Bible* and homosexuality, in his 2001 article, "Christians, the Bible, and Same-Sex Unions: An Argument for Political Self-Restraint."[323] Perry's defense of gay marriage is based on process values and on a liberal unwillingness to coerce others. There is nothing celebratory in Perry.

In general, liberal religious believers have a hard time because the *Bible* contains difficult passages about homosexuality, the rights of women, and other matters. They are like the slavery abolitionists in the nineteenth century, who had a similar problem because the *Bible* seems to accept slavery. The *Bible* does not condemn slavery, at least not in anything like clear terms.

It is this way of looking at the *Bible*—as an objective dogma—that Dietrich Bonhoeffer criticized as "positivism of revelation" in his April 30, 1944, letter to Eberhard Bethge.[324] In this letter, Bonhoeffer attributes this positivistic way of interpreting and understanding the *Bible*, that is, as an objective dogma, to Karl Barth. Bonhoeffer's partial criticism of Barth—he also praises him—is outside my scope, but I have to add that I do not see this in Karl Barth. Karl Barth famously said that the *Bible* is not the Word of God, but becomes the Word of God. Barth seems to me to be the last person to accuse of treating the *Bible* in such a rule-bound way.

In any event Bonhoeffer amplified what he meant by the phrase "positivism of revelation" in another letter to Bethke, on May 5, 1944:

> [It] says in effect, "like it or lump it": virgin birth, Trinity or anything else; each is an equally significant and necessary part of the whole, which must simply be swallowed as a whole or not at all. That isn't biblical. There are degrees of knowledge and degrees of significance; that means that a secret discipline must be restored whereby the *mysteries* of the Christian faith are protected against profanation.[325]

Bonhoeffer is criticizing encountering the *Bible* by simply accepting biblical condemnation of something as a rule In the instance of homosexuality, let's say you know a homosexual couple. They are loving and kind to each other. They are living out a life-long mutual commitment. They express their sexuality in the only way they can. They do not seem to you to be choosing something, but to have been imprinted with something. So you find the biblical condemnation of them to be harsh and unjust, indeed to be incomprehensible, for how could people be condemned for expressing a loving nature with which they were born and which does no obvious harm? Therefore you question the *Bible* on this point. You cannot accept this teaching, though you feel the *Bible* is the most fundamental authority there can be. In the end, like Jesus in regard to the woman taken in adultery, you must come to your conclusion based not on one biblical rule, but on what the *Bible* signifies.

There is no place for your doubts, says a certain kind of Jew or Christian. The *Bible* condemns homosexuality. "Like it or lump it." The *Bible* is all one. You cannot be a Christian or a Jew without buying the whole package, as it is. Nor is there to be any interpretation by the believer when a matter is clearly decided by the Bible. This amounts to what we call in law the parol evidence rule—where there is plain meaning in a written contract, no outside evidence of meaning is allowed. This approach to the *Bible* is what Bonhoeffer was rejecting.

Secularists are put off by religion in general when they see the kind of narrow interpretation Bonhoeffer was criticizing. But that is an overbroad reaction to what is only one kind of biblical religion. It must be the case that a person can be a Jew or a Christian and still support gay rights and gay marriage. There are many believers who do so. Biblical believers are not stuck with what Bohnoeffer calls, critically, "a law of faith." Dietrich Bonhoeffer was just this kind of Christian.

Naturally, there must be some limits in approaches to interpreting the *Bible*. Surely one could not be a believing Jew without believing in God, or a Christian without believing in Christ. In the same letter, Bonhoeffer calls "Christ's incarnation" a "gift for us." Bonhoeffer was not questioning any essential teaching of the *Gospel*.

But the recognition that there are limits to what Jews and Christians can believe leads to a different question. Can one be a *biblical* believer without being a Jew or a Christian? To consider this question, let me take myself as an example of what could be called the biblically oriented secularist. This secularist does not believe in God, meaning he does not believe that there is a separate being, a person, not a part of the observable universe, who has plans, and speaks, and wills. There is no one who could say, "Let there be light" or "This is my beloved son." This places the secularist outside the *Bible*, which seems to begin with just the opposite understanding, although many theologians have taught that God is not a being.

We will return in a later chapter to the question of God, for obviously there are many ways to think about God. Whether a person is a believer in God is not even always clear.

What about the other beliefs of this biblically oriented secularist? He believes that scientific explanations of reality are in general accurate accounts. There are no physical miracles. But scientific explanations leave out the core aspects of reality. They leave out depth and meaning. This secular person does not believe in any continuation of his existence after death, either in Heaven right away or in eventual resurrection. But he believes that he is part of the ongoing stream of life all the same. He does not believe that the world will ever be radically different from the way it is now. But he feels that the world can and should and will become a much better place than it is now. He believes that the creation of the universe was, if not an accident, still not part of what could be called a "plan." Yet what happens in this universe is of incomparable importance. There is nothing arbitrary about it.

Perhaps a person with these beliefs should not be called a Jew or a Christian. That must be decided by Jews and Christians. But could such a person still be considered a believer, in the biblical understanding of faith?

N. T. Wright, in his magisterial and continuing four-volume work describing the early Church and the origins of Christianity—*Christian Origins and the Question of God*[326] makes the point that the *Old Testament* does not plainly include doctrines like life after death, resurrection, and end-of-the-world salvation, although there are hints and clues about such things. He writes of life after death: "The minimal sort of 'life' that the shades had in Sheol, or in the grave, approximated more to sleep than to anything else known by the living."[327] Of resurrection he writes: "[W]ithin the [Jewish] *Bible* itself, the hope of resurrection makes rare appearances, so rare that some have considered them marginal." And of end-of-the-world salvation, he writes: "[I]t is time ... to reject the old idea that Jesus expected the end of the space-time universe.... [Jesus'] warnings about imminent judgment were intended to be taken as denoting (what we would call) sociopolitical events, *seen as the climactic moment in Israel's history*, and in consequence, as constituting a summons to *national* repentance. In this light, Jesus appears as a successor to Jeremiah and his like ..." (italics in original).[328]

The *Old Testament*, and particularly the *Pentateuch*, seem to be concerned not with life in some other realm, but with the working out of God's purpose in history here and now: the Hebrews becoming a people, their enslavement, their liberation, the inheritance of the land and the creation of a holy way of life in that land. There is no eschatological end of history in this understanding. The rejection of some other kind of existence for humankind—that is, the insistence that this life is really all there is for us—does not exclude one from biblical commitment. So, with the obvious exception of nonbelief in God, nothing in the above list of beliefs disqualifies this secular person from considering himself a believer and trying to act accordingly.

Bishop Giampaolo Cripaldi, secretary of the Pontifical Council for Justice and Peace, was quoted in *Zenit*, the Catholic-oriented news agency, on February 2, 2006, describing a sort of religious secularism: "True secularism is the one that not only admits or tolerates transcendence but understands its necessity and promotes it."[329] According to Bishop Cripaldi, secularism must assume at least the postulate of creation, an intelligent design that governs the world.

This intelligent design is creator in the sense that it governs the world. This design might mean only that there is order to the universe. That does not imply a someone who says "Let there be light," but a something, outside of man, that holds sway over the way things turn out. Calling this something a personal God may be too specific. We do not necessarily have the right terms here. What we mean is that there is governing in reality.

Putting things this way may be misleading in terms of the *Bible*. Clearly, the *Bible* cannot be summed up in these terms. As Walter Brueggemann writes of the *Old Testament*: "The hope of Israel is in three dimensions. First, there continued to be alive in Israel hope for a politically serious, Davidic (messianic) recovery. . . . Second, Israel's vigorous hope moved beyond political realism in a transcendent direction, issuing in apocalyptic-visionary expectation of world scope. . . . Third, in a less differentiated way, Israel continued to hope that, in Yahweh's own time and way, the world would be brought right by Yahweh. . . . This latter sort of hope is not messianic . . . but neither is it apocalyptic."[330]

The reason to downplay biblical apocalyptic hints in favor of the world here and now is that this is the general thrust of the *Old Testament*. For too long, believers and secularists have engaged in a kind of joint conspiracy to restrict the radical message of the *Torah/Gospel* for the world here and now.

Let's now add more strokes to the portrait of the secular believer. This person believes that the good has real weight in history—indeed is sovereign in history—and that the world has a tilt in the direction of the good. He believes that this tilt toward the good is not attributable to the will of human beings. He believes that there is a difference between right and wrong, between beautiful and ugly, between true and false, and that these differences are not matters of human judgment, but are real and reliable. He believes that there is significance to the attempt by people to live by love and compassion and that in some sense, the whole universe upholds the righteous ones who live by this path. He believes that holiness has power over everything demeaning, narrow, and small. He believes that those societies that protect the poor and the vulnerable flourish and that those that do not, fail. He believes that slaves are destined to be free. In short, he believes in the blessing and the curse of Deuteronomy 30:19 and he chooses life for himself and his people. All this is governing the world.

Why use the word "tilt" to describe the direction of the good in history? Surely the *Bible* is describing something stronger and more certain and more personal than that. The word "tilt" captures the qualities of both inexorability and indeterminacy. As the *Book of Exodus* tells the story, the Hebrews were slaves in Egypt for 400 years before liberation. The same was true of the slaves in America. It follows from this long period that an individual human life might not experience God's justice. This is the problem of Job. The Hebrews were well aware of these questions, which inevitably arise when we think of God as too much like us. The use of the word "tilt" suggests that there is no doubt that justice will triumph. But there is a large question as to when.

The reference to the blessing in *Deuteronomy* seems to have smuggled religion back in after all. But there is no smuggling here. These are the very understandings and commitments that the Hebrews introduced to the world as God's history. This is the *Bible*. Walter Brueggemann describes the *Old Testament* understanding of reality as follows: "a moral shape to the public process . . . a hidden cunning in the historical process that is capable of surprise." This is the key to biblical belief, not dogmas about the nature of God.

This litany of belief suggests three conclusions. First, it is not easy to be a nonbeliever. There cannot be very many. Most Americans do not accept a purely material interpretation of history. Nor do most Americans believe that the world is chaos, without governance of any kind.

Second, although it is also no mean feat to be a believer, most Americans are. Most Americans believe that injustice is knowable and wrong and that there are social and political consequences that attach to the practice of injustice. Most Americans believe that America is supposed to follow the path of justice and peace and that if we do not, we will suffer as a nation. In other words, most Americans, even those who call themselves secular, believe that society is judged by—that just means "subject to"—transcendent norms. Such people are not secular. They are believers within the biblical tradition.

Third, these beliefs are not matters of "ethics." By ethics, we usually mean what people *should* do. But, in contrast, these beliefs describe what we, as a nation, *must* do if we are to avoid the curse and receive the blessing. It follows, therefore, that we must get the truth of history right. If homosexuality is wrong and we permit it, even encourage it, our nation will be judged. On the other hand, if we behave unjustly to homosexuals, we also will be judged. The stakes of politics are just as ultimate as the religious right says. Compromise is not always the proper course, even in politics. Sometimes inhibiting compromise is the right thing, despite Fareed Zakaria's claim that religion is incompatible with politics because it inhibits political compromise. It does not follow, however, that the conservatives are right in their conclusions, about homosexuality or anything else. These conservatives who condemn gay people for the sin of loving each other do not sound like Jesus. They sound a lot more like the crowd that wanted Jesus' permission to stone the woman taken in adultery.

Ethics are universal and modest. Biblical religion is neither of these things. In a book review in May 2005, in the *New York Times*, Mark Lilla argued that liberal Protestantism collapsed after the 1950s, leading to a more "ecstatic, literalist and credulous" Protestantism—a "dumbing down of American religion" that would have horrified the framers of the Constitution.[331] In typical liberal/secular fashion, his proposed remedy was that "citizens should be more vigilant about policing the public square,"[332] not less so as proposed in this book.

But Lilla acknowledged that liberal biblical religion collapses for a reason. People yearn for "a more dynamic and critical faith, one that would stand in judgment over the modern world . . . an authentic experience with the divine"[333]

That is exactly right. And what Lilla describes is precisely what secularism cannot deliver. But it is also what politics must be capable of. This human yearning cannot be cured by a half-measure quarantine of religion from the public square. This hunger for meaning is a deep religious/political happening that must be expressed, but cannot be expressed through flat, thin, liberal politics. Rawls, and all his process values that refuse to describe the good and meaningful life, are not the answer to our political emptiness. This yearning requires religious democracy based on openness to the radical message of the *Bible*. That openness is much more possible, for many more people, than we realize.

We see the essential nature of biblical belief in the story of Abraham, known in the beginning of the story as Abram, in the book of *Genesis*. This story is foundational for Jews and Christians, as well as for Muslims as the story is retold in the *Q'uran*. The story of Abraham does not contain most of the elements that the secularist cannot accept. Abraham is not promised life after death. He is not promised resurrection. He is not promised salvation at the end of the world. Instead, he is promised that his descendants will be a blessing to all the peoples of the world, in what sounds like the same world, but in a far better condition.

Here is the core of the promise:

> Now the Lord said to Abram, "Go from your country and your kindred and your father's house to the land that I will show you. And I will make of you a great nation, and I will bless you, and make your name great, so that you will be a blessing. I will bless those who bless you, and him who curses you I will curse; and in you all the families of the earth shall be blessed.[334]

The point of the story of Abraham is not that there is a God who speaks in sentences. The point is this: Abraham receives a call. He does not know where or in what particular way he is to be great, but he is told that the way to be great is to be a blessing to the world.

The difference between Abraham and us is not that he receives a call and we do not. A call simply means that one is addressed with a demand that one's life mean something outside one's self-interest and comfort. We all know we have received this call, if we are honest with ourselves. Nor is the point of difference that Abraham is religious and we are secular. Abraham would no doubt have been regarded as antireligious by the people of his time, just as Christians were regarded as atheists in the first century.

The difference between Abraham and us is that, after receiving this call, he responds: "So Abram went, as the Lord had told him . . ."[335] He did not know where he was going but he was faithful.

Is Abraham any different in this regard from Abraham Lincoln? Or Eugene Debs? Or Rachel Carson? Or any other person who has tried to be a blessing to the Earth?

The secular world may be waking up to the importance and richness of religious thinking as well as to its nonideological quality. At least there are now hints in secular culture that the thirst for something deeper may require recourse to religious sources of some kind. In the first volume of the *Mars* trilogy, *Red Mars*, author Kim Stanley Robinson puts the following in the diary of one of the characters:

> The Arabs don't believe in original sin. . . . They believe that man is innocent, and death natural. That we do not need a saviour. There is no heaven or hell, but only reward and punishment, which take the form of this life itself and how it is lived. It is a humanist correction of Judaism and Christianity, in that sense.[336]

We see now that this is no correction to the story of Abraham in the *Old Testament*. It is the story of Abraham. And it is the story of living life well.

Other recent hints of a new openness to religion have appeared in *Harper's Magazine*. *Harper's* has been consistently antireligion and rabidly antireligious right in recent years. Yet, even *Harper's* now seems to be reaching to religion as a basis for a new politics. In August 2005, *Harper's* ran Bill McKibben's article, "The Christian Paradox: How a Faithful Nation Get Jesus Wrong," which was an attempt to enlist Jesus for the environmental left. Then, in the December 2005 issue, *Harper's* ran a piece by Erik Reece about Jesus as reflected in Thomas Jefferson's *Bible* and in the *Gospel of Thomas*. The Jesus that emerges is not just ethical but also mystical and soulful. One can see in this trend a new appreciation by secularists for the depth and popular appeal of religion.

Religious language in the public square actually represents the beliefs described here. This is why Justice O'Connor and Justice Brennan agree that some important matters cannot be readily expressed except through the language of religion. However, Justice O'Connor should not simplemindedly call all this, as she did in *Lynch v. Donnelly*, "confidence in the future." Religious language is an appeal to the transcendent. It is not confidence in the future. We might only have confidence that we are being judged and found wanting—that the future will be dark. We may find that global warming is divine judgment for our selfishness and greed and stupidity.

What is being expressed in religious language is not confidence in the future, but is closer to what Richard John Neuhaus calls theonomy—accountability to transcendent truth. Theonomy is accepted by many who call themselves secular, but are, in fact, religious. The reason we cannot express these ideas without religious language is that they are religious ideas. That is why Robert Bellah's understanding of American civil religion is so genuinely religious. We really are a religious people. When we say the name, God, we are saying these things.

Unfortunately, these insights are often watered down in judicial opinions, though they are rarely disputed directly. They can become so vapid that they are hard to recognize. Thus, Justice Breyer's swing concurrence in *Van Orden* shows that he does not understand the difference between theonomy and ethics. Justice Breyer wrote approvingly that "[i]n certain contexts, a display of the tablets of the Ten Commandments can convey not simply a religious message but also a secular moral message (about proper standards of social conduct)." But the point of the *Ten Commandments*, and what renders all of their content religious, is the understanding that there are consequences, that is, punishments, for their violation. There are consequences when society is unjust. This is why they are not known as the Ten Suggestions. Biblical religion has consequences in history. Most people, unlike Justice Breyer, know that and accept it. In a sense, even secularists accept it.

CHAPTER 15

The Radical Politics of Biblical Religion

The question in American political life is no longer religion or not religion. We have religion now in the public square. We are a religious democracy. The question is: What kind of religious democracy are we to be? Are we going to consider as religion only what is currently denominated such by members of the Republican Party coalition? That would mean a religious democracy primarily concerned with abortion and gay rights and relatively unconcerned with issues of peace and economic justice. How genuinely religious will the religion of the American public square be?

Religious democracy is too new to give definitive answers to these questions. But this chapter will suggest, very briefly and using only four examples, how radical a challenge authentic religious democracy could be to the status quo in America. The challenge is not policy outcomes, but starting points. Authentic religious democracy yields a vantage point for judgment of the modern world. It is not certain that anything else does. Judgment does not mean the usual liberal positions dressed up in religious clothing to attract religious voters. Judgment means letting the *Bible* speak.

TRUTH VERSUS RELATIVISM

Public life in America is now filled with spin. It is easy to imagine that everything is a manipulable matter of opinion. The *Bible* is an antidote to that kind of thinking. The *Bible* insists that there is such a thing as truth. God is called in *Deuteronomy* a God of truth—Ayl Emoonah—and in Psalm 31:5, also translated God of truth, he is called Ayl Emet. Similarly, Jesus is the truth, as we are told in the *Gospel of John*. It is the truth that will set us free.

Nihilism, relativism, and skepticism are surprisingly influential in American life. This can be seen very particularly in the field of law. This is why a conservative, Harry Jaffa, could write in 1994 that Chief Justice Rehnquist "does not, in the least, believe in the principles of the Declaration of Independence as either myth or as reality. He does not believe that we can say that despotism is intrinsically evil. Nor does he believe that we can say that free government and the rule of law are intrinsically good."[337]

Justice Scalia shares the same intellectual heritage as did the late Chief Justice. In his book, *A Matter of Interpretation*,[338] Justice Scalia criticizes the doctrine of substantive due process, not on the ground that it has led to the deaths of innocents in abortion, but that it lacks a "guiding principle." He means by this that the courts will not be able to protect substantive rights against a hostile majority. Because there is no guiding principle, any court applying substantive due process, in the end "will, by God, write it the way the majority wants."[339]

Justice Scalia does not sense the irony in his formulation. Why wouldn't the guiding principle of substantive due process, or any other substantive morality, be "by God,"—that is, that which is true is that which is in accordance with God's will? Why wouldn't God's truth be the guiding principle?

Justice Scalia would respond to this, as he does in regard to substantive due process generally, that there is "no chance of agreement" concerning God's will. That is so, in the present. But it is not so as history plays out over time. Jefferson said that the slaves were destined to be free. It turns out he was right. There was a guiding principle after all. Many people just mistook it. And, even though the South did not agree with this guiding principle, their lack of agreement did not change the guiding principle. The eradication of slavery was not subject to human will anymore than is the reality of global warming. Not everything is spin.

This criticism can also be aimed at liberals like John Hart Ely, who shares the same skeptical worldview. Ely writes of substantive due process in his famous book, *Democracy and Distrust*: "[O]ur society does not, rightly does not, accept the notion of a discoverable and objectively valid set of moral principles, at least not a set that could plausibly serve to overturn the decisions of our elected representatives."[340]

Ely's viewpoint is not something a defender of *Roe v. Wade* ought to endorse. To a defender of abortion rights, the right of choice should be a matter of truth, not just a matter of opinion. Yet, defenders of *Roe* have allowed privacy claims to substitute for claims of substantive right. Justice Blackmun's opinion in *Roe* attempted to avoid all substantive moral judgments through the interpretive strategies of original intent and textualism. It was necessary in *Roe* that the unborn child not be regarded as a human being. But Justice Blackmun made no attempt to defend that view substantially. The fetus was held not to be a person for purposes of the Due Process Clause simply and only because fetuses were not so considered at the time the Constitution and the Fourteenth Amendment were adopted.

Justice Blackmun did not want to decide whether the fetus had a right to life. The question for him was not whether the fetus is a person, but only whether the fetus had been so regarded in the past. Justice Blackmun did not want to treat rights as real. He even called Texas's view in defending its antiabortion statute, "one theory of life." But if there really are human rights, we must decide whether the fetus is a human being with the rights of a human being before abortion can be considered lawful. If the fetus is a human being, abortion is homicide. What happens to a society that lives by homicide?

Now contrast the moral skepticism of Justices Scalia and Blackmun with the comment by Pope Benedict, then Cardinal Ratzinger, in *Truth and Tolerance*, referring to "the Anglo-Saxon trend, which is more inclined to natural law and tends toward constitutional democracy...." Pope Benedict then praises natural law:

> The natural law school of thought criticizes positive law and concrete forms of rule by the standard of the inherent rights of human existence, which are prior to all legal ordinances and constitute their standard and basis.[341]

Yet, not only does American constitutional law now reject natural law as a foundation, the very notion of natural law was considered an insult in Justice Black's dissent in *Adamson v. California* in 1947: "[T]he 'natural law' formula which the Court uses to reach its conclusion in this case should be abandoned as an incongruous excrescence on our Constitution."[342] But, obviously, the generation that referred to self-evident truths in the Declaration of Independence agreed with Pope Benedict rather than with Justice Black.

The commitment to truth does not in and of itself determine the outcome of political and legal issues. The *Bible* does not take a position on abortion, for example. Jewish law, which is based on the *Old Testament*, was not strict about abortion. Susan Looper-Friedman has written that "according to Jewish law there are circumstances when abortion is not only permitted, but may be required to save the life or health of the mother or the well-being of her living children."[343] Nor did Jewish Law consider abortion to be homicide. Rabbi Elliot Dorff explains, "Judaism does not see an abortion as murder, as Catholicism does, because biblical and rabbinic sources understand the process of gestation developmentally."[344] But the *Bible* certainly has an understanding of the value of human life. Human life is precious, much more so than our possessions, including our bodies. The *Bible* would at least be a different starting point for our abortion debates.

Nor does the commitment to truth tell us what the proper role of courts should be in American governance. Maybe judges should be restricted in their appeals to fundamental values in deciding cases. Left and right in American political history have switched sides concerning the powers of the judiciary. During the early twentieth century, business interests favored increased federal court power. Now liberals do. Religious democracy is consistent with either a pro- or antisubstantive due process or fundamental rights position. Whether judges can be trusted to protect human rights, and whether they should be trusted to do so, is a matter of political judgment. Maybe judges are not especially wise in matters of morality, or especially trustworthy. Justice Scalia wrote in the *Cruzan* right-to-die case:

> [T]he point at which life becomes 'worthless,' and the point at which the means   necessary to preserve it become 'extraordinary' or 'inappropriate,' are neither set forth in the Constitution nor known to the nine Justices of this Court any better than they are known to nine people picked at random from the Kansas City telephone directory . . .[345]

The fundamental question, though, is not judicial review, but whether there are such things as human rights. Are there ways of life that are better and worse for people? Are there absolute needs that every human being has a right to have fulfilled? The commitment that there are such needs and rights can no longer be taken for granted, or surrendered. It is something that must be defended.

Because of its commitment to truth rather than to self-interest and advantage, biblical religion has a way of cutting through our ideological coalitions. Over the last few years, for example, the rock star Bono has convinced conservative Christians to become active in the effort to fight poverty in Africa. This was certainly not something that one would have expected.

In an even more startling example, the *New York Times* reported on November 7, 2005, that evangelical groups are pushing for laws creating mandatory controls for carbon emissions in an effort to fight global warming. In the story, Richard Cizik, vice president of the National Association of Evangelicals, cites the biblical obligation to care for God's creation as the basis of this effort.[346]

The response in the news story by Senator James Inhofe, an evangelical himself and a global warming skeptic, was revealing. He was reported to have said that "the vast majority of the nation's evangelical groups would oppose global warming legislation as inconsistent with a conservative agenda that also includes opposition to abortion rights and gay rights."[347]

Senator Inhofe is here thinking in coalition terms rather than in terms of truth. Members of my voting team, he is saying, should vote my way because they are my team. That is why in America, politics is now a place for winning and losing rather than for truth. Religious thinking, in contrast to our politics, must always seek the real.

Secular American society has surrendered truth. That is the hidden secret of advertising gurus and political consultants. Religious democracy could help us find our way toward truth again.

HUMAN SOLIDARITY IN PLACE OF THE MARKET

At some point in history, the biblical religions—Christianity and Judaism—became supportive of capitalism. This makes no sense at all for Christians because Jesus is as far from supporting economic competition as the proper basis of human life as one could be. Jesus doubts that the rich have a place in the kingdom of God. He famously says in the *Gospel of Mark*, that "[I]t is easier for a camel to go through the eye of a needle than for a rich man to enter the kingdom of God."[348] Jesus even suggests in several places that attachment to any possessions is antithetical to his way of life. Jesus teaches not to "lay up for yourselves treasures on earth . . ."[349] If Jesus were taken seriously for one moment, our economic system, based as it is on increasing material consumption, would grind to a halt. As the gorilla teacher says in the book, *Ishmael*, people assume that Jesus could not have meant what he said: "Even the most fundamental of the fundamentalists plug their ears when Jesus starts talking about birds of the air and lilies of the field. They know damn well he's just yarning, just making pretty speeches."[350] It is just a mystery to me how one can be a capitalist and a Christian.

For Jews, the matter of capitalism is not as obvious. Judaism is not as anticonsumption as Jesus is portrayed as being. Nevertheless, the Sabbath itself means that man is not created just to work. The Jubilee year means that debts are forgiven. The gleanings of the field, left for the poor, mean that private property is not absolute. The Earth as the Lord's means that nature is not man's resource. And so forth. Any capitalism that emerges from the *Old Testament* is going to be quite different from our current economic system.

The problem with capitalism from the *Bible's* perspective is not just greed and hyperconsumption. The very logic of winners and losers—the heart of capitalist competition—is the problem. Brueggemann illustrates this point in his interpretation of Psalm 72. The Psalm says of the king:

> For he delivers the needy when he calls, the poor and him who has no helper.
> He has pity on the weak and the needy, and saves the lives of the needy.
> From oppression and violence he redeems their life; and precious is their
> blood in his sight.

Brueggemann interprets this as follows: "The public good requires that active social power must be mobilized to enhance the entire community and to resist personal aggrandizement of some at the expense of others."[351]

Conversely, capitalism requires, as its norm and operating principle, the personal aggrandizement of some at the expense of others. It is true that capitalism promises that, in the end, all will be benefited from its competition, including the losers. Nevertheless, there still are losers, so the aggrandizement is still at the expense of others. This is not an aspect of capitalism. This is its heart.

Actually it is giving capitalism too much credit to even speak of making everyone better off. Capitalism usually leaves much of the winnings where they fall, with the rich and powerful. Ezra Rosser has pointed that the redistributive principle in capitalism is actually hypothetical:

> The Kaldor-Hicks criterion, also called "potential Pareto improvement,"
> slightly modifies Pareto's original idea by saying that if the change resulted
> in "winners" and "losers," and the gain to the "winners" was enough to
> pay the "losers" equal to the loss, then the change is welfare improving.
> Significantly, this Kalder-Hicks improvement is said to hold even where the
> "winners" do not actually pay off the "losers," so long as the winners could
> have done so.[352]

Even worse than the rivalry in the heart of capitalism is the pace of technological capitalism. Religious conservatives now argue that the Ten Commandments should be permitted to be placed on public buildings. This was the issue in a general sense in *Van Orden* and *McCreary*. But have these conservatives read the Ten Commandments? Have they seen its conflict with the market that they so praise? One of the Ten Commandments requires that the Sabbath day be set aside from work—"Six days shall you labor, and do all your work; but the seventh day is a Sabbath to the Lord your God; in it you shall not do any work …" In contrast, the creed of technological capitalism is 24/7/365. Americans are constantly told that we must work harder, better, and faster. Now, as Thomas Friedman points out and justifies in his book, *The World is Flat*,[353] Americans are being told that they must work even harder than even harder because of the economic challenge represented by China and India.

Capitalism in this technological phase is a treadmill. We have been made slaves, not different essentially from the slaves of Egypt. One of the core teachings of the *Bible* is that human beings are not just beasts of burden. Where is the proposed constitutional amendment to reinstitute rest?

There have been such proposals in the past and their biblical resonance has been strongly noted. There have been calls in America for a constitutional amendment instituting rest. There also used to be Blue Laws in many states prohibiting work on the Sabbath. The Blue Laws passed away out of popular indifference, difficulty of enforcement, and judicial invalidation. The very idea of limits now seems quite outdated. We are at the mercy of the technological monster we have created and it does not matter who gets elected.

Whenever criticisms like this are raised, we are told that all of the burdens of the modern market are inevitable. We are at the end of history. Human choice is beside the point. The entire world will be forced to embrace representative government, judicial review, and most importantly, technological capitalism. This is precisely Friedman's point in his book.

It is also Fareed Zakaria's point in his review of Friedman's book in the *New York Times*, book review section on May 1, 2005. Friedman has doubts about whether the emerging economic power of India and China can be good for the young people of the United States. Zakaria comments on these concerns: "[Friedman] ends up, wisely, understanding that there's no way to stop the wave. You cannot switch off these forces except at great cost to your own economic well-being. Over the last century, those countries that tried to preserve their systems, jobs, culture or traditions by keeping the rest of the world out all stagnated. Those that opened themselves up to the world prospered."[354] Or, in other words, I am sorry about the end of your culture and traditions. I'm sure they were lovely.

The *Bible* rejects all such determinism and fatalism. As Brueggemann says, the *Bible* insists that at the heart of history is the capacity for surprise. That is meant to be really and actually true. Humans are not allowed to enslave themselves permanently. The dark future we think we know will not necessarily be that way. That is the *Bible's* promise.

In contrast to religious thinking, it is difficult for a capitalist society to express human solidarity. We can see this in two particular examples. In the Connecticut birth control case, *Griswold v. Connecticut*,[355] the Court held that it was unconstitutional for the State to prohibit the use of birthcontrol devices by a married couple. Later, in *Eisenstadt v. Baird*,[356] the same issue arose with regard to someone who was not married. Justice Brennan had no trouble extending the Griswold decision: "The marital couple is not an independent entity with a mind and heart of its own, but an association of individuals each with a separate intellectual and emotional make-up." These are words to chill any appreciation of a real marriage and it is no surprise, given this understanding, which most Americans share, that divorce rates are so high. The *Bible* has a very different view: "Therefore, a man leaves his father and his mother and cleaves to his wife, and they become one flesh." A marriage is not an association.

We see the same tawdry individualism in the *Casey* abortion case. The most important aspect of the Pennsylvania law that the Court struck down was the spousal notification requirement. The plurality described this holding in the following words:

> The husband's interest in the life of the child his wife is carrying does not permit the State to empower him with this troubling degree of authority over his wife.

I understand the holding. I appreciate the fear of a paternalism that infantilizes a grown woman. I don't understand the description. This man is not a husband in this context; he is a father. And the interest is not in the life of *the* child, but in the life of *his* child. If his child is to be killed, the Court could at least name the father and his child correctly.

TESHUVAH AS A LIMIT ON IMPERIALISM

Politicians like to say that the American people are good. But Jesus' words echo: "Why do you call me good? No one is good but God alone."

The American people are not good. We are no worse than most, but that is all that can be said. We are the people of slavery. We are the people who stole this land from the native people who lived here. We are the people who expanded into Hawaii, Cuba, and the Philippines. We are the people who intervened militarily in the Americas and elsewhere. We are the people who perfected firestorms as a military tactic. We are the only people who ever used an atomic bomb. These are just some of our crimes. No, we are not good.

In the *Naked Public Square*, Richard Neuhaus, citing Reinhold Niebuhr, argues that democracy requires this sort of sense of human sin:

> Democratic discourse ... depends ... upon our agreement about sin—our own sin, and thus our own fallibility, as well as the sin and fallibility of others. Democratic discourse requires that no party fashion itself as the moral majority in order to imply that others belong to an immoral minority.[357]

So, if Neuhaus is right, insofar as we have lost the sense of our own sin, we have lost one of the foundations of democratic life.

When you think you are good, you may end up worse than simply not good. Without a sense of your own sin, there may be no limit to the evil you can do. You might begin to suspend judgment on your own actions because you know you are good. How could a good people do something really evil?

Haven't the crimes committed by the American military during the War on Terror been surprising? Even more amazing than the crimes themselves has been the strong reaction against critics of these crimes. This is what can happen when you think you have no reason to doubt your own motives.

Strangely, the converse is also true. Without a sense of human sin, critics of America also end up supposing that America is unique—not in this case uniquely good, but uniquely evil. That is just as absurd a starting point as the presumption that the American people are good. America's adversaries certainly are not good either. As Barth puts it, in his Commentary on Paul's letter to the Romans, neither the revolutionary nor the conservative is justified. Our political life cannot be understood as "the scene of the conflict between the Kingdom of God and the Anti-Christ."[358]

The *Bible* does not share our illusions about ourselves. The Hebrew nation is not portrayed in the *Bible* as good. But the Hebrews are portrayed as capable of the practice of teshuvah—of repentance. As the prophet Ezekiel says: "Therefore say to the house of Israel, Thus says the Lord God; Repent, and turn yourselves from your idols; and turn away your faces from all your abominations."[359]

So important is teshuvah in the Torah that not only the Hebrews can repent, but pagans can also, as can God. We see this in the story of *Jonah*.

> And word came to the king of Nineveh, and he arose from his throne, and he took off his robe, and covered himself with sackcloth, and sat in ashes. And he caused it to be proclaimed and published through Nineveh by the decree of the king and his nobles, saying: Neither man, beast, herd or flock should taste anything! They should not feed nor drink water! And let man and beast be covered with sackcloth, and cry mightily to God; let them turn everyone from his evil way, and from the violence that is in their hands. Who can tell if God may yet turn and repent, and turn away from his fierce anger, so that we perish not? And God saw   their doings, that they turned from their evil way; and God repented of the evil, which he had said that he would do to them; and he did not do it.[360]

Teshuvah—repentance—is quite different from the notion of an apology, as if we could apologize for the crime of slavery, or for lynchings, as one might apologize for arriving late to a movie. A politics of teshuvah would be open to doubt of our own motives. It would try to look at ourselves as others in the world see us. It would not paralyze us any more than teshuvah now paralyzes any truly religious person. But teshuvah does render all human action ambiguous in moral terms. That is just what America needs.

Our lack of teshuvah is apparent not just in our blind self-righteousness. Imperialism that fails to look at itself critically becomes irresponsible. Our irresponsibility extends to a willingness to unalterably warm the world's climate, with consequences we cannot predict. We irresponsibly insist on an impossible proof of climate change rather than placing the burden on ourselves not to take risks that others—our grandchildren and the people of other nations—will have to pay for.

More simply and obviously, our irresponsibility extends to an unwillingness to pay our bills. Both individually and collectively, both in household debt and in the federal budget deficit, America lives beyond its means. The cumulative federal deficit is estimated to reach $11.2 trillion in 2010, $38,000 for every person in America. In the case of personal debt, as in climate change, a religious opposition is growing. Evangelical Christian Dave Ramsey preaches the gospel of personal industry and spending restraint all across the nation. Eventually, the federal deficit will also be viewed as a religious issue.

Our current religious democracy tends to identify America as the agent of God's will so that America is not called to any kind of judgment. That should not surprise us since religion and blasphemy are routinely linked. What is needed in America is not the banishment of religion but a deeper appreciation of what religion can mean. We need religion that calls us to repent.

The sense of communal and personal repentance is missing from the secular left's critique of America. When Kevin Phillips writes that debt is overwhelming us, in *American Theocracy*, he fails to see the theological foundations of such irresponsibility. He does not see that religion uniquely can help people sacrifice their immediate self-interest. Instead, Phillips says we have too much religion.

When Peter Beinart bemoans the lack of humility in American foreign policy and justice in American domestic policy, he ignores the biblical wellspring from which the American popular commitment to humility and justice were grounded.

The key to accepting limits on ourselves, which is necessary to control the imperial instinct, is not this or that policy prescription. Rather, the key is to see ourselves in a different way. But this means doing away with all of the "us versus them" mentality. The *Bible* teaches that all humans are brothers and sisters and that all of us sin. This means that neither President Bush nor former President Clinton are or were all good or all evil. It also means that the men who crashed planes into the World Trade Center on 9/11 were not absolutely evil. Absolute categories are not for humans to use.

Biblical living is very hard. It is just as hard for those who think they are believers as it is for the rest of us. But it is necessary to make the attempt to live this way if we are to have a decent world.

FREEDOM VERSUS SLAVERY

Passover is the Jewish holiday that celebrates the liberation of the Hebrew slaves from Egypt highlighted by a ceremonial meal, called the

Seder. Jews like to say at the Seder table that there are many kinds of slavery. It is a cliché. But, like many clichés, it is true. What the *Bible* ultimately
promises is freedom from all slavery. Jesus proclaims in his first public
utterance in the *Gospel of Luke* that the task is "to set at liberty those who
are oppressed." Jesus was reading from the *Prophet Isaiah*. Freedom is the
Bible's major theme in both the *Old* and *New Testament*.

In an early work, *The Prophetic Imagination*, Walter Brueggemann describes the new way of life that Moses brought to the Hebrew slaves, in
contrast to the Egyptian paradigm of life. This new prophetic conscious-
ness mixed religion and politics: "a religion of God's freedom as alternative to the static imperial religion of order and triumph and a politics of justice and compassion as alternative to the imperial politics of
oppression."[361] God's freedom, in other words, is the ground of justice.

The secularist knows nothing of all this. The secular voter thinks of the
Bible as oppressive—as filled with rules that must not be broken, some of
which are unjust. It is true that the *Bible* is filled with rules and, further,
that some of them are unjust. That is why the *Bible* is not to be regarded as
a rule book.

But the secularist who says this about the *Bible* is, as Jesus says in the
Gospel of Matthew, pointing to the speck in his brother's eye and overlook-
ing the log in his own. Perhaps some parts of the *Bible* are oppressive, but
who is forced to live in accordance with all of its teachings? On the other
hand, what we can be certain about is the oppressive nature of this modern world that men and women have made, which, unlike the *Bible*, we
actually are forced to live under. The oppression by the modern world—
economic, political, social, and military—is causing enormous suffering.
The *Bible* is the best starting point for us to understand the oppression
to which we are now subject and, perhaps, to defeat it. Or, if we cannot
defeat it, at least by using the *Bible's* vantage point, we might challenge it.

The *Bible* is a source of hope. The *Bible* sees the world as good—"And
God saw everything that he had made, and behold, it was very good." The
Bible regards injustice and suffering as illegitimate—almost inconceivable.
The *Bible* trusts the universe. The *Bible* is open to all things.

This openness of the *Bible*—this freedom—may sound strange, since
some religious conservatives want to banish the teaching of evolution and
other aspects of knowledge. How open is that? Certainly it is not biblical
to imagine God unable to work through evolution. Science is not a threat
to biblical belief.

Yet, it must be added that there is a sense in which evolution, if it is
understood as a complete explanation of all life, must be false. And the
believer is right to say so. For no such reductionist and mechanical explanation of reality is possible. Science seems to be catching up to the notion
that the sum of reality is, if not greater, at least not exactly the same as its
parts added together. This is the recognition by science of what are called
"emergent properties." Emergent properties refer to the "more" that an

integrated system yields over the sum of the different parts of a system that has not been integrated.

Freedom in the *Bible* denotes the rich and unexpected possibilities of human existence. Freedom like this is quite different from the secularized version of freedom that we call choice. Choice is a concept from the market. It suggests a selection from a given array. We have a choice to buy or not to buy. We have a choice to buy one product as opposed to another.

Choice of this kind cannot change the world. The background context is what actually controls choice. The consumer imagines that there is freedom in this consumer sovereignty, but that freedom is an illusion.

It is a perfect reflection of this illusion to call the decision to have an abortion a matter of choice. Women are not given the option to choose a world without the old sexual double standard that still controls. They do not have access to a world of loving relationships, stable partners, well-paying jobs, and a family oriented economic and social life. Abortion is a response to these realities. It is chosen because life would be even more bleak and unforgiving without it. Abortion is usually coerced in one way or another. It is not really chosen. This is not freedom.

We are free when we can imagine human life as it might be. This is what the slave dreams of. Then he is reminded that his master is still in control. But, as Brueggemann says, the *Bible* promises that no human project— no human control—is absolute. So history cannot be at an end. Current political, legal, and economic organization cannot be the last word. That is freedom. That is grace. The *Bible*, not the Constitution or the courts, is our real guarantee of freedom.

CHAPTER 16

God, the Secular Voter, and American Political Life

I said in an earlier chapter that I would return to the question of God. To have healthy political life, America must have a variety of religious expressions in the public square. We should not continue to imagine that we have one God party and one anti-God party. But the Democratic Party contains a substantial number of secular voters who say that they do not believe in God or that they are not sure whether God exists and that they do not think God is a suitable subject for involvement in political life. Lack of belief in God would seem an insurmountable barrier to the embrace of religious democracy that this book promotes. How can this logjam be broken? In other words, how exactly would a secular voter join religious democracy? What would that mean?

The answer to that question has to do with a new understanding of God. Obviously this chapter does not try to say precisely who or what God is. That would be impossible. Karl Barth said, simply, that "[E]very theological statement is an inadequate expression of its object."[362] God is not another thing, like a tree, to be described. Nor is God another human being, even in Christian orthodoxy. No words can describe God. Negative theology, which describes God by negation, reflects that reality, as does process theology, which describes God as radically immanent in the world process itself, without endorsing God as a being. Paul Tillich wrote of "the God above the God of theism,"[363] similarly to avoid the conception of God as another being.

But if God cannot really be described, then believing, or, for that matter, not believing, in God is neither simple nor obvious. For someone to say, "I am not religious" is the beginning of discussion and conversation

rather than the end. The secular voter who believes everything else outlined above concerning truth and history is not outside religious democracy simply because he asserts that God does not exist. Karl Barth, here as
usual is ahead of us, anticipating and rejecting such a Jonah-like attempt to
flee from God. Barth said to the trade unionists, no doubt many of whom
thought they were secularists:

> If you understand the connection between the person of Jesus and your
> socialist convictions, and if you now want to arrange your life so that it
> corresponds to this connection, then that does not at all mean you have to
> "believe" or accept this, that, and any other thing....And as an atheist, a
> materialist, and a Darwinist, one can be a genuine follower and disciple of
> Jesus.[364]

Or, as Jesus said directly, "Not everyone who says to me 'Lord, Lord,' shall
enter the kingdom of heaven, but he who does the will of my Father . . ."[365]
The *Bible* helps us to see what that will is. For the most part, the *Bible* does
not attempt to convince us that there is someone doing the willing. That is
taken for granted, not a matter for argument or proof. Disagreement about
the existence of God is no excuse for failure to act. It is not an excuse
to ignore the depth and richness of human life. More importantly, lack
of belief is not an excuse to scoff at believers, because what the believer
means by God may be believed by the atheist as well.

But does it make sense to say that there can be a way of life for me to follow without a person or an intelligence willing this way for me? How can
there be obedience without someone commanding? On the other hand, belief in a personal God who wills and commands leads to problems. When
I was an undergraduate at Georgetown, this was called, in a mandatory
course for all first-year students, the Problem of God.

The problem of God was illustrated on November 10, 2005, when Pat
Robertson warned the City of Dover, Pennsylvania, of potential disasters
after the City voted their pro-intelligent design school board out of office.
Dover had been the site of intense publicity after the Board ordered that
biology students be told of possible doubts about evolution. A lawsuit, of
course, followed, with days of testimony during fall, 2005. Apparently, the
voters of Dover had had enough and voted out the School Board. Robertson had this to say on his *700 Club* television program:

> I'd like to say to the good citizens of Dover: if there is a disaster in your
> area, don't turn to God, you just rejected Him from your city, and don't
> wonder why He hasn't helped you when problems begin, if they begin. I'm
> not saying they will, but if they do, just remember, you just voted God out
> of your city. And if that's the case, don't ask for His help because he might
> not be there.[366]

Robertson was widely attacked for these comments. But what is wrong with them exactly? The God of the *Bible* is not too loving to destroy Dover. The *Bible* shows God physically punishing sin. In fact, God is portrayed as very specifically promising rain in due season if the children of Israel obey Him and drought and famine if they do not. Why would it not be the same for Dover?

The problem is not that God cannot do these things in traditional theology, but that the clown Robertson purports to speak for God. I expected to hear in the media some serious theological objections raised by religious leaders against Robertson's presumption, especially from the Protestant community to which he belongs. But liberal Protestantism does not seem capable of calling Robertson the blasphemer that he is. The theological objection to these comments is that God is not on call to back up Robertson's particular political commitment to intelligent design. Robertson does not know, unless God has spoken to him as to a prophet, that the people of Dover voted God out of Dover. They may have reclaimed God from political hacks like Robertson. Or, they may have acted out of mixed, sinful motives, just like the rest of us.

The secular voter responds to Robertson differently. The secular voter says that there is no God who acts like that. There is no God who responds to human actions with plans and irritation. The natural world goes its own way. Hurricanes do not hit Florida because of a gay rights parade, as Robertson had once also warned.

What then about global warming? Plenty of liberals who make fun of Robertson are happy to harp about the disasters man is causing because of our selfish misuse of the natural world. Environmentalists who say there is no God sound like fundamentalist preachers when the subject is judgment for the sins of industrialism. This way of thinking by environmentalists is not foreign to a man like Robertson. This environmental thinking is biblical. The disagreement between Robertson and the environmentalists is simply the old one—who is on God's side? Which of us, if either of us, is doing God's will?

Many environmentalists would say that they are not speaking of God. They just mean that there are consequences for behavior that misuses the natural world. Maybe that is exactly what the biblical writers meant. Maybe they were describing in their terms the way reality works.

In other words, God acts in history as the tilt in the universe described above. Or, if even that sounds too religious, one could say that for many secular voters, history happens in a certain direction. History is not chaos. History tells a tale. And the fight about evolution and about global warming may be part of that tale. But God does not respond to particulars. Judgment and reward happen on a large and impersonal scale. It rains on the just and the unjust. The first-born of both the good and the bad Egyptians die.

This point of the structural quality of reality is important, particularly as concerns the natural world. Nature is both regular and unpredictable. That means that nature will both regularly and unpredictably be deadly to people. Storms and sickness are more or less predictable dangers, and, for the moment, tsunamis and earthquakes are unpredictable. But, none of these result from some outside intervention. The secular voters emphasizes that there is no one who can be called on to intervene in these natural processes.

Even true catastrophe, like an asteroid hitting the Earth, would just be one of those things. Nature goes its own way. But this is not a new, secular insight. There were rabbis in the classic Jewish tradition who said the same thing.

So, where is God in natural processes? Both blessing and judgment, life and death, come from the human response to nature. Sin, in this context, is usually the more visible human response. Man can greedily abuse nature rather than living within the limits of the bounty that nature provides. When man sins in that way, the response of natural processes is likely to increase their danger. This seems to be happening now with global warming and its magnification of droughts and storms.

Humans also respond to natural processes by trying to mitigate their harmful impact. That is a faithful response that tries to protect my neighbor. Sin in this context has to do with the failure to devote human resources to this work of mitigation. New Orleans could have been saved much of the damage from Katrina through long-term responsible planning and engineering, including conservation of wetlands to prevent flooding. The failure to do this led to tragedy that fell with particular harshness on the poor.

God's judgment comes in the suffering human sin brings. God's blessings come from the humble acceptance of nature's gifts, which is everything we have really, when nature is not abused and when care is exercised regarding nature's dangers. Nothing supernatural is needed here. All of this is built into the universe in which we have been placed. It is part of the tilt of history. God is in our relationship to nature, though nature is not God. The human response to nature can be understood as emanating from the God of history.

Is this God of history what Barth and Jesus are trying to help us see when they say that a person can be a disciple without a particular orthodox belief? Certainly they both worshiped a personal God. But they may have meant that the fundamental task of man is not to believe that God exists but to do his will. The fundamental question is not whether there is a God who is Lord of history but whether history has an order. If history has a shape and that shape is good and a person tries to support that shape, then that person is a believer. That person is one of the people of

God. If someone believes in the promises of the *Bible*, and its warnings, that person is a follower of the way of the *Bible*.

Imagine the opposite. Imagine a person who believes in the personal God absolutely but who does nothing to live that belief. Whom would Jesus condemn? Who would he think was a neighbor?

Avery Cardinal Dulles wrote something akin to this understanding in November 2005, in the magazine *First Things*:

> The Catholic Church clearly teaches that no one will be condemned for unbelief, or for incomplete belief, without having sinned against the light. Those who with good will follow the movements of God's grace in their own lives are on the road to salvation.[367]

There is a book in the *Old Testament* that illustrates biblical belief for someone who does not believe in God. It is the *Book of Esther*, the only book in the *Old Testament* that does not contain the word God.

In the *Book of Esther*, a decree has been issued by the Persian King, at the behest of the high official Haman, authorizing the deaths of all the Jews in the kingdom. Queen Esther, who is a Jew, though this was not widely known, is requested by her cousin Mordecai to intercede with the King on behalf of the Jews. She is afraid to do so because there is a penalty of death for an uninvited approach to the King, unless the King accepts the entry. Mordecai sends the following response to Esther:

> [I]f you keep silence at such a time as this, relief and deliverance will rise for the Jews from another quarter, but you and your father's house will perish. And who knows whether you have not come to the kingdom for such a time as this?[368]

Mordecai does not say, God made you Queen for this occasion. Rather, he asserts, simply, that she *is* Queen for just this moment. In other words, Esther's life has this certain shape. This is the moment for the fulfillment of the purpose of her life. This is her destiny. Esther is to respond in faithfulness to the reality that she has been placed where she now is.

All meaning in human life comes from the perception that our lives have a meaningful shape. This is the sense I have in my vocation or in my art or in going to war to end slavery or to fight fascism. Unless we deny meaning itself, we must accept, or search for, a shape for our own lives. There are some people who say they deny meaning but they are few in number and, as such, they are not an issue in our politics. Most secular voters are not like that. They do not deny meaning. They accept and search for meaning in public life. In fact they do this enthusiastically.

Just as Esther's life has this shape, so history has a shape as a whole. This is Brueggemann's understanding of the message of the *Old Testament*. There is a moral shape in history. Who in this culture denies that? Someone would have to say that human history is just one thing after another. Who, in denying the shape of history, would want to live out of that denial? What would a human life look like that was lived out of the understanding that the history of life lacks meaning? The sense of meaningfulness extends from my individual life to the sense of human life as a whole.

There was a story in the *New York Times Magazine* in July 2006, about the songwriter and singer, Katell Keineg. She spoke about her music and this sense of meaning:

> Well, for me, listening to music is akin to a religious experience; it's the closest thing to a religion I have. I mean, I wouldn't put it in terms of *God*, because I'm an atheist, but I think humans are hard-wired for religion, hard-wired with a sense of divinity, however you interpret that. There's probably some evolutionary advantage to it—this urge for *meaning*.[369]

This is the perfect expression of the religious secularist. It can be very important to such a person not to use the language of God. But for the rest of us, the presence of God in the life of such a person is palpable.

One can say, and some do, that man makes up meaning—puts it, so to speak, into the world. Man is the being who must have meaning. But why should man be like that? Why should the universe have selected for meaning? After all, if meaningfulness sustains human life, that is not a chimera, but a fact. It is a fact that the secularist must come to terms with.

When a scientist asserts that evolution shows there is no design in the universe, as Richard Dawkins does in his book, *The Blind Watchmaker*, he is not speaking of the shape of his own life. Dawkins says that "Darwin made it possible to be an intellectually fulfilled atheist." But Dawkins is not arguing that there is no meaning in life. He is not speaking of the history of science, for example. And he certainly is not speaking of history itself. Dawkins does not live a life of chaos or materialism, whatever he says about these matters. His life is driven by meaningfulness.

The history of science has a very certain and meaningful shape. It describes the unfolding knowability, if I may use that term, of the universe. Dawkins would not deny that. History as a whole, though it may not show progress overall, similarly shows bits of progress in terms of human growth in wisdom.

The rejection of intelligent design in the evolution debate, or the more general claim that there is no God, are merely assertions that there is not a being who planned all this. There is not a God who is a person like you and me. That may be. But there is significance and meaning and direction in our lives all the same. Perhaps that meaning is simply built into the hidden structure of the universe. But of course that may be what God is—the hidden unfolding of meaning in the universe. As a definition of God, that will do.

Can one have a personal relationship with the workings of history? That is a harder question. God in the *Bible* is not just destiny for an individual life or history for a people or humanity as a whole. God is a relationship to something like a person. In the *New Testament*, that person is Jesus. In the *Old Testament* as well, the moral process in history is not indifferent to human beings.

Esther is invited to participate in the meaning of her life. The universe is not indifferent to her response. We all do, or can, have that same experience of connection. That is what it means to be part of something larger than yourself. We are invited to participate. We are called, just like Abraham. We are called by something that is more than ourselves or other people. Esther is called by Mordecai, it is true, but the call goes deeper than that. In answering such a call, we are promised, if not a happy life, at least a life of significance. Perhaps that is also what we mean when we say the word God.

There does not need to be a supernatural entity for God's actions in history to be recognized. There could simply be a tilt that acknowledges me not at all. There does not even have to be a divine entity for me to personally experience the call to participation in God's work in the world. This too could simply be something—a structure or a process—built into the universe.

But there is yet a deeper and more personal level of the interaction of the human and the divine. That level is the nearness of God. We experience the nearness of God in prayer. How can God be there for me in prayer if there is no God?

There is no doubt of God in history in the sense of the shape of history. There is no real doubt of my call to participation in this shape. We have all felt it. But many would deny the reality of a presence in response to prayer. This is difficult for me because I have myself experienced divine help in response to prayer and the forgiveness of sins in response to repentance. How could such things be, if, as I have said, there is no God?

I do not have an answer to that question. I know that the power of God to act goes beyond human capacity in both the social/historical and the personal realms. That is, the slaves are freed when history does not appear to support freedom. The slaves are freed against all odds. I am called to a meaningful life though I am nothing. My life matters, though there is no reason it should. And, the hardest of all in terms of the reality of God, my sins are forgiven when I could not possibly forgive myself. Human psychology is not the only reality. There is God acting in these three ways.

But in my own experience, it is not a person who acts but something different from anything we know as personal. There is a response to me and it is individual and that response is beneficent, but it is not detailed.

Judaism and Christianity, and other religions, leap from these mysteries to a full and confident account of the reality, nature, and will of God. Thus we end up with heaven, angels, resurrection, Messiah, and policy blueprints, like the condemnation of gay marriage. All this seems much too determined and detailed. We could not know or even be told these things. In order to avoid that kind of leap, I can only say that divine help and forgiveness are near—not that God exists.

Karl Barth, though he would have rejected what I have just said, has nevertheless said this better than anyone else: "as that reality by which men know God, lay hold of Him, and cling to Him, as the Unknown, Hidden God, as the final 'Yes' in the final 'No' of all concrete, observable life."[370]

There is no reason why the universe should not be a final "No" to man. But it is not. The universe is a "Yes" to man instead, at the cosmic and historical and personal levels. My main criticism of the Richard Dawkins of the world is that they show so little gratitude for this and so little interest intellectually in explaining the astounding fact that the universe says "Yes" to man.

Recently I heard another expression of the reality of God that reminded me of this "Yes" in the universe. The writer Ivan Doig has a Web site in which he refers to the deeper level of writing in novels as "that poetry under the prose." That is what we mean by depth—the poetry under the prose. For me, that is God—the presence of poetry everywhere, and especially in those places where at first we see only prose.

And prayer? Prayer is not submission to an alien sovereign. It is recognition, celebration, and thanks for a poetry we do not create. And punishment? That has many forms, but its basic reality is to be cut off from the poetry.

In 1968, in *Reason and Responsibility*,[371] the philosopher Anthony Flew asked what would count to the believer as disproof of the reality of God's love. The implication was that nothing would disprove God and, therefore, that belief was meaningless, or was assuming the improvable. But, if the universe is a "Yes" to man, overall and despite its negative aspects, then this is the source of belief. And if the nonbeliever should respond—"Well, of course the universe is a 'Yes' to you; of course you experience response and help; because you evolved here, you are suited to this universe"—we could ask, who is assuming the improvable now?

Metaphysics used to ask, why should there be something rather than nothing. If we cannot answer the "why" question, we should at least acknowledge that in the existence of something rather than nothing, a claim is made on us. We may respond to that claim by hostility, or selfishness, or indifference. We may even scoff at those people who respond with gratitude and piety. All these responses have been made by people throughout human history. It has always been true that some reject and revile God and do not experience wonder and thanks. Still, we cannot avoid response of some kind. We are part of the something that exists and that by itself makes a claim.

The above discussion shows the difficulty of trying to speak of God. It is easier to say what this understanding of reality does not include. First, this is not pantheism. The world and the universe are not God. Not everything that is, has an equal normative claim. God is what is coming to fruition, and what is promised to us, not what is already here.

Second, this is not man's creation of the power of the ideal, which John Dewey champions in *A Common Faith*. Dewey believed that while the "advance of culture and science" had discredited the supernatural, not everything of a religious nature had been discredited. Dewey understood "the religious" as "experiences having the force of bringing about a better, deeper, and enduring adjustment in life . . ."[372] Such an experience could be brought about from many sources, from poetry to philosophy. What Dewey was particularly interested in was the "moral faith" in which an "ideal end" makes "its rightful claim over our desires and purposes."[373]

This is not really criticizing Dewey, for, as is probably clear, in some ways this book is a continuation of his program. We can only pick up where Dewey left off. But it was very important to Dewey to deny that the ideal has reality and power apart from man's convictions and strivings. He denied what this book asserts—that "justice is embedded in the very make-up of the actually existent world." Everything for Dewey begins with man's striving. While I agree with Dewey that there is no supernatural power, I believe that the ideal, as he calls it, is embedded in reality apart from man's recognition and conviction. We do not call it into being; it calls us into being.

For similar reasons, this is not any other sort of humanism. Man is not reliable, as the twentieth century surely proves. We must not start with man, but what is beyond man.

Third, and at the other extreme, this is not a denial that God acts in our lives. The denial that God acts, the assumption that man is on his own, is illustrated in one of the most important stories in the *Talmud*—the Jewish books of law and learning compiled between 200 and 500 c.e.—in the story of the Oven of Aknai.[374] In a dispute between Rabbi Eliezer and the other scholars on a point of law concerning the ritual purity of an oven, Eliezer appeals to natural phenomena as witness to his position—a carob tree flies for example—but the rest of the rabbis deny that nature can bear witness in this way. Eventually, a voice from heaven endorses Eliezer's view. But even heaven is not permitted to interfere with the workings of human reason. Rabbi Joshua famously rejects the testimony of the voice of heaven with the phrase, "It is not in heaven." Once the *Torah* was given to man, humans by its guidance must find their own way. No doubt this language—that it is not in heaven—was meant to echo Moses.[375] But this is a conclusion in a context Moses would not have endorsed.

Aknai can be understood as the banishment of God from the affairs of men—a kind of nascent deism. Instead of winding up the world like a clock to run by natural law, God winds up the world to run by rabbinic reason, which draws its principles from the *Torah*.

In the Aknai story, the result of the defeat of Eliezer by the rabbis is death and destruction. The *Talmud* tells the Aknai story, but the *Talmud* does not endorse the position of the rabbis. Although so subtle that many readers misread the text, the *Talmud* condemns such human presumption. And it predicts what we have seen—man on his own is in misery.

So I do not mean to be heard as describing a divine passivity. The acts of God are clear. Man cannot live on his own and need not do so.

This book is proposing that the *Bible* be taken as a starting point for personal and public life, but not as a rulebook. The most impressive aspect of the *Bible* is its reliability. The promises of the *Bible*, in the case of divine help, and its warnings, in the case of divine judgment, come true. These promises and warnings, however, are just not as particular and detailed as some believers like to say. Slavery, for example, is condemned by the *Bible*, but not unambiguously. The South thought slavery was endorsed by the *Bible*. But, then, they needed to think so. Abortion is condemned by the *Bible*, but certainly not clearly. Gay marriage may be said to be affirmed by the *Bible*, but also not in unambiguous language. Indeed, there are a number of condemnations of homosexual activity, in the *Old Testament* especially. People might reasonably claim that the *Bible* opposes gay marriage. But to think that misses the *Bible's* underlying message of love and caring, which characterizes the gay couples I know.

The *Bible* teaches change in the name of justice. For example, there were the daughters of Zelophehad in the *Book of Numbers* who, upon the death of their father, asked that they receive the inheritance in the absence of a male heir. God told Moses that the claim was just and this new law was established. Gay marriage will eventually be seen as fundamentally just in this way.

The opposite of the reliability of the *Bible* is the unreliability of everything human. As Brueggemann says, all human programs, from Communism to Capitalism, and including Democracy, always prove false in some critical respect. None of them is reliable. Only living biblically promises a truly human life.

This is, in some sense, the opposite of Pascal's wager. We do not believe because it might be true, does us no harm, and might do us a great deal of good if it turns out to be true. Rather, we believe because to do so does us good, period. And it is good even when we are under judgment.

But this belief is not in the supernatural. It is not a belief in a God who exists as a being. It is not an acceptance of either the *Old* or *New Testament* accounts of who God is.

This is a belief that the secular voter can accept, indeed accepts already. Perhaps in this way, the secular voter can participate in American religious democracy. The word God need not be a fairy tale when understood this way. Nor need the use of the word God, in the sense used here, grant political power to certain religious and political groups.

CONCLUSION

The Coming Religious Renewal
of the Democratic Left

America is a religious democracy now. The secular consensus has ended. This change does not appear to be temporary. The change has centered in the actions of voters rather than acts of government. Therefore, even if religious democracy were something the courts wanted to alter, they would be unable to do so.

Religious democracy, however, is not something we should wish to alter. It opens a depth of political life that secular politics cannot reach. For that reason, religious democracy might help America to become a better democracy.

Clearly, there are questions that religious democracy will have to answer. A significant one is whether religious democracy can practice true pluralism at home and abroad. Can religious democracy deal with nonbelievers and dissenting believers fairly? This is a vital question, but it is not the greatest challenge facing religious democracy.

American political life is crippled today by a false dualism between religious voters and secular voters. This divide has led to a narrow expression of religion in America's public square. The challenge to religious democracy is not ultimately its relationship to our many religious traditions or even its relationship to secularism. The greatest challenge to religious democracy will be to bring about religious renewal in American political life.

AFTERWORD

The 2006 Midterm Election

This book was written before the 2006 Midterm Election on November 7, in which Democrats gained majority control of both the House of Representatives and the Senate. The day after that election, Amy Sullivan, an editor of *Washington Monthly*, wrote in the New Republic's online edition that the election had erased the "God gap" between the two parties. Sullivan reported that in 2004, weekly churchgoers voted for President Bush 58 to 41 percent, but in 2006, weekly religious worshipers voted for Republicans over Democrats by only 51 to 48 per cent, "a statistically meaningless difference."

This election result obviously reflects an important change in attitude by religious voters, although it also shows that these voters still tend to favor Republicans over Democrats. The significant question is, how should this political shift be interpreted?

On one level, religion and the issues directly associated with it, such as abortion, stem cell research, and gay rights, receded in importance in the 2006 election in light of other national problems. The Democrats succeeded in making the 2006 election a referendum on the policies of the Bush Administration by emphasizing the war in Iraq, the federal response to Hurricane Katrina, government spending and the resulting federal deficit, Republican corruption and scandals, and, overall, by linking Republican candidates to President Bush. President Bush treated the election result as a judgment by the voters on his policies by firing Secretary of Defense Donald Rumsfeld the day after the voting.

On another level, however, religion receded in importance in 2006 because the Democrats ran more conservative candidates, at least away from the coasts and in the South and West. These Democratic candidates were more pro-life, pro-gun, and pro-God, or some combination of these, than Democrats had tended to be in the recent past. Certainly without this strategy, Democrats would not have gained as much support as they did.

On the religion front in general, Democratic candidates basically accepted the central premise of this book, the end of secular politics, by not running on a secular agenda—the separation of Church and State, and government religious neutrality—really anywhere in the country. There was little or no talk about getting God out of public life. Even issues indirectly associated with the religious divide, such as school vouchers, abortion, and gay rights, were downplayed during the campaign. For one election at least, the Democratic Party accepted American Religious Democracy.

This Democratic Party strategy of accommodating conservative voters, however, will not work in the long run. Picking more conservative candidates to run, without addressing the underlying issues, could be done in 2006 because midterm congressional elections are played out locally—State by State. So, running some candidates who probably disagreed with their fellow Democrats almost as much as they did with Republicans, was not viewed by the electorate as incoherent. But 2008 will be a national election with a presidential candidate and a national party platform. The Democrats, therefore, will have to return to the debate over the proper role of religion in public life, among other divisive themes.

On the other side of politics, Republicans in 2006 also had little or nothing to say about religion. The Republican Party basically took the support of religious voters for granted and worried only about turnout. Nor did conservative religious leadership present any proposals during the campaign concerning the future of religion in America. They supported President Bush and most Republican candidates based on their past relationship.

So, in the end, the future of religion in American public life lies before us much as it did prior to the 2006 election. In the minds of religious voters, the word "God" in the public square still evokes a kind of partisan response. On election night, Senator Rick Santorum of Pennsylvania gave a gracious concession speech and then clearly meant to say that he and his family thanked God for the past opportunity to serve. His supporters, however, interrupted him with applause right after the word God, as if Senator Santorum had just renewed a campaign pledge. They were applauding the use of God language in the public square. These voters do not realize that the fight over that issue is done and that they have already won.

For secular voters, despite the appearance of more conservative Democratic Party candidates, the dream of secular politics is still alive. The steady drumbeat of popular books bashing religion continued throughout

2006, with Richard Dawkins' *The God Delusion* and Sam Harris' *Letter to a Christian Nation* both published in September and, on the secular right, Andrew Sullivan's *The Conservative Soul* in October. No doubt some secular voters imagine that the Democratic Party's victory in 2006 presages a return to judicial and other victories ensuring the separation of Church and State. These voters do not know that they have already lost.

But these conclusions say little about what the future of religion in American public life will look like. Religious voters must finally admit that religion in the public square is established and healthy. No one is going to put God back in the political closet. The question is, however, what comes next? Just how religious do American religious voters want our public life to be? They must be willing to tell the rest of us what their ultimate goal really is.

For secular voters, the challenge is to surrender childish views of religion and to reengage the Western tradition of robust thought about religious language. It makes no more sense for secularists to oppose the word "God" in politics, and the notion of meaning beyond man, than it does for religious voters to deny biological evolution. Almost uniformly, it is a particular understanding of God, rather than any possible understanding of God, that the secularist is opposing. In other words, there are few atheist-materialists in America and we must stop pretending that our religious differences are a chasm.

I hope that this book will help clarify these matters for both religious and secular voters. The results of the election of 2006, as surprising and important as they may have been in other ways, did not change the fundamental American religious and political tasks.

Notes

1. Mark Danner, "How Bush Really Won," *New York Review of Books*, January 13, 2005, http://www.nybooks.com/articles/17690 (accessed, September 13, 2006).

2. Dick Meyer, "Moral Values' Myth," *Pittsburgh Post-Gazette,* December 12, 2004, J1.

3. *Bradwell v. Illinois*, 83 U.S. 130, 141 (1873) (J. Bradley, concurring).

4. Daniel Eisenberg, "Lessons of the Schiavo Battle," *Time*, April 4, 2005, 22.

5. Adam Nagourney, "G.O.P. Right Is Splintered on Schiavo Intervention," *New York Times*, March 23, 2005, A14.

6. David Van Biema, Cathy Booth-Thomas, Massimo Calabresi, John F. Dickerson, John Cloud, Rebecca Winters, and Sonja Steptoe. "The 25 Most Influential Evangelicals in America," *Time*, February 7, 2005.

7. A.O. Scott, "Reading Hollywood from Left to Right," *New York Times*, September 25, 2005, http://www.nytimes.com/2005/09/25/movies/MoviesFeatures/25scot.html (accessed, September 5, 2006).

8. Terence Samuel and Dan Gilgoff, "At the Brink," *U.S. News & World Report*, May 30, 2005, 32–33.

9. Kevin Phillips, *American Theocracy: The Peril and Politics of Radical Religion, Oil, and Borrowed Money in the 21st Century* (New York: Viking Adult, 2006).

10. Frank Rich, "The Passion of the Embryos," *New York Times*, Week in Review, July 23, 2006.

11. *Poe v. Ullman*, 367 U.S. 497, 522-555 (1961) (J. Harlan, dissenting).

12. David Novak, "Religion, Faith, and Elections," in *One Electorate Under God?: A Dialogue on Religion and American Politics*, ed. E. J. Dionne Jr., Jean Bethke Elshtain, and Kayla M. Drogosz, 159–163. (Washington, DC: Brookings Institute Press, 2004).

13. David R. Dow, "The End of Religion," *Journal of Law and Religion* 16 (2001): 881.

14. Noah Feldman, *Divided by God: America's Church-State Problem and What We Should Do About It* (New York: Farrar, Straus, and Giroux, 2005), 223.

15. Richard John Neuhaus, *The Naked Public Square: Religion and Democracy in America* (Grand Rapids, MI: Wm. B. Eerdmans Publishing Company, 1984).

16. Ibid., 175.

17. Thomas L. Friedman, "Two Nations Under God," *New York Times*, November 4, 2004, A25.

18. CNN.com Election 2004, CNN.com [hereinafter Election 2004], at http://www.cnn.com/ELECTION/2004/pages/results/states/US/P/00/epolls.0.html (last visited Sept. 12, 2005).

19. Michael McGough, "Mission Critical," *Pittsburgh Post-Gazette*, October 24, 2004, B1 (interviewing David Domke).

20. Ed Vitagliano, "Now What?" *American Family Association Journal*, http://www.afajournal.org/2005/february/2.05now_what.asp (accessed September 5, 2006.)

21. Michael Jonas, "Sen. Clinton Urges Use of Faith-Based Initiatives," *Boston Globe*, January 20, 2005, B1.

22. Burt Neuborne, "Courting Trouble," *American Prospect*, January 2005, A18.

23. Hendrik Hertzberg, "Blues" *New Yorker*, November 15, 2004, 33.

24. Neuborne, "Courting Trouble," A17.

25. Russell Shorto, "What's Their Real Problem with Gay Marriage? It's the Gay Part," *New York Times Magazine*, June 19, 2005, 36.

26. 410 U.S. 113 (1973).

27. Mike Allen, "DeLay Wants Panel to Review Role of Courts," *Washington Post*, April 2, 2005, A9.

28. 542 U.S. 1 (2004) (case dismissed for lack of standing).

29. *Van Orden v. Perry*, 125 S.Ct. 2854 (2005).

30. *McCreary v. ACLU*, 125 S.Ct. 2722 (2005).

31. Carol Eisenberg, "Reawakening Pop Culture Says Americans More Religious, But States Tell Different Story," *Journal Gazette* (Fort Wayne, IN), May 1, 2004, 1C.

32. Andrew Delbanco, "Lincoln and Modernity," in *Knowledge and Belief in America* (New York: Woodrow Wilson Press, 1995), 267 n. 38 (quoting Lincoln).

33. *Lynch v. Donnelly*, 465 U.S. 668, 688 (1984) (J. O'Connor, concurring).

34. Peter Carlson, "Taking the Bob Out of Bob Jones University," *Washington Post*, May 5, 2005, C1.

35. Thomas Frank, "What's the Matter with Liberals?" *New York Review of Books*, May 12, 2005, http://www.nybooks.com/articles/17982 (accessed September 13, 2006).

36. Ibid.

37. Neuhaus, *The Naked Public Square*, vii.

38. Stephen L. Carter, *The Culture of Disbelief: How American Law and Politics Trivialize Religious Devotion* (New York: Anchor Books, 1993), 54.

39. Ibid., at 51.

40. Michael Sokolove, "The Believer," *New York Times Magazine*, May 22, 2005, 59.

41. Julia Duin, "Faithless: God under Fire in the Public Square," *Washington Times*, April 13, 2005, A1.

42. Saikrishna Praksh and John Yoo, "Against Interpretive Supremacy," *Michigan Law Review* 103 (2005): 1542.

43. John Rawls, *Political Liberalism: The Supreme Court as Exemplar of Public Reason* (New York: Columbia University Press, 1993), 237–238. I am indebted to my colleague Bruce Antkowiak for bringing this quotation to my attention.

44. H. Jefferson Powell, *The Moral Tradition of American Constitutionalism: A Theological Interpretation* (Durham, NC: Duke University Press, 1993), 11.

45. David Brooks, "How Niebuhr Helps Us Kick the Secularist Habit: A Six-Step Program," in *One Electorate Under God? A Dialogue on Religion and American Politics*. Edited by E. J. Dionne Jr., Jean Bethke Elshtain, and Kayla M. Drogosz, 2004, 67.

46. Ibid., 67.

47. David Brin, "The Real Culture War," http://www.davidbrin.com/realculturewar1.html (accessed September 7, 2006).

48. David R. Dow, "The End of Religion," *Journal of Law and Religion* 16 (2001): 879.

49. 403 U.S. 602 (1971).

50. John Rawls, *A Theory of Justice* (Cambridge, MA: The Belknap Press of Harvard University Press, 1971), 212.

51. Rinker Buck, "Alito's Yale Years: Early Years of Brilliance in a Shy, Religious Scholar," *Hartford Courant NE Magazine*, November 20, 2005.

52. Robert M. Cover, "The Supreme Court, 1982 Term-Foreword: Nomos and Narrative," *Harvard Law Review* 97 (1983): 4.

53. Suzanne Last Stone, "Pursuit of the Counter-Text: The Turn to the Jewish Legal Modal in Contemporary American Legal Theory," *Harvard Law Review* 106 (1993): 816.

54. Richard John Neuhaus, *The Naked Public Square: Religion and Democracy in America* (Grand Rapids, MI: Wm. B. Eerdmans Publishing Company, 1984).

55. Howard J. Vogel, "A Survey and Commentary on the New Literature in Law and Religion," *Journal of Law and Religion* 1 (1983): 79.

56. Ronald Dworkin, *Taking Rights Seriously* (Cambridge, MA: Harvard University Press, 1977), 250.

57. Kathleen Sullivan, "Religion and Liberal Democracy," *University of Chicago Law Review* 59 (1992): 211.

58. Ibid., 201.

59. David S. Douglas, "Holding America Together," Harvard Civil Rights-Civil Liberties Law Review 21 (1986): 338-39.

60. Edward B. Foley, "Jurisprudence and Theology," *Fordham Law* Review 66 (1998): 1195.

61. At least that is the title on the book cover. At the same time the book has been listed by the title, *Rights from Wrongs: The Origin of Human Rights in the Experiences of Injustice*. The clash can be observed at http://www.barnesandnoble.com/(accessed September 10, 2006). Alan Dershowitz, *Rights from Wrongs*. (New York: Basic Books, 2005).

62. *Cruzan v. Director, Mo. Dep't of Health*, 497 U.S. 261, 293 (1s990) (Scalia, concurring).

63. Pope Benedict XVI, *Truth and Tolerance: Christian Belief and World Religions.* Translated by Henry Taylor (San Francisco, CA: Ignatius Press, 2004), 238.

64. Nathan Schleuter and Robert H. Bork, "Constitutional Persons: An Exchange on Abortion," *First Things* (January 2003): 28–36.

65. Phillips, *American Theocracy: The Peril and Politics of Radical Religion, Oil, and Borrowed Money in the 21st Century,* 2006, 172.

66. Isaac Kramnick and R. Laurence Moore, *The Godless Constitution: The Case against Religious Correctness* (New York: W.W. Norton & Company, 1995).

67. 472 U.S. 38 (1985) (striking down period of silence statute for prayer in public schools).

68. Ibid, 113-114 (J. Rehnquist,dissenting).

69. Kent Greenawalt, "Religious Convictions and Lawmaking," *Michigan Law Review* 84 (1985): 396

70. Michael J. Perry, "Why Political Reliance on Religiously Ground Morality Is Not Illegitimate in a Liberal Democracy," *Wake Forest Law Review* 36 (2001).

71. Ibid., 222.

72. Ronald Thieman, *Religion in Public Life: A Dilemma for Democracy* (Washington DC: Georgetown University Press, 1996).

73. Feldman, *Divided by God: America's Church-State Problem—And What We Should Do about It,* 2005, 222.

74. Ibid.

75. Daniel C. Dennett, *Breaking the Spell: Religion as a Natural Phenomenon* (New York: Viking Adult, 2006).

76. Francis Fukuyama, "The Calvinist Manifesto," *New York Times Book Review,* March 13, 2005, http://www.nytimes.com/2005/03/13/books/review/013FUKUYA.html (accessed September 8, 2006).

77. Ibid.

78. *Lochner v. New York,* 198 U.S. 45 (1905).

79. 300 U.S. 379 (1937).

80. 301 U.S. 1 (1937).

81. Rebecca French, "Shopping for Religion: The Change in Everyday Religious Practices and Its Importance to the Law," *Buffalo Law Review* 51 (2003): 192.

82. Polling Report.com, "Religion (p. 2)," Polling Report.com, http://www.pollingreport.com/religion2.htm (accessed September 6, 2006).

83. Ibid.

84. Ariel Levy, *Female Chauvinist Pigs: Women and the Rise of Raunch Culture* (New York: Free Press, 2005).

85. Pamela Paul, *Pornofied: How Pornography is Transforming Our Lives, Our Relationships and Our Families* (New York: Times Books, 2005).

86. Melissa A. Dalziel, "The Tension between a Godless Constitution and a Culture of Belief in an Age of Reason," *Brigham Young University Law Review* 1999 (1999): 872 n.50.

87. Michael Berg, "The Religious Right, Constitutional Values, and the Lemon Test," *N.Y.U. Annual Survey of American Law,* 1995 (1995): 39.

88. Kramnick and Moore, *The Godless Constitution: The Case against Religious Correctness,* 1996.

89. Stephanie Simon, "Grooming Politicians for Christ," *Los Angeles Times*, August 23, 2005, http://pewforum.org/news/display.php?NewsID=5256 (accessed September 9, 2006).

90. Ibid.

91. Jeffrey Hart, "The Evangelical Effect," *Pittsburgh Post-Gazette*, April 17, 2005, J1.

92. Jim Wallis, *God's Politics: Why the Right GETS It Wrong and the Left Doesn't Get It* (San Francisco, CA: Harper, 2005).

93. *Employment Division v. Smith*, 494 U.S. 872 (1990).

94. *Locke v. Davey*, 540 U.S. 712 (2004).

95. *City of Boerne v. Flores*, 521 U.S. 507 (1997).

96. *Zelman v. Simmons Harris*, 536 U.S. 639 (2002).

97. *Van Order v. Perry*, 545 U.S. 677 (2005).

98. *McCreary v. ACLU*, 545 U.S. 844 (2005).

99. John Roberts, "The Ethics of Conviction: Marxism, Ontology and Religion," *Radical Philosophy* 121 (2003), http://www.radicalphilosophy.com/default.asp?channel_id=2188&editorial_id=13669 (accessed September 10, 2006).

100. John D. Caputo, *The Prayers and Tears of Jacques Derrida: Religion without Religion* (Bloomington, IN: University of Indiana Press, 1997).

101. Stanley Fish, "One University, under God?" *Chronicle of Higher Education*, January 7, 2005, C1.

102. Arthur Leff, "Unspeakable Ethics, Unnatural Law," *Duke Law Journal* 1979 (1979): 1229.

103. Ibid.

104. Samuel W. Calhoun, "Grounding Normative Assertions: Arthur Leff''s Still Irrefutable, But Incomplete, 'Sez Who?' Critique," *Journal of Law and Religion* 20 (2004–2005): 31.

105. *Jewish Political Tradition*. Edited by Michael Walzer, Menachem Lorberbaum, Noam J. Zohar, and Yair Lorberbaum. vol. 1 (New Haven, CT: Yale University Press, 2000).

106. *Dred Scott v. Sanford*, 60 U.S. 393 (1856).

107. Neuhaus, *The Naked Public Square: Religion and Democracy in America*, 1984, 26.

108. Robert Audi, *Religious Commitment and Secular Reason* (New York: Cambridge University Press, 2000).

109. Paul E. Salamanca, "The Liberal Policy and Liberalism in Religious Traditions," *Barry Law Review* 4 (2003): 97.

110. Marci A. Hamilton, *God vs. the Gavel: Religion and the Rule of Law* (Cambridge; New York: Cambridge University Press, 2005).

111. Paul F. Campos, "Secular Fundamentalism," *Columbia Law Review* 94 (1994): 1814.

112. Franklin I. Gamwell, *Democracy on Purpose: Justice and the Reality of God* (Washington, DC: Georgetown University Press, 2000).

113. Marci A. Hamilton, "Direct Democracy and the Protestant Ethic," *Journal of Contemporary Legal Issues* 13 (2004): 413.

114. John 8:32 (Revised standard version).

115. Deut. 32:4 (Revised standard version).

116. Pope Benedict XVI, *Truth and Tolerance: Christian Belief and World Religions.* Translated by Henry Taylor (San Francisco, CA: Ignatius Press, 2004), 117.

117. Jeremiah 31:33 (Revised standard version).

118. *Congressional Globe*, 30th Cong., 1st Sess., 1848, 872.

119. Daniel L. Dreisbach, "In Search of a Christian Commonwealth: An Examination of Selected Nineteenth-Century Commentaries on References to God and the Christian Religion in the United States Constitution," *Baylor Law Review* 48 (1996): 994.

120. Hannah Arendt, *On Revolution* (New York: Viking Press, 1965), 190.

121. Richard John Neuhaus, *The Naked Public Square: Religion and Democracy in America* (Grand Rapids, MI: Wm. B. Eerdmans Publishing Company, 1984), 53.

122. Daniel Quinn, *Ishmael: An Adventure of the Mind and Spirit* (New York: Bantam/Turner Books, 1992).

123. Christopher D. Stone, *Should Trees Have Standing? Toward Legal Rights for Natural Objects* (Los Altos, CA: W. Kaufmann, 1974).

124. *Sierra Club v. Norton*, 405 U.S. 727, 741-42 (1972) (J. Douglas, dissenting).

125. Quinn, *Ishmael: An Adventure of the Mind and Spirit*, 1992, 62–63.

126. James W. Gordon, "Religion and First Justice Harlan: A Case Study in Late Nineteenth Century Presbyterian Constitutionalism," *Marquette Law Review* 85 (2001): 342–43.

127. Office of the Press Secretary, President Sworn-in to Second Term, The White House, http://www.whitehouse.gov/news/releases/2005/01/20050120-1.html (accessed September 13, 2006).

128. Michael Maddigan, "The Establishment Clause, Civil Religion, and the Public Church," comment, *California Law Review* 81 (1993): 322.

129. Office of the Press Secretary, President Sworn-in to Second Term, The White House, http://www.whitehouse.gov/news/releases/2005/01/20050120-1.html (accessed September 13, 2006).

130. Robert N. Bellah, *Beyond Belief: Essays on Religion in a Post-Traditional World* (New York: Harper Row, 1970).

131. Steven B. Epstein, "Rethinking the Constitutionality of Ceremonial Deism," *Columbia Law Review* 96 (1996): 2098, n.71.

132. Carl Schmitt, *Political Theology: Four Chapters on the Concept of Sovereignty.* Translated by George Schwab (Cambridge, MA: MIT Press, 1985), 36.

133. Roger Williams, "Mr. Cotton's Letter Examined and Answered (London 1644)," *in Complete Writings of Roger Williams* (New York: Russell & Russell, 1963), 313, 392.

134. John Witte, Jr., "The Essential Rights and Liberties of Religion in the American Constitutional Experiment," *Notre Dame Law Review* 71 (1996): 379.

135. Martin Luther, "The Babylonian Captivity of the Church" and "The Freedom of a Christian," in *Three Treatises* (Philadelphia, PA: Fortress Press, 1960), 274.

136. Elisha Williams, "The Essential Rights and Liberties of Protestants" in *Religion and the Constitution.* Edited by Michael W McConnell, John H. Garvey, and Thomas C. Berg (New York: Aspen Law and Business, 2002), 47.

137. George H. Sabine, *A History of Political Theory* (New York: Holt, 1950), 415.

138. Schmitt, *Political Theology: Four Chapters on the Concept of Sovereignty*, 1985, 36–37.

139. *Youngstown Sheet and Tube Co. v. Sawyer*, 343 U.S. 579 (1952).

140. 542 U.S. 507 (2004).

141. Claude Lefort, *Democracy and Political Theory*. Translated by David Macey (Cambridge, UK: Polity Press, 1988), 222.

142. Ibid., 222–23.

143. Walter Brueggemann, *Theology of the Old Testament: Testimony, Dispute, Advocacy* (Minneapolis, MN: Fortress Press, 1997), 113.

144. Office of the Press Secretary, President Sworn-in to Second Term, The White House, http://www.whitehouse.gov/news/releases/2005/01/20050120-1.html (accessed September 13, 2006).

145. Lefort, *Democracy and Political Theory*. Translated by David Macey, 1988, 232.

146. Ibid.

147. John Rawls, "The Idea of Public Reason Revisited," *University of Chicago Law Review* 64 (1997): 784–85.

148. Ibid.

149. "Scalia Escalates Attacks on Church-State Separation at New York Conference," *Church & State* 58 (2005): 16.

150. Ibid.

151. Letter from Jonas Phillip to the President and Members of the Convention (Sept. 7, 1787), reprinted in Max Farrand, ed., The Records of the Federal Convention of 1787, at 78 (Yale U. Press, 1966 ed.).

152. Ibid., 310.

153. *Everson v. Board of Education*, 330 U.S. 1, 16 (1947).

154. *Reyonlds v. United States*, 98 U.S. 145, 164 (1878).

155. Thomas Jefferson, "Notes on the State of Virginia, Query XVIII," reprinted in *The Portable Thomas Jefferson*. Edited by Merrill D. Peterson (New York: Visiting Press, 1975), 214.

156. John Dewey, *A Common Faith* (New Haven, CT: Yale University Press, 1934).

157. Ibid., 23.

158. 494 U.S. 872 (1990).

159. 536 U.S. 639 (2002).

160. Ibid., at 705 (J. Souter, dissenting).

161. 530 U.S. 793 (2000).

162. 463 U.S. 783 (1983).

163. 465 U.S. 668 (1984).

164. 492 U.S. 573 (1989).

165. 124 S.Ct. 2301 (2004).

166. 125 S.Ct. 2854 (2005).

167. 125 S.Ct. 2722 (2005).

168. *C.H. v. Oliva*, 195 F.3d 167 (3d Cir. 1999), aff'd on other grounds, 226 F.3d 198 (3d Cir. 2000) (en banc), cert. denied, 533 U.S. 915 (2001).

169. *Engel v. Vitale*, 370 U.S. 421 (1962).

170. *School Dist. v. Schempp*, 374 U.S. 203 (1963).

171. *Zorach v. Clausen*, 343 U.S. 306, 325 (1952) (J. Jackson, dissenting).

172. 472 U.S. 38 (1985).

173. 530 U.S. 290 (2000).

174. 125 S.Ct. 2722, at 2733 (quoting *Epperson v. Arkansas*, 393 U.S. 97, 104 (1968) (opinion of J. Souter, joined by Stevens, O'Connor, Ginsburg, and J. J. Breyer).

175. Justice Kennedy did not join this portion of the dissent.

176. 125 S.Ct. at 2753, (J. Scalia, dissenting).

177. 505 U.S. 577, 590 (1992).

178. 530 U.S. at 307.

179. 494 U.S. 872 (1990).

180. 508 U.S. 520 (1993).

181. 540 U.S. 712 (2004).

182. 521 U.S. 507 (1997).

183. 494 U.S. at 879 (quoting *Minersville School Dist. Bd. of Ed. v. Gobitis*, 310 U.S. 586, 594–95 (1940)).

184. *New York Times*, "Bill-Signing at Religious School Is at Issue," June 5, 2005, 34.

185. Ibid.

186. Shailagh Murray, "Dean's Words Draw Democratic Rebukes," *Washington Post*, June 9, 2005, A6.

187. Greeley, "The Puritans and American Politics," in *One Electorate Under God? A Dialogue on Religion and American Politics*. Edited by E. J. Dionne Jr., Jean Bethke Elshtain, and Kayla M. Drogosz, 2004, 106.

188. 60 U.S. 393 (1856).

189. *Plessy v. Ferguson*, 163 U.S. 537 (1896).

190. *Debs v. United States*, 249 U.S. 211 (1919).

191. *Korematsu v. United States*, 323 U.S. 214 (1944).

192. *Dennis v. United States*, 341 U.S. 494 (1951).

193. 198 U.S. 45 (1905) (striking down maximum hours for bakers).

194. Michael W. McConnell, "The Role of Democratic Politics in Transforming Moral Convictions into Law," *Yale Law Journal*, 98 (1989): 1536.

195. *Lawrence v. Texas*, 539 U.S. 558 (2003).

196. 347 U.S. 483 (1954).

197. 367 U.S. 497 (1961).

198. *Poe v. Ullman*, 367 U.S. 497, 542 (1961) (J. Harlan, dissenting).

199. Ibid., 542–43.

200. Ruth Bader Ginsburg, "Constitutional Adjudication in the United States as a Means of Advancing the Equal Stature of Men and Women under the Law," *Hofstra Law Review* 26 (1997): 268.

201. 163 U.S. 537, 552 (1896) (J. Harlan, dissenting).

202. 347 U.S. 483 (1954).

203. Robert Post, "Fashioning the Legal Constitution: Culture, Courts, and Law," Harvard *Law Review* 117 (2003): 8.

204. *Dickerson v. United States*, 530 U.S. 428, 464–65 (2000) (J. Scalia, dissenting).

205. Abraham Lincoln, "First Lincoln-Douglas Debate, Ottawa, Illinois," in *Abraham Lincoln: Speeches and Writings, 1832–1858*. Edited by Don E. Fehrenbacher (New York: Viking Press, 1989), 495, 524–35.

206. Bruce Ackerman, *We the People: Foundations* (Cambridge, MA: Belknap Press, 1991), 9.

207. Bruce Ackerman and James S. Fishkin, *Deliberation Day* (New Haven, CT: Yale University Press, 2004).

208. 347 U.S. 483 (1954).

209. "Public Gets Credit for School Bias Ban," *New York Times*," September 7 (1954): 10.

210. Michael W. McConnell, "Originalism and the Desegregation Decisions," *Virginia Law Review* 81 (1995): 952.

211. 404 U.S. 71 (1971).

212. 384 U.S. 436 (1966).

213. 530 U.S. 428 (2000).

214. Ibid., 443.

215. Bruce Ledewitz, "When Federal Law Is Also State Law: The Implications for State Constitutional Law Methodology of Footnote Seven in *Commonwealth v. Matos*," *Temple Law Review* 72 (1999): 592.

216. 410 U.S. 113 (1973).

217. 505 U.S. 833 (1992).

218. Alexander Bickel, *The Supreme Court and the Idea of Progress* (New York: Harper & Row, 1970), 239.

219. *McCreary v. ALCU*, 545 U.S. 844, 125 S.Ct. 2722, 2752 (2005) (J. Scalia, dissenting).

220. 530 U.S. 914 (2000).

221. Sam. 8:7 (Revised standard version).

222. Amy Chua, *World on Fire: How Exporting Free Market Democracy Breeds Ethnic Hatred and Global Instability* (New York: Doubleday, 2003).

223. Fareed Zakaria, *The Future of Freedom: Illiberal Democracy at Home and Abroad* (New York: W.W. Norton & Company, 2003), 114.

224. Lee Travis, "Corporate Governance and the Global Social Void," *Vanderbilt Journal of Transnational Law* 35 (2002): 498.

225. Ibid.

226. Salman Rushdie, "Yes, This is about Islam," *New York Times*, November 2, 2001.

227. Michael Ignatieff, "Iranian Lessons," *New York Times Magazine*, July 15, 2005, 46.

228. Reza Aslan, *No God But God: The Origins, Evolution, and Future of Islam* (New York: Random House, 2006).

229. Jack Nelson-Pallmeyer, *Is Religion Killing Us?: Violence in the Bible and the Quran* (Harrisburg, PA: Trinity International Press, 2003).

230. Martha Minow, "Governing Religion," in *One Electorate Under God? A Dialogue on Religion and American Politics*, edited by E. J. Dionne Jr., Jean Bethke Elshtain, and Kayla M. Drogosz, 2004, 148.

231. E-mail from Not In Our Name, e-mail message to author May 24, 2005 (quoting New Not in Our Name Statement of Conscience available at http://www.notinourname.net/soc-jan05.htm).

232. Phillips, *American Theocracy: The Peril and Politics of Radical Religion, Oil, and Borrowed Money in the 21st Century, 2006.*

233. *Thornburgh v. American College of Obstetricians & Gynecologists*, 476 U.S. 747, 778 (1986) (J. Stevens, concurring).

234. *Elrod v. Burns*, 427 U.S. 347 (1976) (unconstitutional to dismiss nonpolicy-making employee on ground of nonmembership in political party); *Branti v. Finkel*, 445 U.S. 507 (1980) (applying *Elrod* to dismissal of assistant public defender);

Rutan v. Republican Party of Illinois, 497 U.S. 62 (1990) (extending *Elrod* and *Branti* to hiring decisions).

235. Thomas Nagel, "Rawls and Liberalism," in *The Cambridge Companion to Rawls*. Edited by Samuel Freeman (New York: Cambridge University Press, 2003), 73.

236. Ibid.

237. M. Ozonnia Ojielo, "Human Rights and Sharia'h Justice in Nigeria," *Annual Survey of International and Comparative Law* 9 (2003): 135.

238. Matt. 4:8–10 (Revised standard version).

239. Neuhaus, *The Naked Public Square: Religion and Democracy in America*, 1984, 215.

240. Michael Lerner, *The Politics of Meaning: Restoring Hope and Possibility in an Age of Cynicism* (Reading, MA: Addison-Wesley, 1997).

241. Wallis, *God's Politics: Why the Right Gets it Wrong and the Left Doesn't Get It*, 2005.

242. Feldman, *Divided by God: America's Church-State Problem—And What We Should Do about It*, 2005, 237.

243. Richard Rorty, "Religion as a Conversation Stopper," in *Philosophy and Social Hope* (New York: Penguin, 1999), 171.

244. Steven Gey, "Unity of the Graveyard and the Attack on Constitutional Secularism," *Brigham Young Law Review* 2004 (2004): 1024.

245. Edward B. Foley, "Jurisprudence and Theology," *Fordham Law Review* 66 (1998): 1195.

246. *Lee v. Weisman*, 505 U.S. 577, 646 (1992) (J. Scalia, dissenting).

247. *Newdow v. U.S. Congress*, 328 F.3d 466, 487 (9th Cir. 2003).

248. Huston Smith, *Why Religion Matters* (New York: HarperCollins, 2001), 222–23.

249. James Whitehurst, "Hawaii's Domestication of Shinto," *Christian Century*, November 21 (1984): 1100.

250. Ibid.

251. *Lee v. Weisman*, 505 U.S. 577, 589 (1992).

252. Thomas Nagel, "Rawls and Liberalism," in *The Cambridge Companion to Rawls*. Edited by Samuel Freeman, 2003, 77.

253. Richard D. Parker, "Homeland: An Essay on Patriotism," *Harvard Journal of Law and Policy* 25 (2002): 418 n.30.

254. The Communitarian Network, October 29, 2004, "Not Destiny, but Responsibility," at http://commlaw@hermes. gwu.edu, excerpts adapted from Amitai Etzioni, *From Empire to Community: A New Approach to International Relations* (New York: Palgrave Macmillan, 2004) (accessed September 13, 2006).

255. Rumu Sarkar, "Critical Essay: Theoretical Foundation in Development Law: A Reconciliation of Opposites?" *Denver Journal of International Law and Policy* 33 (2005): 368.

256. Francis Fukuyama, *The End of History and the Last Man* (New York: Free Press, 1992).

257. Francis Fukuyama, "After Neo-Conservatism," *New York Times*, February 19, 2006, at *http://www.nytimes.com/2006/02/19/magazine/neo.html* (accessed September 14, 2006).

258. G. Edward White, "The Arrival of History in Constitutional Scholarship," *Virginia Law Review* 88 (2002): 502.

259. Michael J. Perry, *The Constitution, the Courts, and Human Rights* (New Haven, CT: Yale University Press, 1982), 98–99.

260. Neuhaus, *The Naked Public Square: Religion and Democracy in America,* 1984, 173, 188.

261. Ibid., 188.

262. Wallis, *God's Politics: Why the Right Gets It Wrong and the Left Doesn't Get It,* 2005.

263. Steven C. Rockefeller, *John Dewey: Religious Faith and Democratic Humanism* (New York: Columbia University Press, 1991), 475.

264. Khaled Abou El Fadl, "Islam and the Challenge of Democratic Commitment," *Fordham International Law Journal* 27 (2003): 71.

265. M.A. Muqtedar Khan, "The Myth of Secularism," in *One Electorate Under God? A Dialogue on Religion and American Politics.* Edited by E. J. Dionne Jr., Jean Bethke Elshtain, and Kayla M. Drogosz, 2004, 138.

266. Neuhaus, *The Naked Public Square: Religion and Democracy in America,* 1984, 10.

267. N. T. Wright, *Paul in Fresh Perspective* (Minneapolis, MN: Fortress Press, 2005).

268. Mario Cuomo, "In the American Catholic Tradition of Realism," in *One Electorate Under God? A Dialogue on Religion and American Politics.* Edited by E. J. Dionne Jr., Jean Bethke Elshtain, and Kayla M. Drogosz, 2004, 14.

269. Karl Barth, "Jesus Christ and the Movement for Social Justice," in *Karl Barth and Radical Politics.* Edited and translated by. George Hunsinger (Philadelphia, PA: Westminster Press, 1976), 19.

270. Ibid., 37.

271. John C. Whitcomb and Henry Morris, *The Genesis Flood: The Biblical Record and its Scientific Implications* (Philadelphia, PA: Presbyterian and Reformed Publishing Co., 1961).

272. Karl Barth, *Church Dogmatics,* pt. 2. Edited by G. W. Bromiley and T. F. Torrance. Translated by G. W. Bromiley (New York: T & T Clark International, 2004), 6–7.

273. Pope John Paul II, "Magisterium is Concerned with Question of Evolution for It Involves Conception of Man," Message to the Pontifical Academy of Sciences: on Evolution, http://www.ewtn.com/library/PAPALDOC/JP961022 .HTM (accessed September 13, 2006).

274. Nicole Winfield, "Vatican: Faithful Should Listen to Science," *USA Today,* November 3, 2005, http://www.usatoday.com/tech/science/ethics/2005-11-03-vatican-science_x.htm?POE=TECISVA (accessed September 13, 2006).

275. Bill McKibben, *Enough: Staying Human in an Engineered Age* (New York: Times Books, 2003).

276. Antonio F. Perez, "International Antitrust at the Crossroads: The End of Antitrust History of the Clash of Competition Policy Civilizations?" *Law and Policy in International Business* 33 (2002): 552, n.73.

277. Barth, *Church Dogmatics,* part 2. Edited by G. W. Bromiley and T. F. Torrance. Translated by G. W. Bromiley, 2004, 4.

278. Donella H. Meadows, Dennis L. Meadows, Jorgen Randers, and William W. Behrens III. *The Limits to Growth: A Report for the Club of Rome's Project on the Predicament of Mankind* (New York: Universe Books, 1972), 154.

279. 268 U.S. 510 (1925).

280. Donna J. Sullivan, "Gender Equality and Religious Freedom: Toward a Framework for Conflict Resolution," *N.Y.U. Journal of International Law and Policy* 24 (1992): 795.

281. Levy, *Female Chauvinist Pigs: Women and the Rise of Raunch Culture*, 2005.

282. Paul, *Pornofied: How Pornography is Transforming Our Lives, Our Relationships and Our Families*, 2005.

283. Mackenzie Carpenter, "The Rise of Raunch Culture Feminists Are Torn: Is It Porn or Liberation of Women's Sexuality?" *Pittsburgh Post-Gazette*, October 12, 2005, http://www.post-gazette.com/pg/05285/586648.stm (accessed September 12, 2006).

284. Ibid.

285. Francis Fukuyama, "The West Has Won," *Guardian Unlimited*, October 11, 2001, http://www.guardian.co.uk/waronterror/story/0,1361,567333,00.html (accessed September 9, 2006).

286. Hagigah, 3b, *The Babylonian Talmud*. Translated and edited by I. Epstein (London: Soncino Press, 1938), 11.

287. David R. Dow, "The End of Religion," *Journal of Law and Religion* 16 (2001): 885.

288. Raymond Bonner, "Islamic Cleric Gets Mixed Verdict in Indonesian Trial for Terrorism, "*New York Times*," September 3, 2003, A1.

289. Pew Global Attitudes Project, "The Great Divide: How Westerners and Muslims View Each Other. Europe's Muslims More Moderate," http://pewglobal.org/reports/display.php?ReportID=253 (accessed September 12, 2006).

290. CNN.com,"Election 2004," CNN.com. http://www.cnn.com/ELECTION/2004/pages/results/states/US/P/00/epolls.0.html (accessed September 13, 2006).

291. William J. Bennett, "Why We Fight: Moral Clarity and the War on Terrorism" (New York: Random House, 2003).

292. George Packer, "The Fight Is for Democracy: Winning the War of Ideas in America and the World" (New York: Harper Perennial, 2003).

293. Michael Elliott, "If at First You Don't Succeed . . ." *Time*, November 24, 2003, 36.

294. Bob Herbert, "The Latest Overreach from the Pentagon," *International Herald Tribune*, December 28, 2004, 9.

295. Australian Broadcasting Corporation, "'Holy War' General Linked to Iraq Prison Scandal," *ABC News Online*, May 12, 2004, http://www.infoshop.org/inews/article.php?story=04/05/12/5560892 (accessed September 14, 2006).

296. Harold Bloom, "The Heretic Jew," review of *Betraying Spinoza*, by Rebecca Goldstein, New *York Times*, Sunday Book Review, June 18, 2006, http://www.nytimes.com/2006/06/18/books/review/18bloom.html?ex=1308283200&en=69d53032b750804e&ei=5090&partner=rssuserland&emc=rss (accessed September 12, 2006).

297. "Democracy in Action," Governor Howard Dean, M.D. Address to California State Democratic Convention Sacramento, California, March 15, 2003," http://www.gwu.edu/~action/2004/cdp0303/dean031503spt.html (accessed September 14, 2006).

298. Chris Hedges, "Soldiers of Christ: II: Feeling the Hate with the National Religious Broadcasters," *Harper's Magazine*, May 2005, 55.

299. Lewis Lapham, "Class Act," *Harper's Magazine*, Notebook, July 2006, 7–9.

300. 367 U.S. 488 (1961).

301. 380 U.S. 163 (1965).

302. Michael Lerner, "After the Fall: Why America Needs a Spiritual Left," *Tikkun*, September 18, 2005, http://www.tikkun.org/ (accessed September 12, 2006).

303. Ibid.

304. Peter Beinart, "A Fighting Faith," *The New Republic*, December 13, 2004, http://www.tnr.com/doc.mhtml?i=20041213&s=beinart121304 (accessed September 10, 2006).

305. Peter Beinart, *The Good Fight: Why Liberals—and Only Liberals—Can Win the War on Terror and Make America Great Again* (New York: HarperCollins, 2006).

306. Peter Beinart, "The Rehabilitation of the Cold-War Liberal," *New York Times Magazine*, April 30, 2006, 41.

307. CNN.com,"Election 2004," CNN.com. http://www.cnn.com/ELECTION/2004/pages/results/states/US/P/00/epolls.0.html (accessed September 12, 2006).

308. E. J. Dionne, Jr., "Faith Full-When the Religious Right Was Left," *New Republic*, February 28, 2005, 12.

309. Howard Fineman and Tamara Lipper, "Scream 2: The Sequel," *Newsweek*, June 20, 2006, http://www.msnbc.msn.com/id/8185333/site/newsweek/ (accessed September 12, 2006).

310. Cary Valyo, "Dems and Life Issues," *Pittsburgh Post-Gazette*, Letters to the Editor, November 19, 2004, http://www.post-gazette.com/pg/04324/414068.stm (accessed September 13, 2006).

311. Rev. Dr. N. Graham Standish, "A Country Divided by Christ," *Pittsburgh Post-Gazette*, June 12, 2005, J1.

312. Ibid.

313. James Carville and Paul Begala, *Take it Back: Our Party, Our Country, Our Future* (New York: Simon & Schuster, 2006), 72.

314. *Associated Press*, "Death Penalty, Bush Loom in Va. Race," October 25, 2005.

315. James Traub, "Party Like Its 1994," *New York Times Magazine*, March 12, 2006, http://www.nytimes.com/2006/03/12/magazine/312midterm1_1.html?pagewanted=1&ei=5088&en=9e99b69689477e33&ex=1299819600&partner=rssnyt&emc=rss (accessed September 13, 2006).

316. Alan M. Dershowitz, *Rights From Wrongs: A Secular Theory of the Origin of Rights* (New York: Basic Books, 2004). At least that is the title on the book cover. At the same time the book has been listed by the title, *Rights From Wrongs: the Origin of Human Rights in the Experiences of Injustice*. The clash can be observed at http://www.barnesandnoble.com/ (accessed September 11, 2006).

317. Smith, *Why Religion Matters: The Fate of the Human Spirit In An Age of Disbelief*, 2001, 273.

318. Dietrich Bonhoeffer, *Letters and Papers from Prison*, 3rd. edn. Edited by Eberhard Bethge (New York: Macmillan, 1967), 153.

319. John D. Barbour, "Niebuhr Versus Niebuhr: The Tragic Nature of History," *The Christian Century*, November 21, 1984, 1097.

320. Francis George, "Law and Culture in the United States," *American Journal of Jurisprudence* 48 (2003): 144.

321. Dewey, *A Common Faith*, 1934, 53.

322. N.T. Wright, *Jesus and the Victory of God* (Minneapolis, MN: Augsburg Fortress Publishers, 1996), 98.

323. Michael J. Perry, "Christians, the Bible, and Same-Sex Unions: An Argument for Political Self-Restraint," *Wake Forest Law Review* 36 (2001): 449.

324. Bonhoeffer, *Letters and Papers from Prison*, 3rd edn. Edited by Eberhard Bethge, 1967, 278–82.

325. Ibid., 286.

326. N. T. Wright, *Christian Origins and the Question of God*, 3 vols. (Minneapolis, MN: Fortress Press, 1992–2003).

327. Ibid., 3: 90.

328. Ibid., 2: 96–97.

329. *ZENIT*, "Secularism Needs Christianity, Says Vatican Official," February 2, 2006, http://www.zenit.org/english/default.htm (accessed September 14, 2006).

330. Brueggemann, *Theology of the Old Testament: Testimony, Dispute, Advocacy,* 1997, 446.

331. Mark Lilla, "Church Meets State," *New York Times*, Book Review, May 5, 2005, 39.

332. Ibid.

333. Ibid.

334. Gen. 12:1–3 (Revised standard version).

335. Gen. 12:4 (Revised standard version).

336. Kim Stanley Robinson, *Red Mars* (New York: Bantam, 1993), 373.

337. Harry V. Jaffa, *Original Intent and the Framers of the Constitution: A Disputed Question* (Washington, DC: Regency Gateway, 1994), 84.

338. Antonin Scalia, *A Matter of Interpretation* (Princeton, NJ: Princeton University Press, 1997), 47.

339. Ibid.

340. John Hart Ely, *Democracy and Distrust: A Theory of Judicial Review* (Cambridge, MA: Harvard University Press, 1980), 54.

341. Pope Benedict XVI, *Truth and Tolerance: Christian Belief and World Religions.* Translated by Henry Taylor (San Francisco, CA: Ignatius Press, 2004), 238.

342. *Adamson v. California,* 332 U.S. 46, 76 (1947 J. Black, dissenting).

343. Susan E. Looper-Friedman, "Keep Your Hands Off My Body: Abortion Regulation and the Takings Clause," *New England Law Review* 29 (1995): 268 n.79.

344. Rabbi Elliot N. Dorff, "Jewish Theological and Moral Reflections on Genetic Screening: The Case of BRCA1," *Health Matrix* 7 (1997): 73.

345. *Cruzan v. Director of Missouri Department of Health*, 497 U.S. 261, 293 (1990 J. Scalia, concurring).

346. Michael Janofsky, "When Cleaner Air is a Biblical Obligation," *New York Times*, November 7, 2005, http://www.nytimes.com/2005/11/07/politics/07air.html?ex=1289019600&en=1de88acf51117734&ei=5088&partner=rssnyt&emc=rss (accessed September 14, 2006).

347. Ibid.

348. Mark 10:25 (Revised standard version).

349. Matt. 6:19 (Revised standard version).

350. Quinn, *Ishmael: An Adventure of the Mind and Spirit*, 1992, 232.

351. Brueggemann, *Theology of the Old Testament: Testimony, Dispute, Advocacy*, 1997, 424.

352. Ezra Rosser, "This Is My Land, This Land Is Your Land: Markets and Institutions for Economic Development on Native American Land," *Arizona Law Review* 47 (2005): 293.

353. Thomas L. Friedman, *The World is Flat: A Brief History of the Twenty-First Century* (New York: Farrar, Straus, and Giroux, 2005).

354. Fareed Zakaria, "The Wealth of Yet More Nations," *New York Times*, Book Review, May 1, 2005, 10.

355. 381 U.S. 479 (1965).

356. 405 U.S. 438 (1972).

357. Neuhaus, *The Naked Public Square: Religion and Democracy in America*, 1984, 53.

358. Barth, *The Epistle to the Romans*, 1933, 489.

359. Ezek. 14:6 (Revised standard version).

360. Jon. 3:6-10 (Revised standard version).

361. Walter Brueggemann, *The Prophetic Imagination* (Minneapolis, MN: Fortress Press, 1978), 18.

362. Karl Barth, *Anselm: Fides Quaerens Intellectum, Anselm's Proof of the Existence of God in the Context of His Theological Scheme*. Translated by Ian W. Robertson (Canterbury, UK: S.C.M., 1975).

363. Paul Tillich, *Systematic Theology* (Chicago, IL: University of Chicago Press, 1957), 12 (referring to another of his books, *The Courage to Be* (London: Collins, 1952).

364. Barth, "Jesus Christ and the Movement for Social Justice," in *Karl Barth and Radical Politics*. Edited and translated by George Hunsinger, 1976, 22.

365. Matt. 7:21 (Revised standard version).

366. Reuters, "Televangelist Warns of Evolution Doomsday: Pat Robertson Says a Vote against Intelligent Design Is a Vote against God," MSNBC.com, Science, http://www.msnbc.msn.com/id/9995578/ (accessed September 10, 2006).

367. Avery Cardinal Dulles, "The Covenant with Israel," *First Things*, November 2005, 16–21.

368. Esther 4:14 (Revised standard edition).

369. Darcy Frey, "Her Lonely Voice," *New York Times Magazine*, July 2, 2006, http://www.nytimes.com/2006/07/02/magazine/02keineg.html?ex=1309492800&en=acff89f2d90f545d&ei=5088&partner=rssnyt&emc=rss (accessed September 12, 2006).

370. Barth, *The Epistle to the Romans*. Translated from the 6th edn. by Edwyn C. Hoskyns, 1933, 493.

371. Anthony Flew, "Theology and Falsification," in *Reason and Responsibility*. Edited by Joel Feinberg (Blemont, CA: Thompson/Wadsworth Publishing, 2001).

372. Dewey, *A Common Faith*, 1934, 14.

373. Ibid., 20.

374. Isidore Epstei, *Baba Mezia 59a–b, Soncino Hebrew/English Babylonian Talmud* Bnpublishing.com; CD-Rom edition (Thousand Oaks, CA: BN Publishing, 2005). CD-ROM.

375. Deut. 30:12–14 (Revised standard version).

Selected Bibliography

Ackerman, Bruce. *We the People*. Cambridge, MA: Belknap Press of Harvard University Press, 1991.

Arendt, Hannah. *On Revolution*. New York: Viking Press, 1965.

Aslan, Reza. *No God But God: The Origins, Evolution, and Future of Islam*. New York: Random House, 2006.

Barth, Karl. *The Epistle to the Romans*. Translated from the 6th edition by Edwyn C. Hoskyns. London: Oxford University Press, H. Milford, 1933.

———. "Jesus Christ and the Movement for Social Justice," in *Karl Barth and Radical Politics*, edited and translated by George Hunsinger, 19–45. Philadelphia, PA: Westminster Press, 1976.

———. *Church Dogmatics*, part 2. Edited by G. W. Bromiley and T. F. Torrance. Translated by G. W. Bromiley. New York: T & T Clark International, 2004.

Beinart, Peter. *The Good Fight: Why Liberals—and Only Liberals—Can Win the War on Terror and Make America Great Again*. New York: HarperCollins, 2006.

Bellah, Robert N. *Beyond Belief: Essays on Religion in a Post-Traditional World*. New York: Harper & Row, 1970.

Bonhoeffer, Dietrich. *Letters and Papers from Prison*, 3rd ed. Edited by Eberhard Bethge. New York: Macmillan, 1967.

Brooks, David. "How Niebuhr Helps Us Kick the Secularist Habit: A Six-Step Program," in *One Electorate Under God?: A Dialogue on Religion and American Politics*. Edited by E. J. Dionne Jr., Jean Bethke Elshtain, and Kayla M. Drogosz, 67–71. Washington, DC: Brookings Institute Press, 2004.

Brueggemann, Walter. *The Prophetic Imagination*. Philadelphia, PA: Fortress Press, 1978.

———. *Theology of the Old Testament: Testimony, Dispute, Advocacy*. Minneapolis, MN: Fortress Press, 1997.

Caputo, John D. *The Prayers and Tears of Jacques Derrida: Religion without Religion*. Bloomington, IN: University of Indiana Press, 1997.

Carter, Stephen L. *The Culture of Disbelief: How American Law and Politics Trivialize Religious Devotion*. New York: Basic Books, 1993.

Carville, James, and Paul Begala. *Take It Back: Our Party, Our Country, Our Future*. New York: Simon & Schuster, 2006.

Chua, Amy. *World on Fire: How Exporting Free Market Democracy Breeds Ethnic Hatred and Global Instability*. New York : Doubleday, 2003.

Cuomo, Mario. "In the American Catholic Tradition of Realism," in *One Electorate Under God?: A Dialogue on Religion and American Politics*. Edited by E. J. Dionne Jr., Jean Bethke Elshtain, and Kayla M. Drogosz, 13–19. Washington, DC: Brookings Institute Press, 2004.

Dawkins, Richard. *Blind Watchmaker*. New York: W. W. Norton, 1994.

Dennett, Daniel C. *Breaking the Spell: Religion as a Natural Phenomenon*. London: Allen Lane, 2006.

Dershowitz, Alan. *Rights from Wrongs*. New York: Basic Books, 2005.

Dewey, John. *A Common Faith*. New Haven, CT: Yale University Press, 1934.

Dworkin, Ronald. *Taking Rights Seriously*. Cambridge, MA: Harvard University Press, 1977.

Ely, John Hart. *Democracy and Distrust: A Theory of Judicial Review*. Cambridge, MA: Harvard University Press, 1980.

Feldman, Noah. *Divided by God: America's Church-State Problem—And What We Should Do about It*. New York: Farrar, Straus, and Giroux, 2005.

Friedman, Thomas L. *The World Is Flat: A Brief History of the Twenty-First Century*. New York: Farrar, Straus, and Giroux, 2005.

Fukuyama, Francis. *The End of History and the Last Man*. New York: Free Press, 1992.

Greeley, Andrew. "The Puritans and American Politics," in *One Electorate Under God?: A Dialogue on Religion and American Politics*. Edited by E. J. Dionne Jr., Jean Bethke Elshtain, and Kayla M. Drogosz, 106–110. Washington, DC: Brookings Institute Press, 2004.

Jaffa, Harry V. *Original Intent and the Framers of the Constitution: A Disputed Question*. Washington, DC: Regency Gateway, 1994.

Khan, M. A. Muqtedar. "The Myth of Secularism," in *One Electorate Under God?: A Dialogue on Religion and American Politics*. Edited by E. J. Dionne Jr., Jean Bethke Elshtain, and Kayla M. Drogosz, 134–140. Washington, DC: Brookings Institute Press, 2004.

Kramnick, Isaac, and R. Laurence Moore. *The Godless Constitution: The Case against Religious Correctness*. New York: Norton, 1996.

Lefort, Claude. *Democracy and Political Theory*. Translated by David Macey. Cambridge, UK: Polity Press, 1988.

Levy, Ariel. *Female Chauvinist Pigs: Women and the Rise of Raunch Culture*. New York: Free Press, 2005.

McKibben, Bill. *Enough: Staying Human in an Engineered Age*. New York: Times Books, 2003.

Minow, Martha. "Governing Religion," in *One Electorate Under God?: A Dialogue on Religion and American Politics*. Edited by E. J. Dionne Jr., Jean Bethke Elshtain, and Kayla M. Drogosz, 144–150. Washington, DC: Brookings Institute Press, 2004.

Nagel, Thomas. "Rawls and Liberalism," in *The Cambridge Companion to Rawls.* Edited by Samuel Freeman, 62–86. New York: Cambridge University Press, 2003.

Nelson-Pallmeyer, Jack. *Is Religion Killing Us?: Violence in the Bible and the Quran.* Harrisburg, PA: Trinity International Press, 2003.

Neuhaus, Richard John. *The Naked Public Square: Religion and Democracy in America.* Grand Rapids, MI: W. B. Eerdmans Publishing Company, 1984.

Novak, David. "Religion, Faith, and Elections," in *One Electorate Under God?: A Dialogue on Religion and American Politics.* Edited by E. J. Dionne Jr., Jean Bethke Elshtain, and Kayla M. Drogosz, 159–163. Washington, DC: Brookings Institute Press, 2004.

Paul, Pamela. *Pornofied: How Pornography Is Transforming Our Lives, Our Relationships and Our Families.* New York: Times Books, 2005.

Phillips, Kevin. *American Theocracy: The Peril and Politics of Radical Religion, Oil, and Borrowed Money in the 21st Century.* New York: Viking, 2006.

Powell, H. Jefferson. *The Moral Tradition of American Constitutionalism: A Theological Interpretation.* Durham, NC: Duke University Press, 1993.

Quinn, Daniel. *Ishmael: An Adventure of the Mind and Spirit.* New York: Bantam/Turner Books, 1992.

Ratzinger, Joseph Cardinal. *Truth and Tolerance: Christian Belief and World Religions.* Translated by Henry Taylor. San Francisco, CA: Ignatius Press, 2004.

Rawls, John. *A Theory of Justice.* Cambridge, MA: Belknap Press of Harvard University Press, 1971.

———. *Political Liberalism.* New York: Columbia University Press, 1993.

Rockefeller, Steven C. *John Dewey: Religious Faith and Democratic Humanism.* New York: Columbia University Press, 1991.

Sabine, George Holland. *A History of Political Theory.* New York: Holt, 1950.

Scalia, Antonin. *A Matter of Interpretation: Federal Courts and the Law: An Essay.* Princeton, NJ: Princeton University Press, 1997.

Schmitt, Carl. *Political Theology: Four Chapters on the Concept of Sovereignty.* Translated by George Schwab. Cambridge, MA: MIT Press, 1985.

Smith, Huston. *Why Religion Matters: The Fate of the Human Spirit in an Age of Disbelief.* New York: HarperCollins, 2001.

Wallis, Jim. *God's Politics: Why the Right Gets It Wrong and the Left Doesn't Get It.* San Francisco, CA: Harper, 2005.

Wright, N. T. *Paul in Fresh Perspective.* Minneapolis, MN: Fortress Press, 2005.

———. *Christian Origins and the Question of God*, 3 vols. Minneapolis, MN: Fortress Press, 1992–2003.

Zakaria, Fareed. *The Future of Freedom: Illiberal Democracy at Home and Abroad.* New York: W. W. Norton & Company, 2003.

Index

Abortion: and America as both Church and World, 136; ban on, based on God's will, 29; to a believer, 56, 127; and the *Bible*, 179–80, 198; Bork on, 19; and the Catholic Church during the election of 2004, 125; and a Christian Left, 34; and a conservative agenda, 181; and constitutional rights, 105; and constitutional theory, 115–16; as a cutting-edge social issue, 4; debate in the public square, 117–18; and Democrats, 159, 161–62, 204; as a dispute between the religiously oriented and the secular, 103; in election of 2006, 203–4; in election of 2004, xii; as an exercise of human autonomy in a religious democracy, 144; George W. Bush as an alternative to John Kerry in 2004, 110–11; and human rights, 179; as an illusory matter of choice, 188; and individualism, 184; judicial activism as code for, 7; to a liberal nonbeliever, 56; as a matter of truth, 178; as a moral issue, 110; in the moral shape of history, 56; in *Planned Parenthood of Southeastern*

Pennsylvania v. Casey, 184; plans to have a Texas bill signing ceremony in a private, Christian academy, 79; as policy division, xvii; political debate and religious opposition to, 23; the political right's religious agenda, 30; positivist right to, 19; and the power of judges and judicial action, 106–7; a religious perspective, 19; and religious involvement in government, 79; and religious voters, 62; religious voters seeking to impose their will through a ban on, 104; and *Roe v. Wade*, 106–7, 116, 178–79; Scalia on, 18, 115–16, 178; Scalia's dissent in *Stenberg v. Carhart* on letting States decide, 97; and secularists, 17–18; secular justifications and genuine religious feelings to change government policy, 108; as a social decision, 67; supporters of, 62; in Virginia Governor's race in 2006, 162; and women's rights in a religious democracy, 145

Abou El Fadl, Khaled, on democracy and Islam, 133

About the Author

BRUCE LEDEWITZ is Professor at Duquesne University School of Law and author of several journal articles and pieces for publications such as *The Wall Street Journal, Pittsburgh Post-Gazette, The Philadelphia Inquirer, The New York Times,* and other news outlets.